FAIR PLAY

FAIR PLAY

The Ethics of Sport
Second Edition

ROBERT SIMON

A Member of the Perseus Books Group

Reprinted courtesy of *Sports Illustrated:* from "An Encounter to Last an Eternity," by Frank Deford, April 11, 1983. Copyright 1983. Time Inc. All rights reserved.

Rev. John Lo Shiavo, "Trying to Save a University's Priceless Assets." August 1, 1982. Copyright 1982 by The New York Times Co. Reprinted by permission.

Michael Oriard, "At Oregon State, Basketball Is Pleasing, Not Alarming." March 8, 1981. Copyright 1981 by The New York Times Co. Reprinted by permission.

Copyright © 2004 by Westview Press

Published in the United States of America by Westview Press, A Member of the Perseus Books Group, 5500 Central Avenue, Boulder, Colorado 80301–2877, and in the United Kingdom by Westview Press, 12 Hid's Copse Road, Cumnor Hill, Oxford OX2 9JJ.

Find us on the world wide web at www.westviewpress.com

Westview Press books are available at special discounts for bulk purchases in the United States by corporations, institutions, and other organizations. For more information, please contact the Special Markets Department at the Perseus Books Group, 11 Cambridge Center, Cambridge, MA 02142, or call (617) 252–5298, (800) 255–1514, or email j.mccrary@perseusbooks.com.

Library of Congress Cataloging-in-Publication Data
Simon, Robert L., 1941-
 Fair play : the ethics of sport / Robert L. Simon.
   p. cm.
Includes bibliographical references and index.
 ISBN 0-8133-6567-8 (pbk. : alk. paper) -- ISBN 0-8133-6597-X (hardcover : alk. paper)
 1. Sports--Moral and ethical aspects--United States. 2. Sports--Social aspects--United States.
I. Title.
 GV706.3.S56 2003
 796'.01--dc21
                                                                 2003006399

The paper used in this publication meets the requirements of the American National Standard for Permanence of Paper for Printed Library Materials Z39.48–1984.

10   9   8   7   6   5   4   3   2

To my grandchildren, Kayla and Jake.
I hope they will enjoy sports as much as I do.

Contents

Preface		*ix*
1	INTRODUCTION: THE ETHICS OF SPORT	1
2	COMPETITION, A MUTUAL QUEST FOR EXCELLENCE	17
3	SPORTSMANSHIP	41
4	DRUGS AND VIOLENCE	69
5	GIRLS AND BOYS, MEN AND WOMEN	109
6	SPORTS ON CAMPUS	137
7	THE COMMERCIALIZATION OF SPORT	171
8	SPORTS VALUES TODAY	199
Notes		*217*
Index		*235*

Preface

Sports play a significant role in the lives of millions of people throughout the world. Many men and women participate actively in sports and still more are spectators, fans, and critics of sports. Even those who are uninvolved in sports, bored by them, or critical of athletic competition often will be significantly affected by them, either because of their relationships with enthusiasts or, more important, because of the impact of sports on our language, thought, and culture.

Because sports are a significant form of social activity that affect the educational system, the economy, and perhaps the values of citizens, they raise a wide range of issues, some of which are factual or empirical in character. Social scientists, historians, physicians, and writers have raised many such issues that concern sports. For example, sociologists may be concerned with whether participation in sports affects the values of the participants, and psychologists might try to determine what personality features contribute to success or failure in competitive athletics.

In addition to factual and explanatory questions, sports also raise philosophical issues that are conceptual and ethical. Conceptual questions concern how we are to understand the concepts and ideas that apply in the world of sports. What are sports, anyway? How are sports related to rules? Do those who intentionally break the rules of a game even play it or are they doing something else? Are there different forms of competition in sports? Is it possible to compete against oneself?

Ethical questions raise the moral concerns many of us have about sports. Should sports be accorded the importance they are given in our society? Is there too much emphasis on winning and competition? Are college sports getting out of hand? Why shouldn't we cheat in a game if it will bring us a championship? What, if anything, makes the use of steroids to enhance performance in sports unethical?

How should men and women be treated in sports if they are to be treated equitably and fairly? Should we be aiming more for excellence in competition among highly skilled athletes or should we place greater value on more participation? Does the commercialization of sports actually corrupt the game? *Fair Play* examines such questions and evaluates the principles to which thoughtful people might appeal in trying to formulate answers.

Not only are questions in the philosophy of sports important in their own right, they can also serve as a useful introduction to broader philosophical issues. Most students come to philosophy courses with knowledge of sports, and many have a deep interest in ethical issues raised by sports. This initial interest can serve as a launching pad to introduce students to the nature and value of philosophical inquiry. For example, questions about whether the use of steroids to enhance athletic performance is fair can lead to broad inquiry into the nature of fairness and the just society.

Perhaps most important, issues in the philosophy of sport are of great intrinsic interest and are well worth our attention. Philosophical questions force us to stretch our analytical powers to the fullest and to question basic presuppositions. Those that arise in the philosophical examination of sports, like any others, require us to test and evaluate fundamental justificatory principles and engage in rigorous critical inquiry.

This new edition of the book incorporates significant changes from earlier editions. Chapter 3, based on my presidential address to the International Association of the Philosophy of Sport in 1998, introduces and evaluates various approaches to understanding the nature of sport and assesses the significance of each approach for ethics. Chapter 7, on the commercialization of sport, is completely new, and discusses a related set of issues arising from considering sports as a business and a commodity that must be marketed to the public. Chapter 6 on gender equity in sport contains a new and much more thorough analysis of Title IX, including the controversy over proportionality; the discussion of intercollegiate athletics has been revised and expanded and now includes a discussion of *The Game of Life*, a widely discussed book critical of the influence of intercollegiate athletics even at the most academically selective colleges and universities. Many other sections also have been revised and new, more contemporary examples introduced whenever possible.

Fair Play never would have been written had it not been for the challenges to my own views of sports put forth by friends, colleagues in the philosophy department at Hamilton College, and especially my students, who have been critical of many of my views but always helpful and insightful. I have also benefited from the tough questions posed by Scott Ketchmar's students at Penn State, who have always presented me with challenging questions whenever I have been able to visit their classes. Although I cannot acknowledge and sort out all my intellectual debts here, I would like to thank the original editors of the first edition of this book, Ray O'Connell and Doris Michaels of Prentice-Hall, for their initial encouragement, and especially Spencer Carr and Sarah Warner of Westview Press for their insights as to how the earlier editions could be expanded and improved upon.

I also express my special appreciation to my wife, Joy, not only for her critical help with the manuscript or for putting up with an abnormal number of fits of abstraction ("Earth calling Bob" became one of the phrases used most often at our dinner table) during the writing of all the editions of the book, but also and especially for her support and encouragement, which were crucial during my treatment for prostate cancer in 1998–1999. (She is also a devoted spectator at numerous golf tournaments in which I have played, rarely successfully, and in spite of past performance is *usually* encouraging about the next competition.) Sports have been one of the major activities my family and I have shared, so I hope they enjoy reading the finished product as much as I enjoyed writing it.

Finally, without the participants in sports who demonstrate the kind of quest for excellence discussed in Chapter 2, much of the subject matter of philosophy of sports would be empty abstraction. I thank past and present staff and players in both the Hamilton College men's and women's basketball programs, not only for getting me away from my computer (in view of my attendance at basketball games, many colleagues will find it miraculous that I was able to complete this project) but also for making the harsh upstate New York winter one of the most exciting and pleasurable times of year. I would like to thank my former players on the Hamilton men's golf team for letting me try to apply some ethical theories on the nature of good competition to them and for keeping their swings grooved anyway.

Robert L. Simon
Clinton, NY

1

Introduction:
The Ethics of Sport

I would like to think that this book began on an unfortunately not atypical cold and rainy late October day in upstate New York. I had been discussing some of my generally unsuccessful efforts in local golf tournaments with colleagues in the philosophy department and let drop what I thought was an innocuous remark to the effect that although winning isn't everything, it sure beats losing. Much to my surprise, my colleagues objected vehemently, asserting that winning means nothing. In their view, all that should matter are having fun and trying to improve, not defeating an opponent. I soon found myself backed into a corner by this unthreatening but now fully aroused assortment of philosophers. Fortunately for me, another colleague entered the office just at the right moment. Struck by the vehemence of the argument, although he had no idea what it was about, he looked at my opponents and remarked, "You folks sure are trying to win this argument." This incident illustrates two important aspects of a philosophical examination of sports. First, issues arise in sports that are not simply empirical questions of psychology, sociology, or some other discipline. Empirical surveys can tell us whether people do think winning is important, but they cannot tell us whether that is what people ought to think or whether winning really ought to be regarded as a primary goal of athletics. Second, the incident illustrated that logic could be applied to issues in the philosophy of sport. Thus, at least on the surface, it appeared that my colleagues were in the logically embarrassing position of trying hard to win an argument to the effect that winning is unimportant.

We will return to the issue of whether winning is important in Chapter 2. For now, let us consider further what philosophical inquiry might contribute to our understanding of sports.

Ethical Issues in Sport

Sports play a major, if sometimes unappreciated, role in the lives of Americans. Most of us are exposed to them as children. As a result of our childhood experiences, many of us become participants or fans for life. Others are appalled by their early exposure to sports and avoid them like the plague later in life. They may have been embarrassed by failures in front of peers and parents or humiliated by an insensitive physical education instructor. Girls may have received less encouragement to participate than boys. Others may just find sports boring.

Most of us, however, retain some affiliation with sports for life, even if only as spectators.[1] Athletes and fans devote so much time and effort to sports at all levels that their involvement is surely one of their most valuable and significant activities. The situation is not unique to the United States. Intense interest in sports is virtually a global phenomenon. Whether it is ice hockey in Russia or soccer in Europe, South America, and Africa, sports play a major role worldwide. Sports were valued by the ancient Greeks, by the Romans, and by Native Americans. Indeed, participation in sports, and the related activity of play, are characteristic of most, if not all, human societies.

Although there is a tendency to regard sports as trivial, it is not clear that such a view is justified. Those critical of sports or bored by athletic competition must admit that sports play a significant role in our lives even if they believe that dominance is misguided or even harmful. At the very least, it is surely worth discovering what it is about sports that calls forth a favorable response among so many people from so many different cultures. Reflection upon sports raises issues that not only have intrinsic interest but also go beyond the bounds of sport itself. For example, reflection on the value of competition in athletics and the emphasis on winning in much of organized sports may shed light on the ethics of competition in other areas, such as the marketplace. Inquiry into the nature of fair play in sports can also help our understanding of fairness in a wider social setting. Indeed, because many of our basic values, such as playing fairly, are often absorbed through involvement in athletic competition, inquiry into values in sports is likely not only to prove interesting in its own right but also to have implications of more general concern.

Sports raise many kinds of philosophical issues. For example, what is a sport? Football, baseball, and soccer clearly are sports. But some have doubts about golf. What about chess and auto racing? How are sports related to games? Is participation in sport always a form of play? Questions such as these raise issues that go well beyond looking up words in a dictionary. To settle them, we will need to rely on a theory of what makes something a game, a sport, or an instance of play. Dictionary definitions often presuppose such theories. But the theories presupposed by the definition may be unclear; they may leave open how borderline cases are to be thought of; or they may just be wrong. For example, one dictionary account of games classifies them as competitive activities. But must all games be competitive? Is "playing house" a game and is it competitive? What about playing catch?

One of the most important kinds of philosophical issues that arise in sport are ethical or moral ones; these are the kinds of issues about which this book will be primarily concerned. Some moral issues in sport concern specific actions, often by athletes. For example, in the championship game of the 1999 World Cup, the American women's soccer team completed regulation and overtime play against China with the score tied. The championship, viewed throughout the world by millions of fans, many of them young American girls captivated by the success of the American women, was to be settled by penalty kicks in a game-ending shootout.[2] The American goalkeeper, Briana Scurry, decided that one of the Chinese shooters, Liu Ying, lacked confidence. When Ying made her move, Scurry took two quick steps forward, in violation of a rule of soccer, to cut off Ying's shooting angle. The tactic worked. Scurry deflected Ying's shot, and the Americans won. But did Scurry cheat by violating a rule? Was Scurry doing what any goalkeeper would do in such a situation by conforming to a convention of the game tacitly accepted by all players? Or was the American victory tainted by unethical behavior in a deliberate violation of the rules?[3]

Other kinds of ethical issues in sport involve the assessment of rules or policies, for example, the prohibition by many sports organizations of the use of performance-enhancing drugs by competitive athletes. What justifies this prohibition? Is it because performance-enhancing drugs such as steroids often have harmful side effects? But why shouldn't athletes, especially competent adult athletes, be free to take risks with their bodies? After all, many of us would reject the kind of paternalism that constantly interferes with the pursuit of our goals whenever risky behavior is involved. Think of the dangers inherent in a typical American diet, which contains a high proportion of unhealthy fat and sugar. Or should performance-enhancing drugs be prohibited because they provide unfair advantages to some of the competitors?

But would the advantages still be unfair if all competitors had access to the drug? Are the advantages any different from those conferred by the legal use of technologically advanced equipment?

Questions of marketing, sports administration, and the formulation of rules also involve moral issues, although the moral character of the questions raised may not always be obvious. For example, consider whether a rule change ought to be instituted that might make a sport more attractive to fans at the professional or college levels yet diminish the skill or strategy needed to play the game. Some would argue that the designated hitter rule in American League baseball, which allows teams to replace their usually weak hitting pitcher with a designated hitter in the batting order, is such a case. The rule may make the game more exciting to the casual fan, who values an explosive offense; but it may also remove various subtleties from the game, such as the decision about when to remove the pitcher from the game for a pinch hitter, or the value of the sacrifice bunt, which weak hitting pitchers might be capable of executing. Although this is not as obvious a moral issue as some of the other examples cited, it does have a moral, or at least evaluative, component. It raises questions about the purposes or goals of sports, what social functions they ought to serve, and whether sports have an integrity that ought to be preserved. Similar issues may be raised by questioning when technological innovations ought to be permitted in sport, and when they ought to be prohibited for making a sport too easy.

At a more abstract level, other ethical issues concern the values central to competitive sport itself. Is competition in sport ethically permissible, or even desirable, or does it create a kind of selfishness, perhaps an analog of a narrow form of nationalism that says "My team, right or wrong?" Does the single-minded pursuit of winning, which is apparently central to competition in sport, help promote violent behavior in fans? Does it teach competitors to regard opponents as mere obstacles to be overcome? Is it related to the anger shown by many parents of participants in youth sports that culminated in 2001 in the killing of a hockey coach by an enraged parent? What kind of competition in sport can be defended morally and how great an emphasis on winning is too much?

Questions such as these raise basic issues about the kind of moral values involved in sport. They are not only about what people think about sports or about what values they hold; rather, they are about what people *ought* to think. They require the identification of defensible ethical standards and their application to sport. Critical inquiry into philosophy of sport consists in formulating and rationally evaluating such standards as well as testing them by seeing how they apply to concrete issues in sports and athletics.

Sport, Philosophy, and Moral Values

Just what does philosophy have to contribute to reflection about sports and moral values? It is evident even to a casual observer of our society that sports in the United States are undergoing intense moral scrutiny. How can philosophy contribute to this endeavor?

Philosophy of Sport

Misconceptions about the nature of philosophy are widespread. According to one story, a philosopher on a domestic flight was asked by his seatmate what he did for a living. He replied, perhaps foolishly, "I'm a philosopher," a statement that is one of the greatest conversation-stoppers known to the human race. The seatmate, apparently stupefied by the reply, was silent for several minutes. Finally, he turned to the philosopher and remarked, "Oh, and what are some of your sayings?"[4]

The image of the philosopher as the author of wise sayings can perhaps be forgiven, for the word "philosophy" has its roots in the Greek expression meaning "love of wisdom." But wisdom is not necessarily encapsulated in brief sayings that we might memorize before breakfast. The ancient Greek philosopher Socrates provides a different model of philosophic inquiry.

Socrates, who lived in the fifth century B.C., did not leave a body of written works behind him; but we know a great deal about his life and thought, primarily through the works of his most influential pupil, Plato. As a young man, Socrates, who was seeking a mentor from whom to learn, set out to find the wisest man in Greece. According to the story, he decided to ask a religious figure, the oracle at Delphi, the identity of the man he was seeking. Much to Socrates' surprise, the oracle informed him that he, Socrates, was the wisest man in Greece. "How can that be?" Socrates must have wondered; after all, he was searching for a wise teacher precisely because he was ignorant.

However, looking at the oracle's answer in light of Plato's presentation of Socrates, we can discern what the oracle meant. In the early Platonic dialogues such as the *Euthyphro,* Socrates questioned important figures of the day about the nature of piety or the essence of knowledge. Those questioned purported to be experts in the subject under investigation, but their claim to expertise was discredited by Socrates' logical analysis. These experts not only failed in what they claimed to know but also seemed to have accepted views that they had never exposed to critical examination.

Perhaps in calling Socrates the wisest man in Greece the oracle was suggesting that Socrates alone was willing to expose beliefs and principles to critical examination. He did not claim to know what he did not know, but he was willing to learn. He was also not willing to take popular opinion for granted but was prepared to question it.

This Socratic model suggests that the role of philosophy is to examine our beliefs, clarify the principles on which they rest, and subject them to critical examination. For example, in science, the role of philosophy is not to compete in formulating and testing empirical hypotheses in biology, chemistry, and physics. Rather, philosophers might try to understand in what sense science provides objective knowledge and then examine claims that all knowledge must be scientific in nature.

If we adopt such a view of philosophy, the task of the philosophy of sports would be to clarify, systematize, and evaluate the principles we believe should govern the world of sports. This task might involve a conceptual analysis of such terms as "sport" and "game," an inquiry into the nature of excellence in sports, an ethical evaluation of such principles as "winning should be the only concern of the serious athlete," and an application of ethical analysis to concrete issues, such as disagreement over whether athletes should be permitted to take performance-enhancing drugs.

This book is concerned primarily with the ethical evaluation of principles that many people apply to sports and the application of the analysis to specific issues. Its major focus is on the nature of principles and values that should apply to sports. Thus, its concern is predominantly normative rather than descriptive. Few people think of sports as activities that raise serious moral issues. They see sports either as mere instruments for gaining fame and fortune or as play, something we do for fun and recreation. However, as the headlines of our daily newspapers show all too frequently, serious moral issues do arise in sports.

But can moral issues be critically examined? Is rational argument even possible in ethics? Aren't moral views just matters of opinion? Can moral principles be rationally evaluated and defended or are they mere expressions of personal feelings that are not even the sorts of things that can be rationally evaluated or examined?

Ethics and Moral Reasoning

If reasoned ethical discourse is impossible, rational inquiry into ethical issues in sports is impossible. Although we cannot consider all possible reasons for skepticism about whether rationally justifiable moral positions can be developed, one widely cited reason for doubting the objectivity of ethics is relativism. Because relativism is so widely suggested as a basis for skepticism about the role of reason in ethics, a brief discussion of it will prove helpful. The remainder of this book attempts to consider moral issues in sports rationally. Clearly, if this attempt succeeds, it counts as an example of reasoned inquiry in ethics.

Relativism

Perhaps the most widely cited position that rejects the rationality and objectivity of ethical discourse is relativism. In his best-selling book, *The Closing of the American Mind*, Allen Bloom blames relativism for much of what he sees as the moral and educational decay infecting American universities. According to Bloom, "There is one thing a professor can be absolutely certain of: Almost every student entering the university believes, or says he believes, that truth is relative."[5] Relativism is so widely supported, according to Bloom, because its opposite is (incorrectly, as we will see) identified with a kind of intolerant and dogmatic absolutism. The price we pay for this misidentification is our inability to formulate, articulate, and defend standards we think are correct. But just what is relativism in ethics?

Actually, no one position has a unique claim to the title of relativism.[6] Rather, relativism is more like a family of related positions that share such features as the rejection of a universal outlook or perspective, and the suspicion of principles that claim to be true or justifiable for all. According to *descriptive* relativism, the moral judgments people make and the values they hold arise from or are relative to their culture, socioeconomic state, or ethnic and religious background. For example, secular culture in the West tends to be permissive of sexual contact between consenting adults; but such contacts have been much more strictly regulated at other times and in other places. In the world of sports, some cultures may place more value than others on winning and less on, say, the aesthetic appeal of play. This form of relativism is descriptive in that it is making a factual claim about the origin or empirical basis of our values. It claims to tell us where *in fact* our values originate, not what we *ought* to think about them.

What does descriptive relativism have to do with whether our moral beliefs and judgments are or can be rationally justified? It is sometimes argued that if descriptive relativism is true, there cannot be objectivity or rationality in ethics. No one's ethical judgments would be any more justifiable or correct than anyone else's. Rather, people's ethical judgments would be mere subjective claims based on their distinct and different backgrounds. In this view, our moral values are the prejudices we absorbed as children. Perhaps they were presented to us as self-evident truths. In reality, they are only the blinders of our particular culture or group.

Accordingly, it is sometimes claimed that skepticism about the rationality and objectivity of ethics follows from descriptive relativism. Skepticism denies that we can know whether ethical beliefs or claims are justified or whether some are more reasonable and more defensible than others. This kind of philosophical skepticism needs to be distinguished from an ordinary and perhaps healthy kind of skepticism in ordinary life that cautions us not to accept the opinions of others at face value but to examine whether they are well supported. Philosophical skepticism of the kind at issue here denies that our ethical or moral views ever can be well supported, or that we can know which moral views are rationally warranted and which are not. Ordinary skepticism cautions us to look for evidence for our views, but philosophical skepticism questions whether it is even possible, even in principle, to provide evidence or rational support for our ethical views.

Others have suggested that descriptive relativism implies not skepticism but ethical (value) relativism. Ethical relativism is the view that each culture's moral code is right for that culture. For example, according to ethical relativism, repressive sexual practices are morally right for cultures that have such practices embedded in their moral codes but not for more liberal cultures or groups. Ethical relativism differs from skepticism in that skepticism denies that any ethical perspective is more justifiable or reasonable than any other. Ethical relativism, on the other hand, endorses an ethical view—namely, what is right is what your culture says is right.

What is the significance of these views for the ethical analysis of sports? If skepticism is correct, it follows that we cannot justify any position on questions of ethics that arise in sports, since skepticism denies that any ethical perspective is more justified than any other. For example, we could not justify either the claim that the use of anabolic steroids to enhance performance is warranted or the claim that it is unwarranted. On the other hand, if ethical relativism is correct, what is morally justifiable depends on the group to which one belongs. Perhaps the use of performance-enhancing drugs is permissible for cultures that find it permissible but not for those that find it impermissible.

Does descriptive relativism really have the skeptical implications examined above? Is relativism acceptable in the forms discussed above?

A Critique of Relativism

First, consider the argument that because the thesis of descriptive relativism—that moral codes of different cultures and groups conflict—is true, therefore moral skepticism is true. To evaluate this argument, we need to consider what general conditions an argument must meet to be acceptable. If the premises of an argument are to justify a conclusion, two fundamental requirements must be satisfied. (1) The premises must be true. False statements cannot be acceptable evidence for the truth of a conclusion. (2) The premises must be logically relevant to the conclusion; otherwise, the conclusion could not follow from the premises because they would be irrelevant to it. For example, we would not accept the conclusion that "The major goal of competitive sports is winning" on the basis of the claim that "Washington, D.C., is the capital of the United States." Even though the latter claim is true, it has nothing to do with the former claim and so cannot support it.

Consider again the argument that because the moral codes of different cultures and groups conflict, no set of moral judgments or principles can be correct, reasonable, or justified. First, the argument assumes that descriptive relativism is true, but is it? If descriptive relativism claims no more than that the moral codes, principles, and judgments accepted in different societies sometimes conflict, it may well be true. But it leaves open the possibility that, behind the apparent disagreement, there is deeper agreement on some morally fundamental values. The area of agreement might constitute the basis of cross-cultural universal values that some social scientists and sociobiologists have claimed to detect. For example, people from a wide variety of cultural, ethnic, socioeconomic, and religious backgrounds condemn incest, torture, and the random killing of members of one's community. Protests against Communist regimes in China and the old Soviet Union and, more recently, against Islamic fundamentalism in Iran are also evidence for the broad appeal of freedom.

This point can be taken further. Apparent surface disagreement can disguise deeper agreement in values. For instance, consider a dispute between a basketball coach and her assistant before a big game. The head coach wants to use a pressure defense to take advantage of her team's agility and the opponent's lack of speed. The assistant argues against this strategy because it may cause overanxious and inexperienced defensive players to commit too many fouls. In this example, there is disagreement over which tactics to follow. But behind the disagreement is a common value, or principle, shared by both coaches. Each is trying to select the strategy that will lead to victory.

A parallel situation is possible in ethics. Suppose culture A believes that old people should be separated from the group and left to die when they can no longer contribute to the general welfare, but culture B disagrees. Clearly, there is a disagreement here, but both cultures might share deeper fundamental values as well. For one thing, the circumstances of each culture might differ. Culture A may barely be surviving at the subsistence level; culture B may be affluent and therefore able to care for its older members. Perhaps culture A consists of nomadic bands that must move fast to keep up with game. Arguably, each culture may accept the same basic principle of promoting the greater good for the greater number, but the principle might apply differently in the different circumstances in which each group finds itself. Accordingly, although the descriptive relativist is undoubtedly correct in pointing to moral disagreement among groups, it remains controversial whether there is fundamental disagreement about all values or whether underneath the surface disagreement most societies have a deeper acceptance of fundamental core values.

Suppose, however, that we concede for the sake of argument that there are no universally accepted values or moral principles. The greatest weakness of the relativist argument is that, even if this point is conceded, moral skepticism does not follow. The premise of descriptive relativism is logically irrelevant to supporting moral skepticism. If cultures or groups disagree about moral problems, this does not mean that there are no correct or justifiable resolutions to the dispute. Similarly, some cultures believe the world is flat and others believe it is round, but this does not by itself establish that there is no correct answer concerning the shape of the earth.[7] Whether a justifiable resolution of a dispute is possible depends on whether justifiable modes of ethical (or scientific) inquiry can be applied to it. Moral disagreement can arise just as much from ignorance of such modes of inquiry, misapplication of them, or factual disagreement (as when one group of athletes denies and one asserts that steroids cause harmful side effects), as it can from the impossibility of distinguishing reasonable moral claims from those that are less reasonable. Disagreement alone is not sufficient to show that no rational modes of inquiry exist, let alone that they are insufficient to resolve the issue at hand. (Similarly, moral agreement that some values are justified does not establish by itself that they are justifiable; that depends on the reasons that can be provided in their support. In disagreement or agreement, justification depends on the kinds of *reasons* that can be provided to support our moral views, not simply on whether others share our values.)

Of course, the failure of descriptive relativism to establish moral skepticism doesn't show that there is a correct resolution to moral controversies, only that the presence of cultural or group diversity does not rule out such a resolution in advance of inquiry.

Does descriptive relativism do any better in establishing ethical relativism—the thesis that what your group or culture says is right or wrong for you is really right or wrong for you? For example, is it morally right to take anabolic steroids to enhance your performance in sports just because your peer group or even your culture says it is right?

Once again, no such implication follows. For reasons similar to those outlined above, just because groups may disagree on ethical issues does not show that each group's moral views are right for its members. One might just as well argue that if your culture believes the earth is flat, you ought to believe the earth is flat as well. If such an absurd view were correct, we would never be justified in trying to correct or change the view of our culture or peer group even if we had strong reasons for thinking their views were unfounded. Ethical relativism has the unacceptable implication that the views of our culture or of other groups to which we belong are acceptable just as they are. But surely, even if our peer group does advocate the use of performance-enhancing drugs in sports, they are not automatically correct to do so. We need to engage in ethical inquiry and argument to see whether the best reasons support their view rather than to accept it merely because it is the view of the group to which we belong.[8]

Therefore, moral disagreement among cultures, or other kinds of groups, should not deter us from engaging in a moral inquiry designed to subject moral claims in sports or elsewhere to rational criticism and evaluation. Moreover, such a view does not make us dogmatic or intolerant of the views of others. Indeed, tolerance and the avoidance of dogmatism are themselves values, and many think they have objective support. If moral skepticism were true, there would be no rational basis for tolerance if cultures disagreed about its value. Accordingly, commitment to rational inquiry in ethics does not make us arrogant dogmatists; if anything, it makes us open to the insights of those who may be different from us so long as we are willing to subject their views as well as our own to the test of reasoned inquiry in ethics. Thus, commitment to moral inquiry can help free us from insular prejudices and allow us to test our views by seeing whether they can stand up to the reasoned criticism of others.

Absolutophobia: The Seductive Appeal of Crude Relativism

In spite of such serious intellectual weaknesses, crude forms of relativism and skepticism appeal to many, especially to some college students. This subgroup of students seems unwilling to make moral judgments and views those who do as opinionated or "judgmental." I saw an extreme version of such an attitude some years ago when one of my own students wrote on an examination, "Of course I don't like the Nazis, but who am I to say they are wrong?"[9]

Why do so many people, particularly students, believe that some of the greatest crimes in human history, including genocide and slavery, should not be morally
condemned? I doubt there is one root cause of such attitudes, but I do suggest that
certain intellectual errors contribute to such an attitude.

First, moral language is sometimes misused to bully or intimidate people into
accepting the speaker's position. Moreover, moral positions that are held fanatically
and asserted dogmatically leave no room for reasonable response. Morality may
then be seen as a refuge for dogmatists who assert but never question their own absolutes and use the fear of being labeled immoral or unfair to force people to adopt
favored views. Part of the reaction against "political correctness" on college cam-
puses perhaps reflects resentment against ardent activists trying to impose their
views on others. Moral language is also the weapon of religious zealots and extreme
right-wing politicians.

However, such misuse of moral language does not imply that moral judgments
cannot be justified. Indeed, to favor tolerance, judiciousness, and appeal to reason
over dogmatism and zealotry is to favor one set of values over another and therefore
makes a moral judgment. Respect for the views of others and willingness to reason
with them about values is as much a moral outlook as dogmatism and fanaticism.

Second, many reject "absolutes." But moral judgments about what is right or
wrong, fair or unfair, or just or unjust seem to presuppose the very absolutes we are
told do not exist. The first thing to note about rejecting absolutes is we don't really
know what an "absolute" is supposed to be. But if it means that a simple rule is self-
evident and immune from rational scrutiny, it is far from clear that moral judgments are absolutes. But if an absolute is a reasonable claim well supported by
evidence, surely we are all committed to absolutes. (The denial that absolutes exist
in this sense seems itself to be one, since presumably it purports to be reasonable,
well supported, and true.)

Whether moral claims can be supported by critical rational inquiry can best be
seen by exploring moral issues and not by dismissing moral claims through fear of
committing an absolute (absolutophobia), no matter how murky that concept may
be.

Perhaps another reason for reluctance to make moral judgments is an interpretation (or misinterpretation) of multiculturalism. Although "multiculturalism" stands
for a family of related positions, not just one central doctrine, most multiculturalists
hold that we should learn to understand and respect cultures other than our own.
But sophisticated multiculturalists ought not to blur this claim by asserting that we
should not criticize the moral views of others. This second claim would prohibit

them from criticizing opponents' views of multiculturalism, or from objecting to intolerance of others. Since multiculturalists want to assert that their approaches are morally more acceptable than those they reject, they would undermine themselves by embracing extreme forms of moral relativism and skepticism.

I suggest that many who express skepticism about morality are not true skeptics or relativists but instead hold a disguised morality that tolerates and respects diversity. By denying the moral basis to condemn evils such as the Holocaust, slavery, and racial oppression, such people are unable to condemn any wrongdoing; they cannot even defend the values that lead them to tolerate and respect diversity to begin with. If the legitimate desire to avoid moral fanaticism drives us to see the condemnation of any evil, however great, as an unwarranted intellectual arrogance, then the truly arrogant and the truly fanatical will never fear moral censure, no matter what evil they choose to inflict.

Moral Reasoning

Dogmatism and fanaticism can be avoided if we base our moral views on reasoning and encourage critical examination of them. But how are we to distinguish cogent from weak or incorrect moral reasoning? Philosophers and ethicists have not agreed that any one theory of moral reasoning is the correct one or even whether theories of moral reasoning are morally neutral or are themselves part of a substantive code of ethics. Some philosophers have serious doubts about the objectivity of moral judgments, although not on the crude grounds criticized in earlier sections. Perhaps the best way to determine whether moral judgments can be rationally assessed is to examine moral issues in detail. We will do that, in connection with sport, in subsequent chapters. The following comments may be helpful in assessing moral judgment and argument.

At a minimum, it is doubtful that one can evaluate moral arguments with the precision and rigor appropriate to mathematics. This does not mean that we cannot recognize the difference between well-supported and poorly supported positions. As Aristotle suggested, we should "look for precision in each class of things just so far as the nature of the subject admits; it is evidently equally foolish to accept probable reasoning from a mathematician and to demand from a rhetorician scientific proofs."[10] This does not mean that ethical reasoning must be imprecise; it may resemble a sound case made by a skilled judicial scholar rather than strict mathematical proof.

Although good moral reasoning cannot be totally uncontroversial, the following three criteria will prove especially helpful. First, moral reasoning must be impartial. In evaluating a moral issue, we are not asking "what's in it for me?" We want to see what position is supported by the best reasons, impartially considered. Moral deliberation has a broader perspective than self-interest. Thus, we cannot justify the claim that "the use of steroids by Olympic athletes to enhance their performance is morally legitimate" simply by claiming "the use of steroids will help me gain a gold medal in the Olympics." The latter claim may show that the use of steroids is in the speaker's interest; it does nothing to show that personal interest is the only relevant moral factor.

Philosophers have proposed various models or theories of impartial reasoning. For example, R. M. Hare has suggested that impartial moral reasoning requires that we imagine ourselves in the place of all those affected by the action or policy being evaluated, giving no special weight to any one perspective.[11] John Rawls of Harvard, author of the important book *A Theory of Justice,* has suggested that in thinking of social justice we must reason as if we were behind a veil of ignorance that hides from us the knowledge of our individual characteristics or social circumstances.[12] Thus, impartiality prohibits us from arbitrarily assigning special privileges to our own race or ethnic group because it would be irrational to do so if we had to consider such a policy impartially from the perspective of all affected, as Hare requires, or in ignorance of our own group membership, as Rawls suggests.

Regardless of the similarities and differences between philosophical accounts of impartiality, the core idea of impartiality is that we are prohibited from arbitrarily assigning special weight to our own position or interests. Thus, a referee in a basketball game, to be impartial, must make calls in accord with the rules, not in accord with the team he or she likes better.

Second, the positions we take must be systematically consistent. For example, if one holds that it is wrong to assault another person but that it is permissible for a professional hockey player to assault another player during a game, one's position appears inconsistent. Unless one can show that the two situations are relevantly dissimilar, one or the other position must be given up. If the two situations are similar in the relevant moral respects, assault in one cannot be permissible and assault in the other impermissible because there would be no difference between them to justify the difference in judgment made about them.

Third, the principles one uses in making moral decisions must account for reflective judgments about clear moral examples. Thus, if one believed it was permissible to turn in a wrong score in a golf tournament merely to benefit oneself, and thus essentially win by lying, that would normally be grounds for rejecting, or at least questioning, that principle in the first place. That is because we start with a firm conviction that competitors in a golf tournament should not lie about their scores. Of course, and this is what makes our third criterion controversial, we must be sure that our reactions to situations are critical and reflective, not merely unanalyzed, culturally conditioned responses. It is all too easy to be influenced by cultural, social, and even biologically based presuppositions. For example, our initial reaction that it is permissible for hometown fans to boo and wave while an opposing basketball player shoots a crucial foul shot may simply be a prejudice we share with other hometown fans. However, some of our judgments about particular situations may be reflective and unbiased and therefore allow us to check our principles.

Thus, our reflective reaction to actual and hypothetical examples may be a useful guide for moral inquiry; without such consideration, our principles would be empty abstractions. Conversely, we can criticize an abstract principle by showing that its application would lead to unacceptable consequences for concrete action.

The more an ethical theory survives counterexample and criticism, the more confidence we would seem to be entitled to place in it. Just as we expose our scientific theories to test, so we should test our moral perspectives by exposing them to the criticism of others. It may make us feel good to cling to our entrenched moral views by never exposing them to opposing views. The price we pay for such a policy is to prevent ourselves from discovering errors that might be recognized by others. We also lose opportunities for confirming our views when we refute the objections of our critics. Just as a scientific theory gains credibility by surviving tests, so may a moral view gain credibility by surviving criticism in the crucible of moral debate.

From a critical perspective, a moral view can be undermined by at least three strategies. We can argue that such a view would not be held if impartially considered, that its various parts are inconsistent or inharmonious, or that the view has unacceptable implications for action. Nothing said so far implies that only one moral perspective, code of ethics, or set of principles will survive moral criticism. It is possible that all who go through an extended process of moral inquiry will hold the same moral view; but it is equally possible that a kind of moral pluralism will flourish as well. It is unlikely that serious and extended moral inquiry will rate all moral perspectives as equally justified. Some will be rejected as inconsistent, biased, vulnerable to counterexample, or deficient on some other appropriate ground. Thus, although there is no guarantee that our criteria of moral reasoning are the only defensible ones or that they will yield strictly determinate results for all investigators, they at least provide guidance in the rational evaluation of moral issues. By applying them, we employ reason in ethics.

Let us turn now to moral issues in sports. The discussion will ask us to make and evaluate moral judgments about controversial cases; hence the importance of the discussion about the justifiability of moral judgment. The challenge will be to develop positions that we can impartially affirm, that are consistent with our views in related areas, and that rely on principles whose consequences for action are acceptable. We will begin by examining a fundamental issue: the importance that should be assigned to competition and winning in sports.

2

Competition, a Mutual Quest for Excellence

Winning is not the most important thing; it's the only thing." This widely cited claim, often attributed (perhaps falsely) to the late Vince Lombardi, famous former coach of the Green Bay Packers, raises a host of issues that are central to the moral evaluation of sports.1 What importance should be assigned to winning in athletic competition? Consider sportswriter Grantland Rice's declaration, "When the one Great Scorer comes to mark against your name, He writes not that you won or lost but how you played the Game," and the rejoinder by coach Forest Evashevski that one might as well say of a surgeon that it matters not whether his patient lives or dies but only how he makes the cut.2

Questions about the importance of winning are closely tied to but not identical with questions about the value of competition. Should we be concerned primarily with winning or with competing well? Is competition in sport a good thing or can it be harmful or even immoral? Should winning be the most important goal of an athlete? What degree of emphasis should be placed on competitive success and winning in athletics?

Competition in Sports
At first glance, competition seems to be the very nature of sports. We speak of sporting events as competitions or contests, evaluate athletes as good or bad

competitors, and refer to other teams as opponents. But perhaps the connection between sports and competition is far looser than the initial reaction might suggest. Thus, someone can play golf or run a marathon just for the enjoyment of the activity. Indeed, all sports can be played noncompetitively. Men and women may participate for exercise, to forget about work, to enjoy the company of friends, and to enjoy the outdoors. Another goal of participation might be improvement. Such players, often described as competing with themselves, aim not at defeating opponents but at improving their own performances. Still others may have the aesthetic goal of performing the movements of their sport with skill and grace. For example, playground basketball players may value outstanding moves more than defeating their opponents. A leading amateur golfer, after years of hard practice, says she wants "to make a swing that you know is as close to perfection as you can get. And you say, 'Boy, look at what I did.' That's all it is."[3]

But just because a player does not aim for competitive success or is not motivated by it, it doesn't follow that competition isn't part of the sport. A group of people may play softball just to interact with friends, but the point of the game, as defined by the rules, is to score more runs than the opponent. Even if the principal desire of the participants is to get exercise, they are doing so by trying to achieve the goals of the game as prescribed by the rules. For example, even if the outfielder is playing primarily to escape from pressures of work, she tries to catch a fly ball rather than just let it drop because a successful catch may prevent the opponent from scoring. We need to distinguish, then, two different kinds of questions. First, should the principal goal or motives of participants in sport be competitive and, if so, to what degree? Second, do sports, in so far as they are games, structurally involve a competitive element?

Critics of competition in sports do not object so much to games that have an internal competitive element; rather, as we will see, they object to the defeat of an opponent as a main desire or goal. Critics also object to institutionalizing this attitude and to making competition in sports a social practice.

Competition in sports in the fullest sense can be thought of as participation in sports contests with the intent or major goal of defeating an opponent. In such clear cases, competition seems to be a zero-sum game. Because not all competitors can defeat an opponent, defeat by one precludes a like attainment by the other in the same contest.

Further, the clearest examples of athletic competition involve structured games such as baseball, football, basketball, and tennis, all of which are governed by a set of rules defining permissible moves. For example, the rules of basketball that stipulate what it is to score, foul, or travel are *constitutive* rules. If players were unaware of such rules or made no attempt to follow them, they could not be playing basketball (although minimal modifications might be acceptable in informal play). Constitutive rules should be distinguished from rules of strategy, such as "dribble only if there is no faster way of advancing the ball up court." Rules of strategy are general suggestions about how to play the game well; constitutive rules determine what counts as a permissible move within the game itself.

Accordingly, competition in sports is the attempt to secure victory within the framework set by the constitutive rules. Some philosophers of sport, as we will see in Chapter 3, argue that cheaters cannot really win, since when they cheat they go outside the constitutive rules that define the game, and therefore do not even play it. In this chapter, we will explore the ethics of playing to win. Can a morally acceptable defense of competitive sports be developed? If such an ideal of competitive sports can be defended, we will be able to separate instances of competition in sports that are ethically defensible from those that are not; this knowledge can be applied in later chapters to concrete issues in sport.

The Critique of Competition in Sports

Why is it even necessary to make a moral evaluation of competition in sports? Isn't it enough to say simply that participants and spectators alike enjoy such competition? To critics of competition in sports, that is not enough. They argue that such competition is either inherently immoral or that it reinforces other social values that are undesirable. Many persons, including some professional athletes, who have criticized competition and overemphasis on winning have proposed a more relaxed attitude toward sports, at least at most levels of amateur play, than sanctioned by the competitive creed.

On the other hand, proponents of competition in sports have argued for its moral value. General Douglas MacArthur, an American hero of World War II, may have overstated the case when he maintained that participation in competitive sports "is a vital character builder" that "molds the youth of our country for their roles as custodians of the republic."[4] Overstated or not, that view is widely shared.

A moral evaluation of competition in sports is necessary if we are to make a rational assessment of such conflicting views. It is not enough to assume uncritically that competition in athletics must be morally permissible simply because one enjoys it. After all, a racist majority may enjoy terrorizing members of the minority racial group, but that doesn't make it right. Perhaps competition in sports is harmful or unjust in ways not acknowledged by many of its proponents; for this reason, the critics' views need rational examination.

It will be useful to divide the arguments about the morality of competition in sports into two kinds. The first is concerned with the good or bad consequences of competitive practices, either to competitors themselves or society at large. The second is concerned not with the effects of competition but with its intrinsic character.

The Consequences of Competition

One way of evaluating competition in sports is to assess its consequences. Surely, whether a practice has good or bad effects on other people is relevant to moral evaluation. Yet, although the strategy of evaluating consequences is sound, acting on it may be more difficult.

First, are we to look only at the effects upon ourselves or our team, or are we to look more broadly at the consequences for all participants, or for everyone affected by athletic competition, including long-term social effects on society at large? The important ethical theory known as utilitarianism holds that an action or practice is morally justified only if it has better consequences for all affected than the alternatives.[5]

Utilitarianism sounds like a relatively simple approach to ethics. Just do a cost-benefit analysis on the effects of the act or practice being evaluated. But utilitarianism raises complex issues of theory and practice before it can even be applied to a problem. For example, what are we to count as a good or bad consequence? In economic analysis, costs and benefits can often be measured in monetary profits and losses, but what is to count as a cost or benefit in ethics? Should pleasure and pain be the criteria, as classical utilitarians such as Jeremy Bentham and John Stuart Mill suggest? Are there other criteria, such as excellence in performance, achievement, or knowledge, that should also count? For example, is a well-played game of greater intrinsic value than a poorly played game even if the participants of both games experience the same levels of pleasure and pain? If we say that only pleasure and pain count, our theory may be too narrow. If we add other goods, such as excellence of performance, how are we to aggregate them with pleasure and pain to reach an overall total?

Moreover, even if we can agree on criteria of good and bad consequences, they may admit of different interpretations. For example, should we identify benefits with what actual participants seem to want or with what they would want if they were better informed and more rational? Suppose, for example, that Jones, who sees herself as a potential superstar, despises practices because of her coach's emphasis on teamwork, but would value the practices if she were better informed about the benefits of teamwork and more honest about her own abilities. Are the practices beneficial to Jones or not?

None of this totally discredits utilitarianism. We all sometimes assess the consequences of behavior on our own lives and others. An ethical theory that ignored the consequences of actions or practices on human life would be hard to defend. How many of us, for example, would advocate an action, however noble, knowing that one of its consequences would be the painful death of millions? But even though any satisfactory ethic must give some weight to the effects of acts or policies on human life, the choice of what framework we should adopt for evaluating the consequences will often be controversial.

In addition, if we are to evaluate the effects of competition in sports, another problem arises. Just what practices are we evaluating? Competition in sports can range from professional athletic contests to interscholastic competition to backyard contests among friends. Moreover, it is important to distinguish competition as it is practiced and as it ought to be practiced. Thus, even if competitive practices often have bad consequences, we should not necessarily conclude that competition in sports is morally indefensible. Perhaps competition in sports as carried out has harmful consequences that could be avoided if sports were properly conducted.

Accordingly, any utilitarian evaluation of competition in sports will rest on sometimes unstated and often controversial assumptions. In assessing a utilitarian evaluation's significance, we should identify just what presuppositions have been employed. For example, suppose a study shows that participation in sports has little positive effect on character development. To evaluate the significance of the study, we would need to know what traits of character are considered positive, what forms of competition have been studied, and whether the study has considered only competition as actually practiced or as it should be practiced from the moral point of view.

An exhaustive analysis of the consequences of competition in sports is beyond the scope of this study, but it is important to remember the philosophical and methodological assumptions underlying such work. Given that the presuppositions of any utilitarian analysis are likely to be controversial, utilitarianism by itself probably cannot provide a decisive evaluation of competition in sports.

For example, we know that proponents of competitive sports claim that participation promotes loyalty, discipline, commitment, a concern for excellence, and a "never say die" attitude. These views are often expressed by well-known slogans, sometimes posted on locker room walls, such as "a winner never quits, a quitter never wins" and "when the going gets tough, the tough get going." That athletics offer unique opportunities for character development is a common general assertion.

Even if we restrict ourselves to effects upon competitors, such claims are difficult to document. Thus, with regard to altruism, one recent study concludes: "Most athletes indicate low interest in receiving support and concern from others, low need to take care of others, and low need for affiliation. Such a personality seems necessary to achieve victory over others." More generally, the authors reported: "We found no empirical support for the tradition that sport builds character. . . . It seems that the personality of the ideal athlete is not the result of the molding process, but comes out of the ruthless selection process that occurs at all levels of sport. . . . Horatio Alger success—in sport or elsewhere—comes only to those who already are mentally fit, resilient, and strong."[6]

Although no study is by itself decisive, this passage does have significant methodological implications. In particular, even if participants in competitive sports do manifest desirable character traits to an unusual degree, it does not follow that participation in sports caused these traits to develop; they may have been there all along. Correlation should not be confused with causation.

This point is forcefully made in a widely discussed study by officers of the prestigious Mellon Foundation called *The Game of Life*. The authors, James L. Shulman and William G. Bowen, rely on an extensive database that allows them to compare student athletes from highly selective colleges and universities with other students from the same institutions. Bowen and Shulman argue that although athletes may well show especially high levels of teamwork and ability to cooperate with others to achieve a common goal, the athletes had tended to exhibit these traits before participating in college athletics. Therefore, the traits help account for athletic success, not the opposite.[7]

This point, even if correct, does cut in different directions. If we must not take for granted that positive character traits associated with participation in sports are caused by such participation, we must be equally cautious in assuming that negative character traits associated with participation are caused by it as well. Thus, it has been suggested that "athletes whose sense of identity and self-worth is entirely linked to athletic achievement often experience an identity crisis when the athletic career has ended, and it becomes necessary to move on to something else."[8] This statement may be true generally of hard-driving individuals who face significant career changes in fields other than sport. Would anyone be surprised by the claim that "executives whose sense of identity and self-worth is entirely linked to achievement in business often experience an identity crisis when their careers end and it becomes necessary to move on to something else"? Perhaps anyone sincerely committed to an endeavor would feel a sense of loss over change, which is not necessarily bad.

Moreover, even though there may be no direct and demonstrable connection between participation in competitive sports and desirable character development, there may be more subtle and indirect connections. Harry Edwards, while acknowledging that competitive sports do not build character from scratch, suggests that participation may reinforce and encourage the development of preexisting character traits.[9]

It is not easy, then, to show that participation does or does not promote specific character traits. Similarly, although it is not easy to show that a liberal arts education affects the values of students, we do not conclude that there are no effects. Do the alumni of the highly selective colleges and universities studied in *The Game of Life* tend to succeed in their careers because of their fine education? Or do the colleges and universities in question merely preselect those applicants whom anyone would predict as the most likely to succeed? We surely need to be careful about a double standard in attributing the positive character traits of athletes to preselection yet refusing to apply the same argument to our own favorite social and educational practices.

Even if competitive sports have less impact on character development than many have claimed, they still may play a major role in expressing and illustrating our values; we might call this the expressive function of sports.[10] For example, athletic competition may illustrate the value of dedication and teamwork by publicly manifesting the excellence attained through the cultivation of those traits. Close contests can bring out courage and loyalty. By welcoming challenges in sports, participants and spectators can affirm and exhibit such virtues.

Critics of competitive sports may reply that athletic competition can also illustrate indefensible values, such as the commitment to win at all costs. When applied to actual competitive practices, this response sometimes has force; and if competition is *inherently* immoral, competitive sports may express that inherent immorality as well.

Evaluating the social practice of competitive athletics by seeing whether its consequences are harmful or beneficial raises such complex issues that a decisive and uncontroversial consequential analysis is currently unavailable. However, consequences may not be the most significant part of the ethical story. Competition, the critics contend, cannot satisfy legitimate ethical requirements that are nonconsequential in character. Are they right?

Competition As a Mutual Quest for Excellence
Competition, Selfishness, and the Quest for Excellence

Perhaps the most important criticism of the moral worth of competition is that it is inherently selfish and egoistic. Because competitive activities are zero-sum games, one person's victory is another's defeat. As we have seen, the internal goal of competition is to defeat an opponent and win the contest.

Some critics of competition throughout society, among them political theorist John Schaar, see the competitive society as a very unattractive place. It reduces human interaction to "a contest in which each man competes with his fellows for scarce goods, a contest in which there is never enough for everybody, and where one man's gain is usually another's loss."[11] Michael Fielding identifies competition with "working against others in a spirit of selfishness."[12]

The critics argue, then, that the goal of competition is to enhance the position of one competitor at the expense of others. Thus, by its very nature, competition is selfish. Since selfish concern for oneself at the expense of others is immoral, it follows that competition is immoral as well. Note that this criticism, unlike utilitarian arguments, is not directed at the consequences of competitive sport but at its very nature.

These nonconsequentialist critics of competitive sports do not argue only against debased forms of competition, such as cheating. After all, virtually everyone acknowledges that competitive sports are morally objectionable when players are taught to cheat to win or when teams are so unequally matched that participants risk injury or are intentionally humiliated by opponents. The critics, however, object to competitive sports at their best. Even supposing that the participants are playing fairly, is competition in sports still not selfish and egoistic?

The argument that competitive sports are selfish by their very nature is not without some intuitive force because, in athletic competition, if X wins, Y loses. If they are good competitors, X and Y each try to win. Nevertheless, even if the argument that competition is essentially selfish is justifiable when applied to economic competition in the market, which is hardly self-evident, it faces special difficulties when applied to sports and athletics.

For one thing, the idea of competition in sports as an unrestricted war of all against all seems grossly inaccurate. Even though team sports involve competition between opponents, they also involve cooperation among team members. In many sports, even at the professional level, it is common for opponents to encourage and even instruct each other in the off season or between contests. This altruism can even be overdone. One widely cited explanation for professional golf star Ben

Crenshaw's slump during the early 1980s was the oversolicitousness of his fellow players, who bombarded him with remedies that many believed confused him still further. Critics might reply that such examples show that even professional athletes find it morally impossible to live according to a strict competitive ethic. But such cooperative behavior can be regarded as part of a defensible competitive ethic, based not on the idea of a war of all against all but on the value of meeting the challenges provided by competition in sports.

As we have noted, competition in sports takes place within a context of binding constitutive rules. Good competition requires competitors to forgo breaking the rules for momentary advantages. Commitment to this ideal is perhaps best illustrated by the behavior of athletes in individual sports, from weekend tennis players to professional golfers, who call penalties on themselves in the heat of competition, sometimes at great financial cost. In many sports, rules are enforced by officials. But although it is legitimate to question the calls of officials, no one believes they ought not to apply the rules at all, or that they should apply them selectively.

In addition to obligations to obey the constitutive rules of the sport, there are obligations of competitive fairness that also restrict selfishness in sports. Thus, competitive success seems insignificant, or even unethical, if it is obtained by stacking the deck against one side, or by scheduling vastly inferior opponents for all or much of one's season.

Finally, selfishness in competitive sports is often criticized. The basketball player who is overly concerned with how many points she scores rather than with whether her team wins is criticized for being selfish, an inexplicable practice if selfishness is the norm in competitive athletics.

At this point, critics might concede that normative restrictions apply to selfish behavior in athletic competition, although they might still argue that just as limited war is still war, so minimally constrained selfishness is still selfishness. To answer this point, we need a fuller account of competition in sports. Let us begin by considering a Yale-Princeton football game played in 1895. Princeton was winning 16–10, but Yale was right on the Princeton goal line with a chance to turn the tide on the very last play of the game:

> The clamor ceased once absolutely, and the silence was even
> more impressive than the tumult that had preceded it. . . . While
> they [Yale] were lining up for that last effort the cheering dies
> away, yells both measured and inarticulate stopped and the place

was so still . . . you could hear the telegraph instruments chirping like crickets from the side. Yale scored to win the game on a brilliant run. It is not possible to describe that run. It would be as easy to explain how a snake disappears through the grass, or an eel slips from your fingers, or to say how a flash of linked lightning wriggles across the sky.[13]

Is the important point here simply that Yale won and that Princeton lost? Edwin Delattre, former president of St. John's College of Annapolis, has drawn a different lesson from this episode and the many like it that take place in all seasons and at all levels of competition:

Such moments are what make the game worth the candle. Whether amidst the soft lights and sparkling balls of a billiard table, or the rolling terrain of a lush fairway, or in the violent and crashing pits where linemen struggle, it is the moments where no letup is possible, when there is virtually no tolerance for error, which make up the game. The best and most satisfying contests maximize these moments and minimize respite from pressure.[14]

According to Delattre, these moments of test rather than victory or defeat are the source of the value of competition in sports:

The testing of one's mettle in competitive athletics is a form of self discovery. . . . The claim of competitive athletics to importance rests squarely on their providing us opportunities for self discovery which might otherwise have been missed. . . . They provide opportunities for self-discovery, for concentration and intensity of involvement, for being carried away by the demands of the contest . . . with a frequency seldom matched elsewhere. . . . This is why it is a far greater success in competitive athletics to have played well under pressure of a truly worthwhile opponent and lost than to have defeated a less worthy or unworthy one where no demands were made.[15]

Delattre's comments suggest that although it is essential to good competition that the competitors try as hard as they can to achieve victory, the principal value of athletic competition lies not in winning but in overcoming the challenge presented by a worthy opponent. On this view, good competition presupposes a *cooperative* effort by competitors to generate the best possible challenge to each other. Each has the obligation to the other to try his or her best. Although one wins the contest and the other loses, each gains by trying to meet the challenge.

If this view has force, competition in sports should be regarded and engaged in not as a zero-sum game but as a mutually acceptable quest for excellence through challenge. Underlying the good sports contest, in effect, is an implicit social contract under which both competitors accept the obligation to provide a challenge for opponents according to the rules of the sport. Competition in sports is ethically defensible, in this view, when it is engaged in voluntarily as part of a mutual quest for excellence.

This does not mean that all competition in sports is ethically defensible; actual practice may not satisfy the requirements of the mutual quest for excellence. It does say that competition in sports is ethically defensible when it does satisfy such requirements.

Competitive sports as a mutual quest for excellence not only emphasizes the cooperative side of athletic contests and the acceptance of the challenge from the point of view of all the competitors but also explains much of our society's fascination with competitive sports. A. Bartlett Giamatti, former president of Yale and Commissioner of Baseball, emphasized the quest for excellence:

> When . . . a person on the field or fairway, rink, floor, or track, performs an act that surpasses—despite his or her evident mortality, his or her humanness—whatever we have seen or heard of or could conceive of doing ourselves, then we have witnessed . . . an instant of complete coherence. In that instant, pulled to our feet, we are pulled out of ourselves. We feel what we saw, became what we perceived. The memory of that moment is deep enough to send us all out again and again, to reenact the ceremony, made of all the minor ceremonies to which spectator and player devote themselves, in the hopes that the moment will be summoned again and made again palpable.[16]

Now critics of competition in sports may become impatient. Sports events, conceived as part of a mutually acceptable quest for excellence, may indeed be ethically defensible, they might reply, but such a view does not justify competition in sports. Rather, they might claim, it replaces competitive sports with something else. What has been done is a verbal trick. "Competition" has been so redefined that it no longer refers to true competition at all, but rather to the quest for excellence, self-improvement, and self-knowledge through exposure to challenge. By emphasizing the quest for excellence, we have changed the aim of the sports contest from that of defeating opponents to the quest for self-development and achievement. The aim is no longer to defeat opponents but to reach certain standards of performance or to gain self-knowledge and development through trying to satisfy those standards. Competition in sports has been replaced by so-called "competition with oneself."

Is this charge correct? Let us consider the issue further.

Self-Development and Competition with Self

"Competition with self" suggests that athletes play against ghostly images of their earlier selves. Because there are no ghostly images and no presently existing earlier selves with whom to compete, this expression is potentially misleading. It is less paradoxical to speak of individuals as striving for self-development or self-improvement, not for self-competition.

Should participants in sports strive mainly for self-development or personal improvement? Is such improvement a more important or more ethically defensible goal than competitive success? After considering such questions, we will then consider whether competition, conceived of as a mutual quest for excellence, really is only a disguised way of talking about the quest for self-improvement.

The claim that improvement is an ethically better or more defensible goal than competitive success in sports presupposes first that an ethically relevant difference exists between the two and, second, that the difference contributes to the ethical superiority of the improvement model. What might that difference be? Perhaps the difference is that in aiming for improvement, we do not necessarily aim to beat others. We can all improve together, so the element of the zero-sum game is missing. Since all can improve together, to aim at improvement does not appear as selfish as intending to beat others seems selfish and egoistic to critics of competitive sports.

There are two defenses against such an approach. The first, as we have seen, is that competition thought of as a mutual quest for excellence is not necessarily selfish or a total zero-sum game. Although only one party can win, each cooperates in providing a mutually acceptable challenge to the other. Although not all competitors can win, there is a sense, as we will see, in which all the competitors in a well-played contest can meet the challenge and achieve excellence.

Second, and perhaps most important, we can question the degree to which the quest for self-improvement differs from competitive sports in an ethically relevant way. At the very least, the two approaches share some central features. For one thing, an especially significant criterion of improvement is change in one's competitive standing when measured against the performance of others. Perhaps the best way of judging one's progress is to see whether one is doing better against opponents now than in the past.

Doing better against opponents is not merely a contingent sign of improvement; often, what counts as playing well is logically determined by what counts as an appropriate competitive response to the moves of opponents. For example, it would be incorrect to say that Jones is playing good tennis if he is hitting crisp ground shots when intelligent play calls for charging the net. Similarly, it would be incorrect to say that Jones is improving if he continues to make such competitively inappropriate moves in match after match.

The conceptual point, then, is that achievement, improvement, or development cannot easily be divorced from comparison with the performance of others. Robert Nozick provided a pertinent illustration: "A man living in an isolated mountain village can sink 15 jump shots with a basketball out of 150 tries. Everyone else in the village can sink only one jump shot out of 150 tries. He thinks (as do the others) that he's very good at it. One day along comes Jerry West."[17]

The example illustrates that what counts as a significant achievement requires reference to the performance of others. What may not be so obvious is that judgments about what counts as a significant improvement also presupposes comparative evaluations about the performance of others. Before the arrival of a great professional basketball player such as Jerry West, the village star may have thought that improving his average to 17 out of 150 shots would constitute significant improvement. After the visit, even if it is acknowledged that no villager can ever match West's skill, the very criterion of significant improvement would have radically changed. At the very least, the more expert villagers should expect that, after reasonable practice, they should make at least 50 shots out of 150 tries. Before the visit, the "30-shot barrier" must have seemed as impossible to reach as breaking the four-minute mile must have seemed to runners of an earlier era.

Does this imply that an athlete seeking to improve really is implicitly competing with others? Such an athlete is striving to reach standards set by an appropriate reference group of others, at least if the improvement is thought of as an achievement. Thus, success or failure is partially determined by how others perform. Accordingly, those who value "competition with self" because it seems not to involve (possibly negative) comparisons with the performance of others may need to rethink their position. Although differences may remain, the quest for improvement and the quest for victory share an element of comparison with the performance of others. That is why the rhetoric of competition with self can be misleading; the appropriate reference group is not only an earlier self but also a reference class of fellow competitors. Even in judging our own performance, we are evaluating it by how it compares to a group with whom we believe it appropriate to compare ourselves.[18]

On the other hand, there are important differences between striving for improvement and striving for competitive success. In particular, the significant improvement of some participants does not preclude the improvement of others and may even facilitate it, as when the whole group improves. The attainment of victory by some, however, does preclude its attainment by the opposition. Although this difference may not be as important as critics allege, since everyone can meet the challenge of competition, it is true that although all participants can improve, not all participants can win. Competition emphasizes meeting the challenge set by an opponent but improvement emphasizes the development of one's own skills. Even if one can measure development only by examining competitive performance, the two goals are conceptually different. One can meet an opponent's challenge without improving one's past performance; and one can improve one's past performance while continuing to lose to a more skilled competitor.

Our discussion suggests three conclusions. First, although the quest for improvement and the quest to achieve competitive success by defeating opponents are different in important ways, they also have much in common. In particular, the attempt to improve involves the performance of fellow athletes, and so reaches beyond the self. Second, because the idea of competition as a mutual quest for excellence sees excellence achieved by meeting the challenge presented by an opponent, it differs from simply trying to improve. However, in both cases, excellence can be achieved through victory in the contest, as when two teams play their very best. Third, and perhaps most important, the defense of competition as a mutual quest for excellence avoids many of the objections to competitive excess that may have made "competition with self" seem more attractive than competition against others. As we have seen, athletic competition, conceived of as a mutual quest for excellence, is significantly cooperative; each competitor contracts to provide a challenge to the opponent, and each opponent can meet the challenge by playing well even though only one can win. So even though the goal or intent of the competitors may be to win, each can meet the challenge by playing well.

A different but significant point should also be considered. Suppose dancers were given the following advice: "It's unimportant whether you are good or bad dancers. Just try to get better and better every day." Surely it is important that dancers improve their performance, but isn't the level of achievement they have already attained also important? In the dance, we appreciate personal development, but we also value achievement and a skilled performance. If athletic performance is regarded as significant, skilled performance is important in sports as well. Competition is the mechanism by which achievement is measured and determined. Improvement is a desirable goal, but achievement is no less important or noble. Improvement, then, is a worthy goal towards which all competitors ought to strive. But it is not the only goal; high achievement in athletics can be equally worthy, and sometimes inspiring, and, as Giametti has suggested, even ennobling as well.

Competition, Selfishness, and Inequality

Let us return to the critics' arguments. Their major charge is that competitive sports are inherently selfish, a criticism that seems to ignore cooperation, a mutual quest for excellence through challenge. According to this conception, opponents cooperate in generating mutually acceptable challenges.

It is true that winning will normally be in a competitor's self-interest;[19] but even if victory is in one's *self-interest,* it does not follow that the pursuit of victory is *selfish.* If we define selfish behavior as self-interested behavior, then the trivial pursuit of victory is selfish because we have stipulated it to be so by definition. But is such a definition or characterization of selfishness acceptable?

Consider the following examples.

1. Jones is playing in a touch football game with friends. Jones says, "I'll be the quarterback." The others declare that they, too, want to be quarterbacks and suggest the position be shared. Jones replies, "It's my football! If you don't let me play quarterback, I'll take my ball and go home!"

2. Jones is in a spelling contest between two teams in her fifth grade class. She correctly spells a difficult word. As a result, her team wins and the other team loses.

The concept of selfishness is stretched too far if it is applied to both scenarios. Isn't there a significant difference between the first, in which Jones disregards the interests of others in favor of his own, and the second, in which each student is given a fair chance to succeed? Similarly, an important difference exists between trying to defeat an opponent within a mutually acceptable framework of rules and simply disregarding the interests of others. Thus, there is a significant, ethically relevant difference between athletic competition and selfishness.

To summarize the discussion of competition and selfishness, the charge that competition is intrinsically selfish faces several weighty objections. It does not take into account cooperation in competition, and it does not appreciate the ethical significance of competition conceived of as a mutual quest for excellence. It also rests on a far too broad conception of selfishness. Accordingly, unless the critic can reply satisfactorily to these objections, we may reject the claim that competition in sports is just another example of selfishness and greed. This is not to deny that competitors sometimes behave selfishly; rather, it is to deny that action within competitive sports must be selfish because of the nature of the activity.

Even if competition in sports is not intrinsically selfish, another feature may worry critics. Competitive sports, according to this second critical view, generate inequalities. We become winners and losers, successes and failures, stars and scrubs. Many of us are all too familiar with the slogans, popular with some coaches, that equate losing with failure, and that virtually assign "losers" to an inferior branch of the human race.

In practice, competition is too often used for making invidious distinctions. Making an error in a crucial game or situation is equated with a lack of drive or courage. One of the sadder features of organized sports for children is the emphasis parents and coaches sometimes place on winning. As a result, young players often become more concerned with avoiding errors, and the criticism and even ridicule that follows, than with enjoying the competition or developing fundamental skills. Thus, there is something to the claim that competitive sports generate inequalities and that these are sometimes harmful or unethical. But before we accept too broad a version of the criticism, some considerations must be examined.

First, we need to distinguish between whether a rule or practice generates a factual inequality or difference and whether that difference is unethical, unfair, or inequitable. Some inequalities may well be fair or equitable, as when an instructor gives a high grade to an excellent paper and a low grade to a poor paper. Whether inequalities or differences exist is one thing; whether they are morally defensible is quite another. Accordingly, it doesn't follow that every inequality generated by competitive sports is unethical, unfair, or inequitable.

It should be acknowledged, then, that competitive sports generate inequalities, and even that some of these inequalities, such as those generated by excessive emphasis on winning and losing in children's sports, are ethically objectionable. On the other hand, not all inequalities generated by competitive sports may be ethically objectionable.

Consider the distinction made by legal scholar Ronald Dworkin between the right to equal treatment, "which is the right to an equal distribution of some opportunity of resource or burden," and the right to treatment as an equal, which is the right "to be treated with the same respect and concern as anyone else."[20] Unlike equal treatment, equal respect and concern do not require the identical distribution of a good, such as playing time on a basketball team. Thus, if one of my children is ill and the other isn't, treatment as an equal does not require that I divide the sick child's medicine in half. Rather, giving all the medicine to the sick child is compatible with and may even be required by equal respect and concern for both children.[21] This suggests, as Dworkin maintains, that the right to treatment as an equal, or the right to equal respect and concern, is more fundamental ethically than the right to equal treatment. This is because factual inequalities in distribution, or what Dworkin calls unequal treatment, may or may not be defensible depending upon whether they are compatible with the showing of equal respect and concern to all affected.

Accordingly, even though competition in sports may lead to unequal treatment, such as different assignments of playing time to better and worse players on a team, this is not sufficient to show that competition in sports is inequitable or unjust. The critic must show not just a distinction between winners and losers but that this distinction violates the right to treatment as an equal or that it is unjustified in some different but equally fundamental moral way.

It is plausible to conclude that if people are treated with equal concern and respect, justified inequalities in distribution will emerge naturally. This is because part of treating persons with respect surely is treating them as beings "who are capable of forming and acting on intelligent conceptions of how their lives should be lived."[22] But people will have different conceptions of how their lives should be led and make their choices accordingly. For example, if critics prefer one novel over another, the author of the first novel may make more money than the author of the second novel. But how can such an inequality be avoided without prohibiting persons from making and acting upon their critical judgments? Inequalities of outcome can be avoided only by failing to treat and respect others as the persons capable of critical choice that they are.[23]

A similar point can be made about many of the inequalities of result that emerge from competitive sports. For one thing, most participants want to compete. They find the challenge posed by competitors worth trying to meet and the competitive sport they play worth their commitment. If respect for persons requires that we respect their conception of how they should lead their lives, the inequalities generated by competition in sports seem no less justified than the inequalities arising from the autonomous choices of those involved in other areas.

Critics might object that treating people as equals involves more than simply respecting their choices. The choices must be reasonably informed and competent; they must not be made if mental illness, depression, or mood-altering drugs are influences. For example, suppose Jones chooses to humiliate himself to gain Smith's affections. Surely, Smith does not treat Jones with respect if she heaps extreme humiliation upon Jones, even though he chooses to leave himself open to such treatment. Rather, Jones is degrading himself, and Smith is contributing to that degradation. Similarly, just because participants in sports agree to compete, it doesn't follow that their choice ought to be respected. It must be shown that the competitive relationship itself is not inherently degrading or incompatible in some other way with respect for persons as equals.

Indeed, competitive relationships are often characterized in derogatory terms. Competitors are often seen merely as obstacles to be overcome. They are to be "destroyed," "humiliated," and "run off the court." Persons are reduced to mere things or barriers standing in the way of competitive success.

For example, in a major college football game, a star running back, playing again for the first time after experiencing a serious knee injury, reported that during a pileup, he felt the opposing players trying to twist his injured knee. Thinking quickly, he yelled out, "You've got the wrong knee! You've got the wrong knee!"[24]

It would clearly be ethically indefensible if competition required that we win by deliberately injuring our opponents. We already know that the ethics of good competition prohibits the intentional infliction of injury. Indeed, if competition is understood as a mutual quest for excellence, competitors should want their opponents to be at their peak so they can present the best possible challenge. Noted golfer and 2001 British Open Champion David Duval expresses how a good competitor should view opponents when he discusses the possibility of contending against Tiger Woods in a major championship: "One of the great things about golf is that you don't have to have any ill-will in this game. If I come head-to-head against him at say, the U.S. Open, I want him to be playing as good as he can play because I want to beat him when he's playing his best. It would be a heck of a lot better, if you know he gave you all he's got, and you beat him."[25]

Significant victory requires outplaying worthy opponents, not deliberately injuring them to prevent them from competing.

In evaluating competition in sports, it is crucial that features central to competition be distinguished from those that are not. Many features of competitive sports that are ethically objectionable are not necessarily part of competitive sports. In particular, the reduction of opponents to mere things, although too often a part of high-pressure athletics, is not a central element of competitive sports and can consistently be condemned by proponents of a defensible competitive ethic.

Inequalities generated by competitive sports, then, need not be ethically indefensible. Participants in competitive sports presumably prefer a life that includes competition, with the possibility of winning or losing, to a life that does not. If treating individuals as equals requires us to react appropriately to the life plans of persons—to treat them as agents "capable of forming and acting on an intelligent conception of how their lives should be led"—inequalities that arise from their decisions in athletics are presumptively fair and equitable.

An even stronger conclusion is supported by our discussion. Each competitor in an athletic contest must respond and react to the choices and actions of fellow competitors, actions manifesting the skills the participants have chosen to develop and the decisions they have made during play. Therefore, competition in sport conceived along lines of a mutual quest for excellence is a paradigm case of an activity in which the participants treat each others as equals. The good competitor does not see the opponent merely as an obstacle to be overcome but as a person whose activity calls for an appropriate response. Rather than being incompatible with equal respect for persons, competition in athletics, at its best, may presuppose it.

Is Winning Important?

If we view competitive sports and athletics as a mutual quest for excellence in the face of challenge, what importance should be assigned to winning? Is simply playing well in an attempt to meet the opponent's challenge all we should strive for? Why should who wins or loses matter at all?

Can't it be argued that winning is significant precisely because it is a criterion of meeting the challenge? To lose is to fail to meet the challenge; to win is to succeed. If competition in sports is justified by attempts to meet challenges, it is surely important whether or not we succeed in meeting them. After all, isn't the principal point of deliberately attempting a difficult task to see whether we can accomplish it?

Although there is much to this position, perhaps it is overstated. Winning is not necessarily a sign of competitive success, and losing is not necessarily a sign of competitive failure. If winning were the only criterion of success, it would be sensible to take pride in consistently defeating far weaker opponents by wide margins. Conversely, if losing were necessarily a sign of competitive failure, a weaker opponent would have no cause for pride after having extended a far superior opponent to the limit before going down to defeat.

This argument suggests that winning is far from everything in competitive sports. Not everyone can win, but each competitor may well meet the challenge set by an opponent, although one wins and one loses. But it is not unimportant who wins or loses. If winning is not everything, it is something. For one thing, if the competition is not one sided, winning will certainly be an important criterion, sometimes the criterion, of having met the challenge of the opposition. Because one is trying to meet the challenge set by the opponent, it seems appropriate to feel elated at victory or disappointed at defeat. Even when opponents are mismatched, pride in victory may be appropriate: The victors rightly may be proud that they played to their potential without the incentive of strong opposition.

It is often far too easy in sports to take pride in defeat on the grounds that the opponents really were better. It is easy enough to make excuses: "We played well but lost to a clearly better team." One may suspect that the truth is this: "If we had played to our potential, we could have beaten them." Sometimes it is appropriate to take pride in a well-played defeat, but often the scoreboard is an important indicator of whether the play was really good.

Finally, we should remember that playing well in some aesthetic sense is not necessarily playing well in the sense of meeting the competitive challenge presented by an opponent. Remember the earlier example of the tennis player who hits ground strokes with beautiful form yet loses because the competitive situation called for aggressive play at the net. Similarly, a 3-point shot from twenty feet may look good but may make no competitive sense if the team with the ball has a 2-point lead and fifteen seconds left on the clock. What may look like good play from an aesthetic standpoint may be poor play given the competitive situation.

Therefore, although winning may not be a necessary criterion of competitive success, it is often the most reliable indicator of it. In many competitive contexts, it won't do to separate winning and losing from how well one played the game, because the outcome of the game is an especially significant indicator of how well one actually played.

But why should success and failure matter at all? After all, "It's only a game." Isn't concern for competitive success overemphasized, given the nature of the activity?

There is no question that competitive success can be overemphasized, especially at the level of children's sports. Certainly, if the slogan "It's only a game" means that extreme depression, abusiveness to others, extended withdrawal from family and friends, spouse beating, and existential anxiety are inappropriate responses to losing, it surely is correct.

On the other hand, if "It's only a game" means that success in competitive athletics shouldn't matter at all, it is far more dubious. Competitive sports provide a context in which we can stretch our bodily skills and capacities to the limits in the pursuit of excellence. The pursuit of excellence in the use of the body is hardly trivial. On the contrary, the meeting of the demands athletes place upon their talents often involves beauty, courage, dedication, and passion. If these things don't matter, what does? Would the critics say to the artist who botches a significant painting or to the dancer who performs poorly in a major performance, "Well, it's only art!" Finally, at the professional level, concern for professional success, which may involve winning, seems no less appropriate than similar concern in other professions.

Our conclusions do not imply that all sporting activity should always be intensely competitive. Not everyone wants or needs a challenge all the time. At many levels of play, the trick for coaches and educators is to balance an emphasis on achievement and competitive success with participation and instruction in developmental skills. On the other hand, insofar as an activity is a sport, then even if played with little emphasis on competition, it will still involve a degree of competitive challenge because the goal of the participants, as players, will be to make correct moves or plays, which in turn will be defined by the moves of the opposing players. If standards of good and bad performance did not apply, the participants would merely be exercising, not engaging in sports.

This point suggests that critics of overemphasis on winning and competitive success may take their points too far by ignoring the perhaps equally deleterious effects of underemphasis. Thus, if participants normally are told that "it doesn't matter how you do, just go out and have fun," the subtle message being conveyed may be that doing well is unimportant. If participation in competitive sports can be a form of human excellence, if it can contribute to self-development and self-expression, and perhaps reinforce desirable character traits, performance may well matter after all.

It is worth considering here William Bennett's description of a rigidly non-competitive softball team that he refers to as The Persons:

> The team is coed, they have no "discrimination" and no "rules.". . . Occasionally, they let one of their dogs . . . "play a position" . . . and the Persons laugh and try to look loose and non-competitive. . . . In the end, the Persons must be judged in their own terms to be insensitive both to the game and to one another as "players"—the cost no doubt of each one's being sensitive to himself exclusively as a Person.[26]

Bennett concludes that

> Charles Reich's ideal in *The Greening of America*—a laughing generation playing football in bell bottom trousers—is one of sheer aimlessness, of distraction pure and simple, doing nothing. Serious playing and watching, on the other hand, . . . are rarely if ever doing nothing, for sports is a way to scorn indifference, and occasionally, indeed, one can even discern in competition those elements of grace, skill, beauty, and courage that mirror the greatest affirmations of human spirit and passion.[27]

The sarcasm Bennett devotes to noncompetitive sport seems overdone, but his suggestion that competitive sports, at their best, involve applying standards of excellence to challenges people regard as worthwhile in themselves should be taken seriously. If competitive sports are understood on the model of a mutual quest for excellence through challenge, they not only can be activities of beauty and skill, but they also represent a striving for human excellence, and in so doing are a paradigmatic way of respecting each other as persons—of taking our status as persons seriously.

Summary

This chapter suggests that competition in the context of sports is most defensible ethically when understood as a mutual quest for excellence in the intelligent and directed use of athletic skills in the face of challenge. Athletic competition of this sort, under appropriate conditions, may have such beneficial consequences as expressing important values and reinforcing the development of desirable character traits. Perhaps more important, competition in sports may have intrinsic worth as a framework within which we express ourselves as persons and respond to others as persons in the mutual pursuit of excellence. Although other such frameworks also exist, few are as universally accessible and involve us so fully as agents who must intelligently use our bodies to meet challenges we have chosen for ourselves.

Competition as the mutual quest for excellence, it must be emphasized, is an ideal. Actual practices may not conform to its requirements. In the real world, winning may be overemphasized, rules may be broken, athletes may be exploited, and unfair conditions for competition may preclude genuine challenge. If so, the ideal provides grounds for the moral criticism of serious deviations from it. In the remainder of this book, the ideal will be applied to the moral evaluation of actual practices in sports.

The ideal of competition in sports as a mutual quest for excellence itself needs to be examined, refined, clarified, criticized, or even replaced with a better conception if sufficiently powerful objections are raised against it; however, without some defensible standards against which actual play can be measured, the valuable aspects of sports cannot be distinguished from the harmful or unfair aspects. Without reasoned standards of evaluation, criticism and acclaim alike would rest on purely emotive reactions rather than upon the results of perhaps the most important quest—the quest for justification through meeting the challenges of open discussion and critical inquiry.

3

Sportsmanship

The victory of the United States women's team in the 1999 World Cup Soccer matches was one of the most exciting events in sports in the last decade of the twentieth century. Not only were the contests leading to this triumph hotly contested, the final game being decided in a shoot-out, but the team was also taken by many to symbolize the emergence of women into the center of attention in athletic competition. The team's stars, popular and highly skilled players such as Mia Hamm and Brandy Chastain, were heroes to many young girls who played in soccer leagues across the country, as well as to adults throughout the United States.

However, the final plays of the world championship game, in which the Americans defeated China, became the center of an important ethical controversy. Regular and overtime play had ended in a tie and the game was to be decided by a shoot-out in which players from each team go one-on-one against the opposing goalie. The team that scored the most goals after a set number of attempts would win the game. Under the current rules, which prevent the goalkeeper from moving forward to cut off the shooter's angle until a shot is launched, the offensive player has a major advantage.

So the world championship was on the line while the offensive players matched each other goal for goal as the shoot-out progressed. The American goalkeeper, Briana Scurry, decided that one of the remaining Chinese players, Liu Ying, seemed to lack confidence. When Liu Ying made her move against Scurry, the American goalie decided on a controversial tactic to stop the shot. As the Chinese player made her move, Scurry, by stepping forward in violation of the rule limiting the movement of goalies in such circumstances, attempted to deprive Liu Ying of the angle she would need to score. The tactic worked, Scurry blocked the shot, and the Americans won. But did they win fairly?

As one view has it, "Its only cheating if you get caught." A more sophisticated and surely more defensible modification of that view is that it is the referee's job to call the game and as long as the player is willing to accept the penalty if detected, no unethical behavior is involved. As another prominent goalkeeper put it, "What Briana did was perfectly normal. She took a step and the referee didn't call it. I don't call that cheating."[1]

Is committing what we will call a strategic foul, an intentional violation of the rules designed to secure a tactical advantage, cheating? What if it is done openly and with willingness to accept the penalty if the referee calls the fouls? What if it is a common practice, known about and accepted by the players, as is fouling at the end of a basketball game to stop the clock? Scurry's move in the World Cup has been defended on exactly such grounds; all goalkeepers do it, players know that goalkeepers do it, and a penalty is prescribed under the rules if the violation is detected. After all, it is not as if Scurry was trying to hide her move from the referee or claim an advantage for herself that she would not accord to other goalies as well. On the other hand, what happens to sport as a rule-governed activity if players decide for themselves when to obey the rules and are encouraged to test referees to see what they can get away with? Do we have a true sports contest if each team plays only by the rules it feels are useful to obey at a given moment?

Consider a second example that raises issues of ethics in competition.

In early October 1990, the highly regarded University of Colorado Buffaloes were playing a home football contest against the University of Missouri. Top national ranking was at stake. The final seconds saw Colorado trailing 31–27 but driving toward the Missouri goal line. Somehow, in the confusion on the field, the seven officials on the field, the "chain gang" working the sideline markers, and the scoreboard operator all lost track of the downs. On what should have been the fourth and deciding down, Colorado failed to score, in part because the Colorado quarterback, mistakenly thinking he had another play left, intentionally grounded a pass. In fact, the officials signaled that Colorado had another chance, unaware that the Buffaloes already had used the four chances to score allowed by the rules. Colorado scored on the illegal but unnoticed fifth down to eke out a 33–31 "victory."

Did Colorado really win? Should the final score have been allowed to stand? It was decided that the officials' mistake was not the sort of error that can be overruled.

But should the University of Colorado have accepted the victory? Is such a "win" meaningful in an important ethical sense?

Consider a third example. A championship basketball game is tied, and only a few seconds remain. A player on the defensive team steals the ball and breaks away for the winning basket. Only one player can catch the streaking guard heading for the winning bucket. The defender realizes she cannot block the shot, but she also knows the opponent is her team's worst foul shooter. She pretends to go for the ball but in fact deliberately fouls her opponent. Is deliberate fouling to gain a strategic advantage ethical? After all, fouling is against the rules. Was committing a deliberate foul in this way a form of cheating? Should one take pride in the resulting victory? Why or why not?

These examples raise questions, not about the general issue we examined in the last chapter of whether competition in sports is ever ethical, but about how to conduct competition ethically. They raise issues of sportsmanship and fair play. By examining them, we can better understand the values that may be used in assessing the behavior of competitors within the athletic contest itself.

Sportsmanship and Fairness in the Pursuit of Victory

What values ought to govern the behavior of competitors in athletic competition? Sportsmanship is one value that is often appealed to in such contexts. Sportsmanship has received relatively little attention by moral thinkers, and probably suffers today because of associations with the morality of an elite upper crust and perhaps by concerns that a male bias is built into the meaning of the term.[2] Nevertheless, sportsmanship is a value frequently cited by coaches, players, and commentators on sports, and should not be dismissed without a hearing.

But what is sportsmanship? Does it apply equally to intense athletic competition as well as to informal games among friends?

James W. Keating has provided a particularly interesting analysis of sportsmanship. Keating properly warns us, first of all, not to make our account of sportsmanship so broad as to make it virtually identical with virtue. Not every virtue is an instance of sportsmanship and not every vice is unsportsmanlike. Thus, one dictionary defines "sportsmanship" rather unhelpfully as "sportsmanlike conduct"; it continues by listing conduct appropriate to a sportsman as exhibiting "fairness, self-control, etc." Keating tells us that a formal code of sportsmanship promulgated earlier in this century included such diverse injunctions as "Keep yourself fit," "Keep your temper," and "Keep a sound soul and a clean mind in a healthy body." The trouble with such broad accounts of sportsmanship is that they do no specific work. We cannot say conduct is ethical because it is sportsmanlike, for "sportsmanlike" has just become another way of saying "ethical." The idea of sportsmanship has been characterized so broadly that there is no particular aspect of morality that is its specific concern.[3]

Keating believes that a more useful account of sportsmanship will develop the rather vague suggestion of the dictionary about behavior expected of a sportsman or sportswoman. To develop this idea, he introduces a crucial distinction between sports and athletics: "In essence, sport is a kind of diversion which has for its direct and immediate end fun, pleasure, and delight and which is dominated by a spirit of moderation and generosity. Athletics on the other hand, is essentially a competitive activity, which has for its end victory in the contest and which is characterized by a spirit of dedication, sacrifice, and intensity."[4]

Sportsmanship, then, is the kind of attitude toward opponents that best promotes the goal of sports as defined by Keating; namely, friendly, mutually satisfactory relationships among the players. "Its purpose is to protect and cultivate the festive mood proper to an activity whose primary purpose is pleasant diversion, amusement, joy."[5] In Keating's view, then, the supreme principle of sportsmanship is an injunction to "always conduct yourself in such a manner that you will increase rather than detract from the pleasure found in the activity, both your own and that of your fellow participant."[6]

Sportsmanship, Keating argues, is a virtue that applies to the recreational activity of sports, as he understands it, but not to the more serious and competitive activity of athletics. To Keating, sportsmanship and athletics do not fit together easily: "The strange paradox of sportsmanship as applied to athletics is that it asks the athlete, locked in a deadly serious and emotionally charged situation, to act outwardly as if he was engaged in some pleasant diversion."[7]

Sportsmanship only applies to athletics in an attenuated way, then, involving adherence to the value of fair play, which to Keating implies adherence to the letter and spirit of equality before the rules. Since the athletic contest is designed to determine which competitor meets the challenge best, fair play requires that competitors not intentionally disregard or circumvent the rules. Broadly understood, perhaps more broadly than Keating would recommend, fair play requires that victory be honorable. So fair play can be expected of the serious athlete in intense competition, but also to require sportsmanship—the attempt to increase the pleasure of the opponent in the contest—normally is to ask too much.

But what is honorable behavior in competitive sport? Is it ethically required? Do we act wrongly, in a way that is morally prohibited, if we behave dishonorably, or do we just fail to live up to an ideal that is above and beyond the call of duty? And what is fair play? Does it mean simply following the rules or does it require more than that? Did Scurry act unfairly in the decisive play in the World Cup championship game? What precisely is the relationship between unfair and unsportsmanlike conduct? Did the University of Colorado act honorably in accepting its disputed victory over Missouri? Even if it didn't, is honorable behavior too much to expect at elite levels of competitive athletics? Finally, is the line between sports and athletics as sharp and as ethically significant as Keating's account suggests?[8]

To answer these questions, and to clarify the relationship between fair play and sportsmanship, we need to say more about how sport is to be understood and the implications of such an understanding for ethics and fair play. For example, if sports are understood simply as rule-governed activities, and fair play is thought of simply as conformity to the rules, any deviation from the rules may be considered unethical. But if common social understandings and conventions accepted in practice by participants are ethically relevant, a more permissive account of ethically acceptable behavior in sport may emerge.

Internalism, Externalism, and the Ethics of Sport

In this section, the view that sport has a kind of internal morality that is tightly (perhaps conceptually) connected with the structural features of athletic competition will be examined. The results then will be applied to the examples cited at the beginning of the chapter.

Externalism denies that sport is a special or fundamental source or basis of ethical principles or values, although sophisticated externalists acknowledge, and even emphasize, that sport plays a significant role in reinforcing values already in the culture and in socializing participants and spectators to accept those values as their own. On this view, the values sport promotes or expresses simply mirror, reflect, or reinforce the values dominant in the wider society. Thus, to take a perhaps too crude example, in a predominantly capitalist society, sports will emphasize such capitalist values as intense competition and rivalry; but in more communal and less individualistic societies, more emphasis will be given to teamwork and the role of opposing players as facilitators who help make good competition possible than to winning and losing.

Internalism, on the other hand, holds that sport is sometimes a significant source or basis for ethical principles and values. Internalists emphasize that sport can have a significant degree of autonomy from the wider society and does, or can, support, stand for, and express a set of values of its own that in particular contexts may conflict with the values dominant in the broader society. Thus, in his important work titled *Leftist Theories of Sport*, William J. Morgan defends the idea of a "gratuitous logic" of sport that does not merely mirror or reinforce the values dominant elsewhere.[9]

Why is this distinction important for the concrete problems we raised earlier, such as the ethics of rule breaking for strategic purposes? Perhaps it is this: If internalism is correct, the ethical principles embedded in or implied by central features of athletic competition may provide a morally relevant framework for adjudicating the cases. Of course, just because some values or moral principles are internal to sport does not mean they are justifiable or well supported by reasons. Nevertheless, they may provide a useful starting point for analysis. Let us begin by considering one form of internalism and the critical response to it.

Formalism

"Formalism" is the name given to a family of positions that characterizes games, such central elements of games as winning and losing, and allowable moves within the activity, primarily in their formal structure and particularly their constitutive rules. Thus, in a narrow sense, formalism has been characterized as the view that such game derivative notions as "a move or play within a game" and "winning a game" are definable by reference to the constitutive rules of the game. In a broader sense, formalism is the view that games (and sports to the extent that sports are games of physical skill) can be defined primarily by reference to constitutive rules. The goals or obstacles of the sport are defined by the rules and are unintelligible outside the context of the rules. A move within a game is what is permitted or required by the constitutive rules and what counts as winning a game also is defined by such rules. For example, using a tank during a football game to run over the opposing team's defensive players is not a move within the sport since such moves may be made only in accord with the constitutive rules. There are different versions of formalism, so "formalism" might best be regarded as an umbrella term covering a family of positions that, although closely related, sometimes differ on points of varying degrees of significance.[10]

Formalism not only is a theory about the nature of games but also has normative implications. Perhaps the best known is the incompatibility thesis: Cheaters violate the rules by failing to make moves within the sport and therefore fail to play it. One can win the game only by playing it, and since cheaters do not play, cheaters can't win.

The emphasis of formalists on the constitutive rules of the game has helped us understand the nature of games. However, formalism lacks the normative resources to address many of the moral problems that arise in connection with sport. (Many versions of formalism were developed to define the notions of "game" and "sport" rather than to resolve ethical issues arising in games and sport.)

Issues of sportsmanship, for example, often go beyond conformity to the formal rules of a sport. Thus, consider the case of clubless Josie, a top amateur golfer who arrives at a national amateur golf championship without her clubs. Clubless Josie has lost her clubs, not because she is clueless but because her airline was careless. Josie's chief rival, Annika, has a spare set of clubs virtually identical to those Josie has lost. Should Annika lend poor clubless but not clueless Josie the spare set of clubs so that Josie can compete in the tournament? Because Josie's problem does not concern the application of rules, it is unclear that formalism addresses this question.[11]

Some formalists might reply that their view, sympathetically interpreted, supports lending the clubs to Josie. If we correctly understand the *spirit* or *point* of the rules, which is to promote competition, we should do what enhances competition. However, in appealing to the spirit of the rules or their underlying point, formalists go beyond a narrow version of formalism and ask *how* we are to understand the spirit of the rules or their underlying point. We will consider this broader form of internalism below.

A second criticism of formalism is that it suggests an implausible account of the ethics of strategic rule violations in certain situations. A strategic foul, as we noted when considering Briana Scurry's behavior during the World Cup, is a rule violation designed to secure an advantage within the sporting contest to the team or individual who fouls. Another widely discussed example is the strategic foul at the end of a basketball game, where the losing team fouls as a strategy to stop the clock and force the team in the lead to make foul shots to maintain its advantage. According to critics of this practice, whom I suggest are influenced by the formalist emphasis on the rules as central to the game, such fouls are intentional violations of the rules and therefore are not legitimate moves within the game. In particular, according to many formalists, they violate the understanding or implicit contract that must hold between opponents to play the game by the rules. On this analysis, strategic fouling is a form of cheating.[12]

Almost all practitioners of the game, especially basketball, consider strategic fouling an established part of the game and deny that it is a form of cheating. And some goalkeepers in soccer maintain that Scurry's behavior reflects common practice within the game. The participants might just be wrong, of course; but if their view can be defended, formalism may not be adequate, even on what seems to be its strongest ground where violating the central rules of the game is concerned.

Formalism also has problems with the ethics of rule change and rule formation. How are proposed changes in the rules, or sets of rules for new sports and games, to be assessed? Formalists might point out that the rules of many sports include what legal philosopher H. L. A. Hart calls "rules of change." A rule of change for golf might state that a proposal becomes a rule of golf if, and only if, it is accepted through established procedures by the governing golf organizations of an area, such as the United States Golf Association (USGA) in the United States and the Royal and Ancient in Britain. But although such rules of change might establish when a rule change becomes official, they do not establish whether the change is good or bad for the game. Consider, for example, the proposed rule that anyone who commits a strategic foul in the last four minutes of a basketball game is thrown out of the game and the opposing team is awarded 30 straight foul shots. Because it is so penal, such a rule might eliminate strategic fouling. But is it a good rule? Is basketball a better or worse game if fouling late in the game to stop the clock is recognized as a legitimate tactic? Similar questions might be raised about the designated hitter rule in baseball or proposals to give the goalkeeper more freedom of movement during shoot-outs in soccer. Although formalists are quite right to emphasize the formal structure of games, it is not clear how their theory might apply to ethical questions in sport that are not necessarily resolvable by formal or structural features alone.

Conventionalism

Many theorists argue that in emphasizing the formal constitutive rules of given sports, the formalists have ignored the implicit conventions that apply to the sports in question. These conventions are sometimes referred to as the "ethos of the game."[13] For example, with respect to strategic fouling in basketball, conventional-ists argue that a convention in basketball permits such fouls as a legitimate strategic move within the game. Since the players all accept the convention, and since each team knows the other team will strategically foul at appropriate points in a contest, no team has a special advantage over others. Therefore, strategic fouling is not cheating, but is justified by practice and the widely accepted social conventions within that practice.

But can social conventions be a source of value in sports? Conventionalists have made a contribution to our understanding of sporting practice by exploring the role of the ethos and cultural context of games. But does the ethos have normative force? Do the conventions express what *ought* to take place as well as describe what *does* take place in sporting practice?

Consider clubless Josie. For one thing, if such a dilemma were highly unusual, there might be no applicable convention. Conventionalism, like formalism, would not tell us what should be done. But suppose there was an applicable convention under which players were not obligated to lend equipment to fellow competitors. Would that settle the issue or would it simply raise the deeper issue of whether that convention was ethical or reflected appropriate standards of fair play? Thus, one major problem with conventionalism is the ethical status of the conventions themselves.

This is true even where conventionalism is plausible; namely, its analysis of strategic fouls in sports such as basketball. But even in basketball, it is unclear that the mere existence of conventions settles the issue of strategic fouling. The critics of strategic fouling acknowledge that they are opposing a widely accepted practice, as well as the conventional understandings upon which practice is based, but they argue that appeal to central values implicit in the logic of sports requires the reform of existing conventional behavior. Unless we are to immunize conventions from criticism, and, in effect, always choose to preserve the existing understandings of sport, challenges to existing conventions cannot be dismissed simply because they counter our present conventional understandings of sporting practice.

It also is unclear whether conventionalism can respond any better than strict formalism to the evaluation of proposed changes in the rules or conventions of a sport. When is a change for the better? How are we to evaluate a proposed change to the conventions of basketball, for example, to the effect that players on a losing team should not foul simply to gain a strategic advantage? Just as appeal to the existing rules alone cannot settle the issue of whether a proposed rule change is or is not an improvement, so appeal to existing conventions cannot be the sole basis for evaluating proposals for reform. Arguments for and against the proposed changes, either in the rules or the conventions, would have to come from elsewhere. But from where?

So far, then, the discussion suggests that both pure formalism, understood as a narrow version of internalism, and conventionalism, a form of externalism (conventions arguably are imported from a social context rather than inherent to competitive sport), lack the intellectual resources to deal with the important ethical issues that arise in sport. It is hard to see how emphasizing either existing formal rules or social conventions can resolve fundamental moral issues in sport or provide the moral and educational development that many expect sport to provide. Perhaps a third position, which we can call broad internalism, can do better.

Broad Internalism: Expanding the Formalist Approach

In a series of writings in jurisprudence, noted legal scholar Ronald Dworkin has criticized legal positivists, particularly the highly influential legal philosopher H. L. A. Hart, for holding too narrow a view of the nature of law. Because legal positivists, particularly Hart, tend to identify law with a formal structure of rules, their views resemble the formalist approach to the analysis of games and sport. According to Dworkin, the positivists have identified law with a model of formal rules. One of Hart's major contributions is to show the diverse rules that make up law; these include criminal sanctions, rules of change and adjudication, and the Rule of Recognition, which identifies the rules of the legal system and distinguishes them from nonlegal rules. Dworkin has argued that in addition to rules, there are legal principles, which have normative force within the legal system. What makes these principles legal ones, rather than simply moral principles imported from beyond the law and applied according to the particular political and ethical commitments of individual judges, is that they are either presupposed by the legal system or are required to make sense of its key elements. In other words, the principles are justified if they must be presupposed to arrive at the most comprehensive, coherent, and morally acceptable account of the law itself, the best interpretation of the legal system.[14]

An analogous position in the philosophy of sport has been developing for some time.[15] Although many writers are sympathetic to various aspects of formalism, or may even view themselves as formalists, they go beyond narrow versions of formalism in developing resources for the ethical assessment of behavior that can be distinguished from rules without being mere conventions. Rather, the considerations they point to seem to be presuppositions of sporting practice in the sense that they must be accepted if our sporting practice is to make sense, or perhaps make the *best* sense. Before developing this view, which we will call broad internalism (those who see it as a version of formalism may prefer to call it "interpretive formalism"), let us consider some examples.

In "Fair Play As Respect for the Game," Robert Butcher and Angela Schneider maintain that "if one honors or esteems one's sport, . . . one will have a coherent conceptual framework for arbitrating between competing claims regarding the fairness . . . of actions."[16] Where does this conceptual framework come from? Butcher and Schneider suggest that sports themselves have interests; athletes show respect for the game when they make its internal interests their own. Thus, they claim that "the idea of the interests of the game provide a means for judging one's own action in relation to the sport. . . . Taking the interests of the game seriously means that we ask ourselves whether or not some action we are contemplating would be good for the game concerned, if everyone did that."[17] Butcher and Schneider illustrate their position by applying it to poor clubless Josie (who in earlier versions of the example is a racquetless squash player rather than a clubless but not clueless golfer): "The notion of respect for the game provides ample reason for lending Josie the racquet. At the personal level . . . you would forgo a valuable experience and personal test if you decline to play Josie. At a more general level, the sport of squash is enhanced by people playing and competing at their best whenever possible. Squash at the institutional level would not be served by neglecting to play a . . . scheduled match. You should want to lend Josie your racquet."[18]

What makes this an example of broad internalism is that appeal is being made to norms or principles internal to the idea of sport. These principles are not mere social conventions and indeed may provide a basis for criticizing existing social conventions that might support requiring Josie to forfeit the match. Neither are they formal rules of the game. Although broad internalists might well want to avoid the metaphysical complications attached to the notion of games having interests— games may not even be the sort of entities that can have their own interests—perhaps all that internalists need to assert is that the point of playing competitive golf would best be made if the match was played.

A second and instructive example of broad internalism is provided by J. S. Russell in an article titled "Are Rules All an Umpire Has to Work With?"[19] Russell, who explicitly appeals to Dworkin's views in jurisprudence, argues against the view that rules are all an umpire has to work with. He discusses various games from American baseball that call on umpires and officials to extend, change, or interpret rules that, by themselves, may be indeterminate when applied to hard cases.

For example, in an 1887 American Association game between Louisville and Brooklyn, a Louisville player named Reddy Mack, who had just scored, jostled the Brooklyn catcher thereby interfering with him and allowed another Louisville player to score as a result. At that time, the rules of baseball stated that no base-runner may interfere with a fielder, but the Louisville player might have reasoned that when he crossed home plate, he was no longer a base-runner. The umpire, Wesley Curry, called Mack out for interfering with the catcher. As the rule technically did not apply once Mack had crossed home plate and ceased to be a base-runner, did Curry make the right decision?

Russell points out that Curry's decision "was not explicitly covered by the rules, but his actions seem irreproachable, were not overturned, and were the basis for a subsequent rule change. . . . Any other decision would have invited a nine-inning . . . wrestling match."[20]

Russell is going beyond explicit formal rules here and offering what might be called an interpretation of baseball. Thus, following Dworkin's suggestions in legal philosophy, Russell suggests that "we might try to understand and interpret the rules of a game, say, baseball, . . . to generate a coherent and principled account of the point and purposes that underlie the game, attempting to show the game in its best light."[21] Russell cites, as an example of a principle that might underlie such competitive sports as baseball, the injunction that "rules should be interpreted in such a manner that the excellences embodied in achieving the illusory goal of the game are not undermined but are maintained and fostered." [22]

Broad internalism, then, is the view that in addition to the constitutive rules of sport, there are other resources connected closely—perhaps conceptually—to sport that are neither social conventions nor moral principles imported from outside. These resources can be used to adjudicate moral issues in sports and athletics. In William J. Morgan's terms, sport has an independent "gratuitous logic" of its own that makes it more than a mirror reflecting the values of society.[23] This underlying logic may be helpful in analyzing concrete ethical issues that arise within competitive sport.

Fair Play in Competitive Sport

The argument of Chapter 2 suggested that competitive athletics is justified morally when conducted as a mutual quest for excellence through challenge. On this view, competitive sport is best understood as a place where we freely test ourselves and attempt to develop excellences at overcoming the obstacles allowed by the rules. On the broad internalist view, this approach to sport is an interpretive theory that attempts to make the best sense out of sporting practice and provide principles for appropriate sporting behavior. This theory, or interpretation, has implications for the cases we discussed earlier.

Winning Versus Sportsmanship and Fair Play

Consider again the dilemma of Annika and clubless Josie. Surely Butcher and Schneider are correct to argue that Annika should lend the clubs to Josie. Sporting contests are designed to be tests, and competitors should not avoid a worthy opponent. However, although Annika should be encouraged to lend the clubs to Josie, and may be subject to moral criticism on the basis of poor sportsmanship for not doing so, she arguably is not morally required to make the clubs available to Josie and should not be formally punished or penalized for failing to do so, at least at the professional or top amateur level. (Presumably, the less competitive the situation, the greater the obligation to lend the clubs to the opponent. Keating's perhaps overdrawn distinction between sport and athletics may well apply here.) Failing to lend her opponent the clubs is in a different moral category than, say, trying deliberately to disable an opponent or bribe an official. External interference with competitors, say by deliberately trying to injure them or by bribing officials, makes the good sports contest impossible and undermines the very point of competitive sports. However, the idea that competitors take positive steps to promote good play on the part of opponents, although worthy, is open ended and not so clearly essential to the good sports contest. Thus, what level of support should be provided in what contexts is controversial—suppose Josie needed a golf lesson from Annika just five minutes before teeing off—so it is unclear when noncompliance is worthy of punishment. We need to distinguish then between prohibited behavior in sport that ought to be penalized or sanctioned from desirable behavior that should be encouraged but the nonperformance of which is not necessarily sanctionable.

Competition as a mutual quest for excellence also suggests the attitudes competitors should have towards each other. Although every participant at some time probably hopes for an easy victory in an important contest, reflective participants should acknowledge that such an attitude should not be prevalent among competitors. Rather, competitors should hope to meet worthy opponents who can provide a true test of the abilities required in the sport being played. After all, as we have seen, if victory is the primary goal, one need simply schedule vastly inferior opponents. (At the time of writing this sentence I am the best basketball player on my street; but, as all the other players are less than eight years old and most cannot even reach the basket, is that anything to take pride in?)

The appropriate attitude towards fellow competitors is well expressed by professional golfer David Duval in talking about the prospects of going head-to-head with Tiger Woods in the last round of a major championship. In a passage also quoted in Chapter 2, Duval makes this remark: "If I come head-to-head against him at say, the U.S. Open, I want him to be playing as good as he can play because I want to beat him when he's playing his best."[24] Duval's attitude seems to be the one that best fits with the conception of sport as a mutual quest for excellence through challenge. Good competitors want to be challenged by worthy opponents. Given that, good competitors should want to promote conditions under which other athletes can play their best. As we have noted, it is unclear just how stringent such a require-ment is and when athletes are encouraged to follow it as an ideal and adopt it as a moral rule they have a duty to obey.

The conception of broad internalism suggests that sport presupposes an at least partial conception of the good life for human beings. According to this con-ception, a significant segment of the good life consists of seeking out and trying to meet interesting challenges, including physical ones. Thus some activities, such as participation in sport, are worth doing, not because of external rewards, but be-cause of the nature of the activity itself.

Of course, some athletes compete for fame, trophies, and incredibly large salaries. But although many professional players may not be motivated by the ideal of meeting challenges for their own sake, their large salaries are still parasitic on that ideal. For if the players did not try to meet the challenges set by the rules of the sport, but instead tried to win through such external means as deliberately injuring opponents or bribing referees, they would undermine the structure of their own practice and perhaps even destroy it. Thus, regardless of the personal motivations of the players, they must meet the challenge set by the sport on its own terms and will be rewarded to the extent that they do so.

Let us now consider how our discussion can help us with the ethical issues raised by behavior such as Briana Scurry's during the World Cup; that is, the inten-tional breaking of a rule for strategic advantage.

Is Strategic Fouling Cheating?

Although moral skeptics often appeal to disagreement on controversial moral issues, not all moral issues are controversial. Thus, most agree that straightforward cheating, which has no moral justification, is to be condemned. Such cheating might include a golfer who deliberately fails to count all her strokes in an important tournament, or a basketball coach who, in the confusion of a last second foul call, intentionally de-ceives referees and opponents by directing his best foul shooter to go to the line even though another player, a particularly poor foul shooter, has been fouled.

What makes these examples paradigm cases of cheating? Since rules can be broken by accident or ignorance, cheating cannot simply involve breaking the rules. Sometimes cheating is identified with deception, as when an unfaithful spouse de-ceives his or her partner; or breaking an explicit or implicit promise, as when someone violates an agreement made with others.

However, as philosopher Bernard Gert has pointed out in a perspicuous analy-sis, cheating does not necessarily involve either deception or promise breaking.[25] A competitor who has power over the other competitors may cheat quite openly. Similarly, a revolutionary who cheats on a civil service examination to attain a powerful position, which can then be used for purposes of betrayal, may deny that he has ever promised, even implicitly, to obey the rules laid down by the very government he despises. More generally, the idea of an "implicit" promise may be too vague to support charges of cheating.

Cheating, Gert suggests, is best identified with the intentional violation of a public system of rules to secure the goals of that system for oneself or for others.[26] Cheating is normally wrong, but not only because it deceives or violates a promise, although these may contribute to its wrongness. The distinctive element in the general presumption that cheating is wrong is that the cheater behaves in a way that no one could rationally or impartially recommend that everyone in the activity behave. Thus, cheaters make arbitrary exceptions of themselves to gain advantages and, in effect, treat others as mere means to their own well-being. Cheaters fail to respect their opponents as persons, as agents with purposes of their own, by violating the public system of rules that others may reasonably expect to govern the activity in question. Thus, a golf tournament would not be an athletic contest if everyone cheated because it would not determine who was the best player. The rules of golf are the public system under which it can reasonably be presumed that the participants expect to compete. It may be difficult to say what is or is not cheating in borderline cases, but in paradigm cases, cheaters arbitrarily subordinate the interests and purposes of others to their own, and so violate the fundamental moral norm of respect for persons.

Strategic fouling is the intentional violation of the rules of a sport for a competitive advantage. Examples of strategic fouling already mentioned include Scurry's save at the World Cup, fouling by the losing team to stop the clock in the last minutes of a basketball game, and a football team that deliberately incurs a delay of game penalty to get a better angle for an attempt at a field goal. Is strategic fouling cheating? If it is not, is it unethical in some other fashion?

Many philosophers would unequivocally assert that strategic fouling is unethical, and perhaps a form of cheating. For example, Warren Fraleigh analyzes the basketball example by maintaining that "intentional holding, tripping, and so on are not part of the game or within the rules of basketball. . . . [Therefore] the 'good' foul is a violation of the agreement which all participants know that all participants make when they agree to play basketball, namely, that all will pursue the . . . goal of basketball by the necessary and allowable skills and tactics and will avoid use of proscribed skills and tactics."[27] In a similar vein, Kathleen Pearson writes that strategic fouling "destroys the vital framework of agreement which makes sport possible."[28] These comments reflect the central emphasis of the formalists on the rules. Indeed, one might go further and argue that cheaters aren't even really playing the game, since the game is constituted by the rules. Be that as it may, the remarks of Fraleigh and Pearson suggest that strategic fouling is a form of cheating because it intentionally violates the framework of rules that make the game possible and that the participants have agreed (either implicitly of explicitly) to obey.

If the analysis of cheating presented earlier is on the right track, this formalist approach to strategic fouling may be seriously questioned. One criticism is that the formalist approach does not give sufficient weight to the conventions associated with specific sports that have been called the "ethos" of the game. Thus, in basketball, players understand that losing teams will foul at the end of the game to stop the clock. Virtually all players expect the losing team to foul to stop the clock when such behavior is strategically appropriate; the players expect it of themselves and of their opponents.

Even though such behavior is conventional does not make it morally right or in the best interests of the game. But if cheating means violating a public set of norms to gain an advantage for oneself or one's team, and these norms include conventions as well as rules, then strategic fouling is not always a form of cheating. This is in part because conventions exist that sometimes make such behavior normal and expected. But, more important, it is also because the strategic fouler acknowledges that such behavior is appropriate for all participants, including opponents. This is quite a different situation from that of the cheater who, say, wants to get an advantage by falsifying the score book, behavior that could not possibly be made universal without destroying the game itself.

Theorists such as Fraleigh and Pearson could object that conventions, unlike rules, are too vague to form a basis of the common understanding presupposed by players who commit themselves to respect the game. For example, is there really a convention in international soccer that goalkeepers can bend the rules as Scurry did in the World Cup? How are we to tell?

This rejoinder surely has force. Nevertheless, it still seems plausible to distinguish the strategic foul from paradigm examples of cheating; strategic foulers, unlike cheaters, are conforming to a general practice they are willing to condone even when it works against them.

But even if strategic fouling is not a form of cheating, it may be morally unacceptable on other grounds. After all, just because behavior is conventional does not mean it is ethical. Strategic fouling may be unethical by being unsportsmanlike or showing disrespect for principles that should govern conduct in competition. Let us explore these possibilities more fully.

Penalties As Sanctions and As Prices

The remarks of Fraleigh and Pearson suggest that players and teams committing strategic fouls violate an implicit social contract according to which players agree to play by the rules. The contest is defined by the rules. By intentionally breaking the rules, the offending players act immorally by unilaterally altering the terms under which the contest is to be played.

As we have seen, one possible reply is that the game is defined by conventions as well as rules, and that conventions sometimes permit strategic fouling. But this reply may not be fully satisfactory because the conventions themselves may be vague or not understood the same way by all, and because the ethical status of the conventions may be questioned.

Perhaps a stronger moral defense of strategic fouling is that such behavior really does not violate the rules to begin with. For example, in basketball, one can argue that the strategic foul is part of the game because an explicit penalty—foul shots—is provided for in the rules.

Pearson has considered this rejoinder and points out that "the obvious rebuttal to this position is that penalties for breaking the law are contained within the law books, but no sensible person concludes, therefore, that all acts are within the law."[29] For example, we surely would not say that murder is allowed by law simply because penalties for murder are prescribed by law. Similarly, we should not say that the strategic foul is allowed by the rules of basketball simply because the penalty is prescribed in the rule book.

But is this reply decisive? Such a question may not admit of a conclusive answer, but we should not accept the affirmative response too quickly. The parallel drawn between sanctions in law, such as punishment for criminals, and penalties for strategic fouls needs closer examination.

In particular, some penalties in sports do not play a role analogous to criminal sanctions in law. A jail sentence for a crime should not be thought of as the price the law charges for a particular act, such as a felony. That would make the felony a permissible option for those criminals who are willing to bear the cost of a jail sentence if caught. Rather, a felony is a prohibited act, and a jail sentence is not the price for allowable commission of the act, but rather is a punishment for committing it.

Not all penalties in sports are punishments or sanctions for prohibited acts. For example, in golf, when balls come to rest in a position from which players judge no shot is possible, as when a ball comes to rest up against a tree, golfers may invoke the unplayable lie rule. According to this rule, the player either may replay the shot from the original location, hit a new shot from two club lengths from either side of the location of the unplayable ball, or hit a new shot from as far behind the location of the ball as the player chooses. The penalty for exercising any of these options is one shot. Here, the penalty clearly is not intended to punish. Rather, the options are there for the player to use. The penalty in this example is the price of exercising the option rather than a sanction for doing what is forbidden.[30] Invoking the unplayable lie option is unlike strategic fouling in that the latter violates a rule and the former is permitted by the rule. The point of the example is not to say the two are totally analogous but only to illustrate the difference between the two functions penalties may have: to function as punishments for impermissible acts and as a price for exercising a strategic option.

Once we distinguish between the two kinds of penalties, sanctions for prohibited acts and prices for options, we do not know for certain that strategic fouling is cheating or whether it is always unethical in some morally questionable way. This is because the penalties for the fouls in at least some contexts can be regarded as prices for exercising a strategy rather than sanctions for violating the rules; indeed, this does seem to be the common understanding of intentional fouling to stop the clock in basketball.

Although it is sometimes difficult to tell whether a penalty should be regarded as a sanction or a price, the notion of a fair price might help us distinguish the two. The intuitive idea here is that if a pricing penalty is fair in sports, violating the rule should be a fair penalty for the infraction. The penalty for intentional fouling in basketball is probably best regarded as a price rather than as a sanction if the foul shots awarded are fair compensation for the violation. Sports authorities can more clearly distinguish sanctions from prices by making the penalty for prohibited acts more severe than mere fair compensation would require. Thus, recent rule changes in college and high school basketball awarding extra foul shots and possession of the ball to the team that is intentionally fouled can be regarded as a step towards making intentional fouling prohibited rather than a strategy with a price. (The distinction between prices and sanctions may remain ambiguous if referees fail to call intentional fouls because they believe the punishment is too severe.)

This analysis of strategic fouling in basketball in effect rests on a (broad internalist) theory of the game that views foul shots as fair compensation for the team that was fouled for strategic reasons. A good team should be able to convert the foul shots and be no worse off than before the infraction was committed. Inability to convert the foul shots indicates a weakness that rightly puts that team's lead in jeopardy.[31]

The strategic violation allegedly committed by Briana Scurry might be analyzed in a similar fashion, but arguably is more complex. The penalty for illegal movement by the goalkeeper allows the shooter to make another attempt to score if the original shot was missed (otherwise the goal stands), so the rules call for restoring the situation to what it was before the infraction was committed. But although this suggests that the prescribed penalty is a price rather than a sanction, it may not demonstrate it beyond reasonable doubt.

Another relevant factor is that officials seldom call the kind of infraction committed by Scurry. In the World Cup finals, the officials should have suspected that the goalkeepers would seek every edge in the shoot-out, but either they did not notice the infraction or deliberately ignored it. Do referees tend not to make this call because they believe the shoot-out is too heavily weighted in favor of the offense and that goalkeepers have no real chance to stop a shot without moving illegally? If so, the referees, by refraining from calling all but blatant violations by goalkeepers, may be trying to restore competitive balance to what they regard as an unfair restriction imposed by the rules. In fact, the reason why an implicit convention allowing goalkeepers to move forward in shoot-outs, even though this involves breaking a rule, is because competitors believe the rule creates a significantly unbalanced competitive match-up. Goalkeepers have only the lowest probability of stopping a shot if they play within the rules. In other words, the convention improves the game.

What does our discussion suggest about the morality of strategic fouling? One conclusion is that strategic fouling often cannot be equated with paradigm cases or blatant examples of cheating, since it rests on implicit practices accepted by all the players. Thus, it differs from behavior where cheaters try to gain an advantage through actions they could not reasonably accept as a universal practice. Moreover, in many contexts in sport, strategic fouling may constitute a strategic option for which the rules exact a price rather than impose a sanction. It might even be argued that sometimes strategic fouling improves the game by creating interesting tactical choices or, as in the example of the movement at issue in the World Cup, even improves the competitiveness of the game.

Whether such considerations show that strategic fouling is *always* morally allowable remains debatable. First, in many instances, it may be unclear whether the penalty for an act should be considered a price for exercising an option or a sanction for prohibited behavior. Normally, the more severe the penalty the more likely

it functions as a sanction; and the more the penalty seems to restore the competitive balance that existed before the behavior that triggered it, the more likely it is to
function as a price.

Second, the appeal to implicit conventions accepted by the players is open to
all sorts of difficulties. Do all players agree that the relevant convention exists and
understand it in the same way, especially in international or multicultural contexts?
Sigmund Loland provides an example of just such a difference in understanding. In a
major soccer competition in England between Arsenal FC and Sheffield United,
when an Arsenal player became injured, a Sheffield United player deliberately
kicked the ball out of bounds, as required by conventions for play, so that the injured player could receive medical treatment. According to the convention, once
the ball is back in play, the receiving team, in this game Arsenal, would turn the ball
over to the opposition so that Sheffield would suffer no competitive disadvantage
for following the convention. But while this was being done, "a new player to the
Arsenal team (a recent recruit from another continent [and presumably different
cultural setting]) intercepted the ball, crossed it to one of his teammates who in-
stinctively (so it is said) . . . scored."[32] Apparently, the understanding of the convention was not common to all players. This possibility of misunderstanding may be
more common in international competition, or when competitors come from different "sport cultures." (This may suggest that Scurry's strategy was ethically more
questionable than our previous discussion suggests because the Americans, the Chinese, and the officials may all have had different understandings of conventional behavior by goalkeepers.)

To conclude, the ethics of strategic fouling is quite complex. For reasons given
above, strategic fouling normally should not be equated with cheating and sometimes may be a legitimate part of the game if the penalty is best regarded as a price
rather than a sanction. Yet it may not always be clear whether a penalty is a price or
a sanction in a given situation. In my view, strategic fouling to stop the clock late in
a basketball game is not unethical, but Scurry's move during the World Cup is more
controversial. The general failure of referees to call movement by the goalkeeper
during shoot-outs, and the appearance that the penalty is restorative rather than
penal, indicates that Scurry's move was within the bounds of ethically appropriate
behavior. But it may be unclear whether the Chinese were playing under the same
understanding of the relevant conventions as the Americans, or whether the referee
simply missed the infraction, rather than, as I have suggested, refusing to call it
(perhaps to make the shoot-out more competitive). It also may be less clear than I
have suggested that the penalty for Scurry's breach of the rules is restorative rather

than penal. If it is debatable just how much to weigh each of the factors bearing on the situation, the moral evaluation of Scurry's strategic violation will remain highly controversial for a long time to come.

The Fifth Down: A Tainted Victory?

There are many other situations in sports where it is unclear whether certain actions are cheating or are unethical in some other way. Is a tennis player cheating if she changes the tempo of her game to upset an opponent who prefers a faster pace? Is a groundskeeper cheating if he wets down the home team's baseball field to slow the opponent's base stealers? Is a pitcher cheating if he slips an illegal spitball past the batter in a crucial game?

Although we cannot explore all these kinds of situations here, we can consider another of the examples with which we began this chapter. It involved a top-ranked university football team winning a game on a "fifth down" play that was run because officials lost count and didn't notice that the allotted number of downs already had been used up. Should the winning team, the University of Colorado, have accepted the victory or, as many critics of the university suggested, have refused to accept a tainted win?

Proponents of one view might begin by appealing to Keating's distinction between sports and athletics. They might argue, first, that since a major intercollegiate football game is clearly an example of athletics, neither team is under an obligation to make the experience pleasurable or enjoyable for the other. Generosity should not be expected, either; after all, if a referee had made an incorrect pass interference call in their favor, Missouri would not have been urged to refuse to accept the penalty.

Second, Colorado did not cheat, as least as we have defined cheating. There was no intent to violate a public system of rules to gain an advantage. The Colorado team seemed unaware of the true situation. Tapes of the game reveal that on the fourth-down play, the Colorado quarterback looked to the sideline, noticed that the play was officially marked as a third down on the official scoreboard, and intentionally grounded a pass to stop the clock. Had the quarterback believed the play was his team's last down, he surely would have gambled by attempting a touchdown pass, perhaps successfully.

Although these arguments cannot just be dismissed, some may think they rest on an indefensible conception of ethics in competition. To begin with, they might reject Keating's distinction between sports and athletics as misleading. In particular, if it is taken as descriptive, it may set up a false dichotomy. Activities need not be classified exclusively as athletics or exclusively as sports but may share elements of each.[33]

More important, we need to ask the normative question. Which conception should apply to a particular activity? Thus, to assume that the Colorado-Missouri football game should be regarded as an example of athletics rather than sports, in Keating's sense, is to beg the question about whether Colorado should have accepted the victory. We would be assuming an answer to the very point that is being debated—namely, whether Colorado ought to have accepted the victory.

Second, critics might maintain that sportsmanship, although certainly not an all-encompassing value, covers more than generosity towards opponents. In particular, if athletic contests ought to be regarded as mutual quests for excellence, along lines argued in Chapter 2, implications follow for sportsmanship. Thus, opponents ought to be regarded as engaged in a cooperative enterprise designed to test their abilities and skills, and, whether or not they are owed generous treatment, they should be treated as partners in the creation and execution of a fair test. To treat them differently is to reject the presuppositions of the very model of athletic competition that ought to be observed.

We can argue that the Missouri team was not treated in such a fashion. The play that won the game was not allowed by the rules of the game. Even though the officials were mistaken about how the rule applied, that does not alter the fact that Colorado did not win the test as defined by the rules. Moreover, there is no common convention acceptable to all participants that covers the situation. According to its critics, Colorado, by accepting the victory, did not treat its opponents as partners or facilitators in a common enterprise but instead treated them as a means for attaining the kind of external rewards that go with victory in big-time college games.

If this point has force, it suggests that the distinction between sportsmanship and fair play may not be as sharp as Keating's account suggests. If by "fair play" we mean adherence to criteria of fairness implied by the idea of a mutual quest for excellence, it is at best unclear whether Colorado's decision was truly fair. If its team did not truly demonstrate superiority by the public code of rules that all parties agree applied to the game, in what sense was the assignment of a victory fair?

In a famous game played forty years before the contest between Colorado and Missouri, a similar incident led to a dissimilar resolution. In the late fall of 1940, an undefeated Cornell team, also in contention for the national championship and a Rose Bowl bid, played a Dartmouth team that was hoping for a major upset. Although trailing late in the fourth quarter, Cornell apparently pulled out a victory with a scoring pass on the game's last play. But did Cornell really win? Film of the game indicated without a doubt that the referee, who admitted the error, had allowed Cornell a fifth down! The game should have ended a play earlier and Dartmouth should have pulled off a major upset.

Although no rule required that Cornell forfeit the victory, soon after the game film's release, "Cornell officials (including the Director of Athletics) telegraphed Hanover formally conceding the game to Dartmouth 'without reservation . . . with hearty congratulations . . . to the gallant Dartmouth team.' Another loss the following Saturday to Pennsylvania helped the Cornell team drop from second to 15th in the Associated Press polls, its season ruined but its pride intact."[34] Should Colorado take pride in its victory? Should Cornell be proud of its loss?

Our discussion so far suggests that some of the distinctions with which we began our discussion may need to be rethought. Suppose we take fair play as a central value to be articulated along lines suggested by a broadly internalist approach to sport that encompasses the principles of athletic competition as a mutual quest for excellence. On this interpretation, fair play would require treating opponents in a way fitting their status as partners in a partially cooperative enterprise; namely, the provision of a challenge so that skills and abilities may be tested. Finally, we can question whether even intense competition at high levels of performance ought to be regarded as pure cases of athletics in Keating's sense. Although some activities, such as major intercollegiate and professional sports, might justifiably tend more in that direction, a strong argument can be made that sportsmanship and fair play should both apply, although perhaps with different emphases, at all levels of sports and athletics. We can argue that athletics, in Keating's sense, ought not to exist at all in its pure form because, unless fair play is understood broadly enough to encompass sportsmanship in the wider sense developed above, "athletics" and the ethic of the mutual quest for excellence are incompatible. Accordingly, the terms "sports" and "athletics" will be used interchangeably in what follows, unless otherwise indicated.

We also need to consider the role of officials and referees in sports. Should we conclude that since opponents in many forms of organized competition delegate responsibility for enforcement of the rules to officials in full knowledge that officials sometimes make mistakes, the decisions of officials should be accepted as ethically final? Alternately, do participants have obligations not to accept unearned benefits arising from particularly egregious official errors, especially those that involve misapplication of the rules rather than "judgment calls" about whether a rule was violated?

Although these questions do not admit of easy answers, an argument can be made that Colorado's victory was tainted. Although there was no intention to violate rules and therefore no cheating in a central sense, and although the referees bear heavy responsibility for what happened, Colorado still had to decide after the game was over whether or not to accept the victory. Although it may not have been morally required for them to forfeit the game, as Cornell did in a perhaps more innocent era of intercollegiate sports, it seems just as clear that Colorado did not meet the test of defeating opponents within the rules. Their victory was therefore less meaningful than it otherwise would have been. It would seem, then, that Colorado's reasons for wanting the full benefits of victory had more to do with securing the external benefits of a win, including national rankings and a bid to a Bowl game, than to intrinsic pride in a well-earned victory. Be that as it may, it is far from clear that Colorado met the challenge set by their opponent, or that Missouri failed to meet it simply because the final score was in Colorado's favor.[35]

Among the tests of a principled ethical approach to sport are overall consistency and compatibility. Relevantly similar situations should be evaluated in similar ways, and responses to one set of issues should fit well with responses to others. Otherwise, the theory appears tailored to the sympathies of its proponents to rationalize the views they personally favor.

Does our discussion of the 1999 World Cup and our discussion of the Colorado-Missouri game fit together coherently? A critic might argue that intentional rule breaking by Scurry seems to have been condoned out of hand, but the unintentional violation of a rule by the Colorado football team is said to have tainted their victory. Are these responses compatible or are they in conflict?

Arguably, there are relevant differences between the two. Scurry's movement to cut off the shooter can be viewed as a strategic foul with a set price rather than a prohibited act. Moreover, it falls under a convention recognized by the players, and perhaps by officials as well. Presumably, if the situation had been reversed, the Americans would have expected the Chinese goalkeeper to act in the same way and would have regarded her behavior as appropriate. And perhaps such movement by goalkeepers alters the competitive balance in the direction of fairness since the shoot-out in soccer seems far too heavily weighted against the defense. On the other hand, although the Colorado team surely did not cheat (they were unaware they had been awarded a fifth play), the rules infraction involved was not a strategic foul with a set price and so was not within the framework of the game.

This reasoning might not convince all readers. Those who are not persuaded that the two accounts are mutually coherent have two options. The first is to come up with a better argument for the overall coherence of the discussion; and the second, of course, is to either reject the judgments that Scurry's act was not unethical or to reject the conclusion that Colorado's victory was tainted. Although these cases are controversial, trying to arrive at principled responses to them allows us to formulate and then test our ethical intuitions about specific cases by trying to place them within the context of an overall theoretical approach to the ethics of sport. Analysis of these cases is of theoretical as well as practical interest because different and sometimes competing factors must all be taken into account before a coherent response to both can be formulated and tested through reasoned dialogue.

Cases such as those discussed here are likely to be controversial, and discussion of them may generate disagreement, but it is important to remember that such disagreement occurs against a general background of deeper agreement on sports ethics. None of the parties to the discussion endorses cheating, blatant examples of unfair play, or unsportsmanlike behavior. Rather, the disagreement concerns "hard cases" that help us define the boundaries of the values we are exploring. Sometimes disagreement over controversial cases is used as a justification for overall moral skepticism, since a rational resolution may seem impossible. This overall drift to moral skepticism should be resisted, however, for often rational adjudication is possible (as application of the model of the mutual quest for excellence to our cases may suggest); or, if it is not, there still remains deeper agreement on the moral fundamentals that are not at stake in the controversies at issue.

Is It Ever Permissible to Cheat?

Is cheating always morally wrong? If our suggestion that cheating normally takes unfair advantage of other competitors is sound, then cheating is morally prohibited except in contexts where there are weightier conflicting factors that might be overriding. For example, if gamblers have kidnapped your family and will kill them unless your team wins, you would seem to be morally justified if you cheated to ensure the victory and save their lives.

Recently, it has been suggested that cheating is not always wrong even if we restrict the kinds of factors at issue to sports. In fact, on this view, cheating, although it may undermine fair play, might make for good sports. As one commentator has maintained: "Many competitions . . . would be more interesting if cheating takes place within it or if several players try to stretch the rules. Such deviant behavior adds a new dimension to the game which can also add to its interest. . . . Insofar as the contest is one of wits as well as one of skill and strategy, it can be exciting to compete with and against someone who uses his wits to try to cheat and it can be exciting for an audience to observe such intelligent behavior."[36]

For example, if the use of the illegal spitball pitch in baseball by a major league pitcher such as Gaylord Perry, who was well known for throwing spitballs, can make the game more fascinating and exciting, isn't its use justified?

This position seems open to the objection that cheating undermines the idea of the sports contest as a test of skill, a mutual quest for excellence by the participants. This is not to deny that sports serve other purposes in our society, such as providing entertainment and the opportunities for professionals to secure financial gains. But these other purposes are parasitic in that what ought to be entertaining about our sports, and what makes them sometimes worth paying to see, is the test of excellence they provide. Gladiatorial contests or the throwing of the politically or religiously unpopular to the lions also may be entertaining to some people. Whether such people ought to be entertained by such behavior is another issue.

Perhaps what is being endorsed are not solitary acts of cheating that deceive opponents or in some other way violate the public system of rules that players are entitled to have apply to the game. Thus, "if . . . cheating is recognized as an option which both sides may morally take up, then in general the principles of equality and justice are not affected."[37] Perhaps the practice of strategic fouling in basketball fits such a description in that players expect other players to foul strategically in appropriate situations.

If the practice is acknowledged and expected, it is far from clear that it is cheating at all. That is, once we realize that all penalties are not sanctions for prohibited activities, it is not clear that all intentional rule violations are examples of cheating. If all players acknowledge that other competitors will engage in the action at issue, and if the rules contain just compensation for violation, why is the act one of cheating? The difficulty for those who believe that cheating in sports is sometimes justified because it makes for better sports is to find behavior that clearly is cheating and that is also morally permissible. Insofar as such activity is acknowledged to fall under the rules, as interpreted by morally acceptable conventions known by participants and officials, it arguably is not cheating. Insofar as the behavior does not fall under such rules, as interpreted by morally acceptable conventions known by participants and officials, it arguably is not permissible. In neither case do we find an instance of behavior that is both cheating and morally acceptable as well.

The Actual and the Ideal in Philosophy of Sports

Our discussion so far has been concerned with standards that should apply to sports. The attempt to find such standards is not only of philosophical interest but also is of great practical importance. It is difficult to understand how we could even identify abuses in sports unless we had some grasp of the ethical principles that were being violated in the first place. Besides, without some standards at which to aim, we would not know the proper recommendations to make for moral change.

Some of the cases we have examined are controversial and reasonable people may disagree over their proper resolution. However, as noted earlier, hard cases are important because they force us to identify the relevant moral factors that bear upon them and also require us to see whether our responses to a diverse set of such cases can fit within a coherent and rationally defensible framework. Hard cases often presuppose a background of agreement on fundamentals. Disagreement may persist over how the University of Colorado should have responded to its victory over Missouri, but surely all parties to the discussion would acknowledge that a victory earned through blatant cheating is unearned and should be disallowed.

The views developed in this chapter do have implications for policy. They indicate that although it is difficult to always draw the line between what sportsmanship and fair play permit and what they forbid, those values are not vacuous and do apply to the behavior of competitors in sports.

If competition in sports is thought of as a mutual quest for excellence, then cheating, disrespect for the game, and bad sportsmanship are in different ways each violations of the ethic that should apply to athletic competition. A defensible sports ethic, one that respects participants as persons, should avoid the twin errors of, on one hand, leaving no room for such tactics as the clever strategic foul or, on the other hand, assuming that any behavior that contributes to victory is morally acceptable. Let us see whether the approach to ethics and sport developed so far can contribute to the analysis of ethical issues that arise not simply within the confines of competition but concern what many would regard as its corruption through the use of performance-enhancing drugs, violence, discrimination, and commercialization in the world of sport.

4

Drugs and Violence

It is the 1988 Summer Olympics at Seoul, Korea. The long-awaited race between Canadian Ben Johnson and American Carl Lewis is about to be run. The muscles on Johnson's almost sculptured body stand out as the gun fires, and the runners are off. In a hard-fought race, Johnson defeats Lewis and apparently wins the gold medal.

Urinalysis tests subsequently reveal that Johnson has been taking the steroid stanozolol to enhance his performance. To the shock of Canadians, to whom Johnson has become a national hero, and to the rest of the sports world, Johnson is disqualified. He forfeits his medal from the race against Lewis and all his other medals from the 1988 Olympics as well. Other athletes are also found to have been using performance enhancers. Indeed, it is alleged that such prohibited use is widespread among top athletes in many sports.

The issue of performance enhancing drugs continues to be a major one within the world of competitive athletics. Testing for drug use is now commonplace, and users and their advisers continually work on ways to fool the tests. The use of performance enhancers is found not only among professional and elite amateur athletes, in spite of rules prohibiting it, but has filtered down to younger and younger athletes at less advanced levels of skill. Even sports not usually associated with drug use seem to have been affected. For example, in an article published in the summer of 2002, a prominent sports publication asserted that steroid use was then widespread among major league baseball players, which may not be surprising since at the time major league baseball had no rules prohibiting the use of steroids to enhance performance.[1]

Is the use of performance-enhancing drugs such as anabolic steroids really unethical? Should use be prohibited in competitive sport? Why shouldn't athletes be allowed to use them if they want to? Does their use somehow undermine competitive sports conceived of as a mutual quest for excellence? Did Ben Johnson cheat, or had he simply found a more effective way to compete, just as some athletes may use more effective programs of weight training than others? Let us consider these questions further.

Performance-Enhancing Drugs and the Quest for Excellence
Excellence and the Ethic of Success

Competition in sports, it has been argued, is ethically defensible when it involves participants in a mutual quest for excellence through challenge. In effect, competitors should view themselves as under moral obligations to their opponents. Competitors are obligated to try their best so that opponents can develop their own skills through facing a significant test. In this view, sports are of interest and significance in large part because they fully involve our minds and bodies in meeting a challenge, one regarded as worth meeting for its own sake.

Although there are different levels of competitive intensity, even the recreational athlete playing in a relaxed and informal atmosphere tries to play well and often fantasizes about making great plays. Whether one is a recreational softball player imagining himself or herself as a major leaguer or a hacker on the golf course who for once hits a perfect shot, participants in sports all take part in the quest for excellence, although with various degrees of intensity. What distinguishes the fun we have through sports from mere exercise is the presence of standards of excellence and the challenge presented by the play of others.

At the professional level, the primary goals of most players and coaches may be financial. However, regardless of the personal goals of the competitors, to the extent that professional sports captures the imagination of players and fans alike, professional athletes are involved in the mutual quest for excellence at the highest level of attainable skill.

Many athletes at the most skilled levels of professional and amateur competition love the challenge provided by sports and seek constantly to improve their performance. Some seem to compete as much for the love of competition as for financial reward. Some professional star athletes, Michael Jordan and Tiger Woods being especially prominent examples, seem to play as much for the love of the challenge and the desire to compete as for external rewards such as fame and fortune. Indeed, could anyone rise to the top in a highly competitive sport unless love of the game and dedication to excellence provided the motivation for the hours of practice, drills, and preparation that are required?

The danger, of course, is that the drive to win will lead some dedicated athletes to use dangerous and arguably unethical means to achieve success. Losing becomes identified with failure, and anything that promotes winning is also seen as promoting success. But is winning achieved by any means always a success worth having?

We need to ask how excellence might be achieved. In particular, is the use of drugs, such as anabolic steroids, an ethically permissible method for achieving excellence in sports, or, as most sports authorities argue, should the use of such drugs be prohibited in organized athletic competition?

Understanding the Problem

Athletes' relatively wide use of such drugs as anabolic steroids dates back at least to the Olympics of the 1960s, although broad public awareness of the problem seems much more recent. Anabolic steroids are a family of drugs, synthetic derivatives of the hormone testosterone, that stimulate muscle growth and repair injured tissue. Although not everyone would agree that the controlled and supervised use of steroids to enhance performance is dangerous, the American College of Sports Medicine, as well as other major medical organizations, warn against serious side effects. Some of these are, at least in high doses, liver damage, arteriosclerosis, hypertension, a lowered sperm count in males, and development of masculine physical characteristics in women. The regular use of steroids is also asserted to produce such personality changes as increased aggressiveness and hostility.

Although the degree to which steroids are used by top amateur and professional athletes is unclear, most observers would acknowledge that their use is not uncommon or infrequent, particularly at elite levels. Users range from weight lifters to football linemen, from track-and-field stars to, more recently, major league baseball players.

What is particularly frightening is that world-class athletes are reported to be taking steroids at dosages so high that it would be illegal to administer them to human subjects in legitimate medical experiments. Some athletes are said to "stack" various forms of steroids in attempts to find the most effective combinations. Moreover, many athletes who use steroids do so without medical supervision. Such athletes are likely to ignore claims that steroids have little effect on performance when such claims are based on studies that administer only low doses of the relevant drugs.

What Is a Performance-Enhancing Drug?

Before we can turn to a discussion of the ethics of the use of performance-enhancing drugs in sports, we need to be clearer about what counts as a performance enhancer. Are vitamins performance-enhancing drugs? What about a cup of coffee that stimulates a sleepy athlete before a match? What about medication that alleviates allergy symptoms, thereby allowing an athlete to compete more effectively? If we want to forbid the use of performance enhancers, what defines these substances?

Unfortunately, there does not seem to be a clear and simple definition that distinguishes the kind of performance-enhancing drugs that officials of major sports organizations want to prohibit from the legitimate use of vitamins or allergy medicine. The situation is complicated further because a substance that might enhance performance in one context or sport may fail to do so, or even harm performance, in another. Thus, moderate use of alcohol normally would affect performance adversely, but it can be a performance enhancer in riflery. This is because alcohol is a depressant and therefore slows the heartbeat, which, in turn, allows for a steadier shooting hand on the rifle range.

Moreover, it is of little help to say that athletes should be permitted to take only what is "natural"; steroids are derivatives of the hormone testosterone, which does occur naturally in the human body, but many legitimate medications that athletes ought to be allowed to take are synthetic and not present in a normal or natural diet. But the term "natural" is too vague and open-textured to be of much help in this area. In addition, what of practices such as blood doping, where athletes inject stored samples of their own blood in an attempt to boost their oxygen carrying capacity? It is doubtful whether one's own blood can be classified as "unnatural," yet major sports organizations regard blood doping as an unethical form of performance enhancement.

Rather than search for a precise definition to distinguish the substances that we intuitively believe are illegitimate performance enhancers from those that are not, it seems more useful to examine anabolic steroids, prohibited by major sports organizations. We can then ask what factors, if any, morally justify this prohibition. If the prohibition is justified, and if we can isolate the moral reasons for it, then any other substances to which the same reasons apply should also be prohibited. Thus, rather than search for an abstract definition, we should first decide what ought or ought not to be allowed to affect athletic performance.

Evaluating the Use of Performance Enhancers

Various reasons are cited as justifications of the claim that competitive athletes ought not to use performance-enhancing steroids. Among the most frequently cited are the following: (a) use of steroids to enhance performance is harmful to athletes, who need to be protected; (b) use of steroids to enhance performance by some athletes coerces others into using steroids; (c) use of steroids to enhance performance is unfair, or a form of cheating; (d) use of steroids to enhance performance violates justifiable norms or ideals that ought to govern athletic competition. Let us examine each kind of justification in turn.

Paternalism, Informed Consent, and the Use of Steroids

Why shouldn't athletes be allowed to use performance-enhancing steroids? According to one argument, steroids, particularly at the high dosages believed necessary to enhance performance, can seriously harm those who use them. Let us accept the factual claim that steroids as performance enhancers can be seriously harmful and consider whether potential harm to the user justifies prohibiting their use.

The principal criticism of prohibiting steroid use to protect athletes from themselves is that it is unjustifiably paternalistic. Paternalistic interference prevents athletes from making decisions for themselves. After all, would any of us want to have our liberty interfered with whenever some outside agency felt that our personal decisions about how to live our lives were too risky? If widespread paternalism were practiced, third parties could prohibit us from eating foods that might be harmful, playing in sports that carried even slight risk of injury, or indulging in unhealthy lifestyles. Our lives would be monitored—for our own good, of course. The difficulty is that we might not conceive of our own good in the same way as the paternalist.

The trouble with paternalism, then, is that it restricts human liberty. We may believe with John Stuart Mill (1806–1873), the great nineteenth-century defender of human freedom, "that the only purpose for which power can be rightfully exercised over any member of a civilized community, against his will, is to prevent harm to others. His own good, either physical or moral, is not a sufficient warrant."[2]

If each of us ought to be free to assume risks that we think are worth taking, shouldn't athletes have the same freedom as anyone else? In particular, if athletes prefer the gains in performance allegedly provided by the use of steroids, along with the increased risk of harm to the alternative of less risk and worse performance, what gives anyone else the right to interfere with their choice? After all, if we should not forbid smokers from risking their health by smoking, why should we prohibit track stars or weight lifters from taking risks with their health in pursuit of their goals?

But although the antipaternalistic considerations advanced above have great force, we need to consider some difficulties before we can dismiss paternalism as a justification for prohibiting steroids as performance enhancers. Even Mill acknowledged that the kind of antipaternalism articulated in his Harm Principle (the principle stating that the only justification for limiting liberty is to prevent harm to others) had limits. Mill excluded children and young people below the age of maturity, and those, such as the mentally ill, who may require care by others. Moreover, Mill would surely exempt those who are misinformed or coerced from immediate protection of the principle. To use one of his own examples, if you attempt to cross a bridge in the dark not knowing that the bridge has been washed away by a flood, I do not violate the Harm Principle by preventing you from attempting the crossing until I have explained the situation to you.[3]

In particular, before accepting the antipaternalistic argument, we need to consider whether athletes who use steroids to enhance performance really are making a free and informed choice. If behavior is not the result of free and informed choice, it is not really the action of a rational autonomous agent. If it is not informed, the person does not truly know what she is doing; but if the behavior is coerced, it is not what the agent wants to do in the first place.

Is there reason to believe that athletes who use steroids are either uninformed about the effects of the drug or are coerced or otherwise incompetent to make rational decisions?

First, those below the age of consent can legitimately be prevented from using performance-enhancing steroids on paternalistic grounds. In the same way that parents can prevent children from engaging in potentially harmful behavior, even if the children want to take their chances on getting hurt, so sports authorities can prohibit the use of harmful performance enhancers by those who are incompetent because of age.

What about the requirement of informed consent? Are athletes who use steroids adequately informed about the serious potential side effects of the drug? Some athletes, particularly teenagers, may be uninformed or skeptical about the information available, but it is hard to believe that most adult users of steroids are ignorant of the risks involved. Even if H. L. Mencken may not have been totally off the mark when he suggested that it was impossible to go broke by underestimating the intelligence of the American people, it is difficult to believe, in view of the amount of publicity devoted to the use of performance enhancers, that the majority of mature athletes are unaware that steroid use can be dangerous. However, even if ignorance about the effects of steroids is more widespread than suggested, antipaternalists still might argue that the remedy is better education so that informed choice becomes possible, not simple prohibition.

Coercion and Freedom in Sports

What about the requirement of free choice? Are athletes really free to not use steroids? At least some analysts would argue that athletes are coerced into using steroids. Consider professional sports. The professional athlete's livelihood may depend on performing at the highest level. Athletes who are not among the best in the world may not be professionals for very long. "Thus," one writer concluded, "the onus is on the athlete to continue playing and to consent to things he or she would not otherwise consent to. . . . Coercion, however subtle, makes the athlete vulnerable. It also takes away the athlete's ability to act and choose freely with regard to informed consent."[4]

Although this point may not be without force in specific contexts, the use it makes of the term "coercion" seems questionable. After all, no one is forced to become (or remain) a professional athlete or to participate at elite levels in amateur athletics. If we want to use "coercion" so broadly, are we also committed, absurdly it seems, to saying that coaches coerce players into practicing or training hard? Do professors similarly "coerce" students into studying hard? Isn't it more plausible to say that although there are pressures on athletes to achieve peak physical condition, these amount to coercion no more than the pressures on law or medical students to study hard? Rather, the athletes (or the students) have *reasons* to try hard to achieve success; the pressures are self-imposed.

At best, it is unclear, in light of various incentives and disincentives, whether top athletes are coerced into using steroids or whether they freely decide that the gains of steroid use outweigh the risks. Surely we are not entitled to assume that professional athletes as a class are unable to give informed consent to steroid use unless we are willing to count similar pressures in other professions as forms of coercion as well. And if we use "coercion" that broadly, it becomes unclear who, if anybody, is left free.

Sometimes athletes may clearly be victims of coercion. Perhaps an athlete who otherwise would not use steroids is threatened with dismissal by an owner who requires such use. Apart from such specific situations, however, it appears doubtful that a general desire by the athlete to be successful at his or her profession can by itself undermine the capacity for free choice.

But is this conclusion too hasty? A critic might point out that even if the athlete's own internal desires for success do not rule out free choice, what about coercion by other competitors? That is, even if we agree that internal pressures generated by the athletes are not coercive, we might suspect that their competitors create external pressures that are. Thus, it is sometimes argued that even if some sophisticated athletes do give informed consent, their drug use may force others into taking steroids as well. Athletes who would prefer not to become users may believe that unless they take drugs they will not be able to compete with those who do. Athletes may believe they are trapped; don't take steroids and lose or take them and remain competitive.

Note that the argument here is no longer that we should interfere with athletes on paternalistic grounds—to prevent them from harming themselves—but rather that we should interfere with them to prevent them from coercing others. Such an argument is in accord with Mill's Harm Principle; liberty is restricted but only to prevent harm to others.

Do pressures generated by athletes who use drugs coerce other athletes into using performance enhancers too? One reason for doubting that they do is that it once again appears as if "coercion" is being used too broadly. One might just as well say that students who study harder than others "coerce" their classmates into studying harder in order to keep up, or that athletes who practice longer hours than others "coerce" their competitors into practicing longer hours as well. The problem with such claims is that all competitive pressure becomes "coercive." As a result, the term "coercion" is deprived of any moral force because virtually no competitive behavior is left over that would not be coercive.

Critics might reply that there is a difference between weight training and extra studying, on one hand, and steroid use on the other. As one writer has pointed out, "Steroids place regard for enhancement of athletic performance above regard for the health of the athletes themselves."[5] Weight training should make athletes stronger and more resistant to injury; studying normally enhances the intellectual ability of students.

These differences are important and suggest that the use of steroids does present athletes with a difficult choice. But is this enough to show that the user coerced others into also becoming users? Much depends upon how we understand the term "coercion."[6] If we understand coercion to involve imposing difficult choices on others when we have no right to do so, and if we assume the user has no right to impose the choice of using or not using on other athletes, then perhaps a strong form of the coercion argument can be defended.

But before any such argument can be made good, we need to consider whether steroid users do have a right to impose the choice of becoming a user on others. Even if they have such a right, would it be wrong for them to exercise it? Rather than focus on conceptual analysis of the notion of "coercion," it will be more profitable to consider directly whether it is morally wrong for athletes who use steroids to place other athletes in a situation where they must choose between be-coming users themselves or becoming competitively disadvantaged.

Unethically Constrained Choice

The appeal to coercion as a justification for prohibiting the use of steroids is open to the charge that it uses the notion of coercion far too broadly. Perhaps the argument can be reconstructed or modified without unacceptably stretching the term "coercion."

Whatever the proper definition of "coercion," what seems to make coercion presumptively wrong is when it unduly, illegitimately, or in some other way, im-properly interferes with the freedom of another. Thus, we are reluctant to say that the student who studies harder than his peers, or the athlete who trains harder than her competitors, coerces them because we don't think the student or the athlete is acting improperly. Both have a right to work harder, so their working harder does not coerce others to do the same; or, if it does, it does not do so improperly or wrongly. Accordingly, we have no reason to prohibit the behavior of the student and athlete (and even have reason to encourage it because it leads to superior achieve-ment).

But consider another situation in which competitive pressures are imposed improperly. Suppose you work in a firm where young employees compete for pro-motions to higher levels. Up to a point, if some work harder than others, no ethical issue is involved because it is not wrong for some workers to try to perform better than others. But now, suppose that some workers work all the time, including weekends. Everyone feels the pressure to keep up, and soon all the workers give up their holidays and evenings for fear that they will lose their jobs if they do not. In this situation, it looks a bit more plausible that the workers are coerced or, if not "coerced," at least unjustifiably pressured into putting in many hours of overtime.

Let us go further. Suppose some of the workers start taking stimulants—drugs having harmful side effects—so they can work even harder. Other workers feel that, to keep up, they too must take the stimulants. They ask the employer to set limits on the amount of time they are expected to work because they are being co-erced into taking the stimulant to keep their jobs.

In this example, it is unclear that the workers who take the stimulants are be-having properly. Arguably, they are putting undue pressure on other workers to risk harming themselves so they can keep their jobs. If so, the workers taking the stimu-lants are violating the freedom of their fellow workers and their behavior may be regulated in the interests of protecting the freedom of all.

Is the practice of steroid use in competitive sports like that of our last example? Do users of dangerous performance-enhancing drugs behave improperly when they put pressure on others to keep up competitively? Some would say "No!" As one writer argues, "The ingestion of steroids for competitive reasons cannot be distinguished from the other tortures, deprivations, and risks to which athletes subject themselves to achieve success. No one is coerced into world class competition. . . . If they find the costs excessive, they may withdraw."[7]

But although such a rejoinder has force, it may not be decisive. Although steroid use is not strictly "coercive" because athletes can always withdraw from the competition, the choice either of using a potentially harmful drug or of being noncompetitive may be unethical if imposed on others. Perhaps a prohibition on steroids can be justified as a means of protecting athletes from being placed in a position where they have to make such a choice. To the extent that we think it is wrong or illegitimate to face athletes with such a dilemma, then to that extent we will find the argument from coercion to have a point. Whether or not we want to apply the term "coercion" in such a context, we need to consider whether it is morally wrong to insist that athletes risk harming themselves to compete. If so, a prohibition on steroid use may be justified as a means of protecting athletes against having such a choice imposed upon them and from competitive pressures that, if unregulated, are far too likely to get out of hand.

Such considerations may not satisfy those who think steroid use is permissible. They would reply that athletes are not considered unethical if they engage in demanding training and thereby impose hard choices on other competitors. How can we justifiably condemn the users of performance-enhancing drugs for confronting competitors with difficult choices when we do not make the same judgment in similar situations?

This rejoinder does need to be explored further but it is far from decisive. Perhaps we can distinguish the risks inherent in stressful training programs from those inherent in the use of steroids. As M. Andrew Holowchak remarked in a passage quoted earlier, we might distinguish between harmful steroid use and training that, if done properly, promotes conditioning and reduces the chances of injury.

Although we have not arrived at an uncontroversial justification for prohibiting the use of steroids in organized athletic competition, we have discovered an argument that is well worth further examination. According to this argument, athletes who use steroids have no right to put other athletes in the position of either damaging their health or competing under a significant disadvantage. Whether it will survive the test of further critical discussion remains to be seen, but perhaps it is strong enough to create at least a presumption in favor of prohibiting steroids in athletic competition. Perhaps this presumption can be strengthened when conjoined with another argument of a different, but not totally unrelated, kind.

Fairness, Cheating, and the Use of Performance Enhancers

Many of those who object to the use of performance-enhancing drugs in sports do so not (or not only) because they believe users coerce others into also becoming users. Rather, they believe that using such drugs is cheating. What reasons, if any, can be given for regarding the use of drugs, such as steroids, as an unfair competitive practice?

Those who assert that users of performance-enhancing drugs are cheating their opponents mean more than that users are breaking existing rules. Of course, if the existing rules prohibit the use of such drugs, then their use is cheating. Those who secretly violate the rules take unfair advantage of those who don't. The interesting philosophical issue is whether the rules should be changed to allow the use of performance-enhancing drugs. According to the approach we will now consider, a rule allowing the use of performance-enhancing drugs would be unfair even if such drugs were available to anyone.

Many of us share the intuition that use of performance enhancers provides an unfair advantage, but we need to ask whether this intuition can be supported by good arguments. We also need to consider just where the unfairness lies. In what follows, it will be useful to keep in mind a perceptive distinction made by Roger Gardner: Is steroid use unfair because of the advantage it provides *against competitors* or is it unfair *to the game* by making success too easy? [8]

One line of argument suggests an analogy with differences in the equipment available to competitors. For example, if one player in a golf tournament used golf balls that fly significantly farther than balls used by opponents even when struck with the same force, the tournament arguably is unfair. One player is able to avoid one of the major challenges of golf not through skill but by using a superior product. Perhaps the use of steroids provides a similar unfair advantage.

The problem with this argument is that it is at best unclear that the golf tournament is unfair. If the ball is acceptable under the rules and available to other competitors, the user indeed has an advantage over players using ordinary equipment, but what makes the advantage unfair? Other players could use the same brand of golf ball if they wished to do so. There are all sorts of differences in equipment, background, training facilities, coaching, and diet that can affect athletic performance but are not regarded as unfair. Until we can say why the advantages provided by steroids are illegitimate and the advantages provided by other conditions are le-gitimate, the charge of unfairness must be dismissed for lack of support.[9]

A similar difficulty affects the view that performance enhancers make sports too easy. Thus, we might say the trouble with the "hot" golf ball is not that it gives some competitors unfair advantages over others but that it makes golf significantly less challenging. Similarly, perhaps the trouble with steroids, we might claim, is that they reduce the challenge of sports by making achievement the result of taking a pill rather than skill. But as Roger Gardner points out, the same claim can be made about equipment, such as perimeter-weighted golf clubs that expand their "sweet spot," thereby reducing the skill needed for a desirable shot, as well as about diets promot-ing carbohydrate loading, high-tech running shoes, and top-of-the-line practice facil-ities, all of which are regarded as acceptable parts of athletic competition.[10]

The difficulty, then, is that of finding a principled way of drawing the line be-tween the illegitimate use of steroids and other performance enhancers and factors that provide legitimate competitive advantages.

After all, some advances in equipment can make the game too easy and should be prohibited in the interest of preserving the game's inherent challenge, but other innovations should be allowed. (We will return to this issue in Chapter 7 when we discuss the potential conflict of interest between equipment manufacturers and sports organizations whose role is to safeguard the interest of the sport.) Perhaps steroid use is on one (prohibited) side of the line and effective dieting is on the other (permissible) side. The problem is to draw the line properly in the first place. Just when does an innovation make the game too easy?

Although a simple answer to such a question is unlikely, the charge of unfair-ness should not be dismissed too quickly. Perhaps by expanding considerations mentioned in our discussion of potential coercive effects of steroid use we can de-velop a different analysis of the unfairness involved. This analysis may be able to help us develop a reasonable although perhaps not conclusive case that steroid use should be prohibited in competitive sport.

That steroid use by some athletes created a situation of unpalatable choices for others was suggested earlier: Either use steroids and risk harm or cease to be com-petitive. In a sense, the steroid user, if perhaps not like the robber who demands your money or your life, at least creates a dilemma like that facing the workers who must use harmful stimulants to keep pace with the drug-induced energy of col-leagues. We may conclude that neither athletes nor workers should face such choices and that we should enact legislation to protect them from such a cruel dilemma.

Does a similar line of argument also suggest that the use of performance-enhancing steroids is *unfair*? Suppose we ask whether it would be rational for all athletes to support either the rule "use of steroids should be prohibited in athletic competition" or the rule "use of steroids should be permitted in athletic competition"? Let us stipulate one artificial but plausible and morally justifiable limitation on their choice; namely, the athletes vote as if in ignorance of how the use or nonuse of steroids would affect them personally but with knowledge of the general properties of steroids. The use of this limited "veil of ignorance," suggested by John Rawls's theory of justice, forces the athletes to be impartial and unbiased rather than voting according to personal self-interest.[11] How would rational and impartial athletes vote?

Can it be established that a vote for the rule permitting steroid use would be irrational under such circumstances? One might argue for such a view by pointing out that all athletes would know of the general harmful effects of steroids, but, because of the requirement of limited ignorance, none would have any reason to believe that steroids would be especially beneficial. Widespread use would at best yield only minimal gains for any one competitor, since the advantages gained by some would be largely cancelled out by roughly similar advantages gained by others. However, the risk of serious effects on health would be significant for all.

Under such circumstances, a rule allowing the general use of steroids seems collectively irrational. Why would rational individuals choose to run great risks for minimal gains, gains that, from behind the veil of ignorance, they have no reason to believe will benefit them rather than their competitors? It seems that significant competitive advantage can be secured only if some athletes use steroids covertly. Allowing steroid use would not be supported by the informed impartial choice of all athletes and would provide only minimal gains relative to the risk of serious harm. The use of steroids as performance enhancers is unethical precisely because rational and impartial athletes would not agree to it as a universal practice.

Thus, steroid use may seem rational if users think only about themselves and hope to secure advantages over nonusers. But if they must think impartially about what is an acceptable universal practice, steroid use no longer seems rational. This is why the use of steroids seems to many to be a form of cheating. The user operates from principles that could not be consented to as principles applying to all.

In effect, this argument appeals to a hypothetical contract among rational and impartial athletes. It is hypothetical because it attempts to specify what would be agreed to under specified but not necessarily real or actual conditions of choice. Although hypothetical rather than actual, writers such as Rawls have suggested that such a contract nevertheless is binding on us in that the hypothetical conditions reflect considerations we think ought to apply to moral reasoning. The veil of ignorance, for example, reflects our belief that moral reasoning should be impartial rather than biased in our own favor and should not be unduly influenced by our social class, race, gender, religion, or genetic endowment.

Unfortunately for those who oppose the use of performance-enhancing steroids, this argument is hardly free from criticism. In particular, it assumes, perhaps incorrectly, that the only outcomes athletes would consider behind the veil of ignorance would be risks to health versus competitive gains over other athletes. Some athletes might consider other issues; for example, some might consider that a universally higher level of competition generated by using steroids more than compensates for health risks, personal advantage not being an issue. Others may value their greater strength as a result of steroid use, regardless of competitive gain over others.[12] Thus, it is not as uncontroversial as it first appeared to suppose that impartial and reasonable athletes would unanimously agree to prohibit steroid use; their deliberations behind the veil might even be indeterminate because of conflicting views.

This objection indicates that even the contractual version of the argument from fairness is open to reasonable objection, although further development of the argument may undermine some of the objections to it. For example, we might consider whether the official rule-making bodies of sports, such as the NCAA (National Collegiate Athletic Association) or the IOC (International Olympic Committee) are obligated to ignore the idiosyncratic values of individual athletes and simply consider steroid use from the point of good competition. If we can justifiably rule out the preferences of athletes who value increases in strength or in overall athletic achievement over risks to health, and only consider the issue from the point of competitive advantages and disadvantages (which arguably is the point of view that rule-making bodies should take), then our original conclusion seems to follow. From the standpoint of collective impartial choice about the conditions of competition, users of steroids are exempting themselves from rules to which they would not consent under conditions of free impartial choice. Because they are making exceptions of themselves arbitrarily, can their behavior be regarded as justifiable or fair? Users who engage in a policy they could not rationally endorse for others treat their fellow athletes merely as a means to their own success.[13]

This conclusion, as we have seen, may not follow if we allow that athletes may take a point of view based on some value not directly connected to competitive success, such as raising the limits of human performance; but because sports organizations regulate competition, it seems reasonable for them to ignore such idiosyncratic values when making regulations about steroid use.

Performance-Enhancing Drugs, Respect for Persons, and the Ethic of Competition

Even if the contractual version of the argument from fairness has force, it may seem to miss part of the issue raised by the use of performance enhancers. For one thing, it depends heavily on the harmful effects of prolonged steroid use to the user. But we may believe that the use of performance-enhancing would be wrong even if the drugs were not harmful. If there were a "magic pill," which if taken properly would improve athletic ability without risks to health, would using such a pill be ethical? Doesn't the use of steroids run counter to the ethic of good competition outlined in earlier chapters.

To many people, steroid use seems a way of avoiding the challenges presented by sports rather than overcoming them. This belief does not seem to rest upon claims that the use of steroids is coercive or that such use is unfair but seem to arise independently from concerns about the basic ethic of athletic competition. Can such intuitions about the wrongness of performance-enhancing drugs be justified?

If competition in sports is supposed to be a test of the athletic ability of persons, isn't the very heart of competition corrupted if results are affected by performance-enhancing drugs? Presumably, we would not accept a new high-jump record if the winner wore special mechanical aids that added spring to her shoes. Similarly, consider home runs produced by use of a high-tech baseball bat programmed to make square contact with the ball (perhaps through an implanted sensor and computerized control chip) so that it will fly out of the park regardless of the batter's skill. In all these examples, we are inclined to say that success does not reflect the skill of the athlete but is the result of special equipment.

Isn't it the same with the use of performance-enhancing drugs? Where such drugs lead to improved play, it is not the person who is responsible for the gains. Rather, it is the drug that makes the difference. Isn't this similar to the examples of the mechanical track shoes and the high-tech baseball bat? Isn't the ethic of competition violated because the skills of the athlete are replaced by technological aids that turn the contest from one of competing persons into one of machines? The logical extension of such a route would be to replace flesh-and-blood athletes by robots designed to maximize performance in every category. What we would have, if such a nightmare ever became reality, might be enhanced performance, but would it be sport?

Those who believe the use of performance-enhancing drugs should be permitted would not be convinced by such an argument. They might raise four important objections. First, we do allow new equipment in sport, even if such equipment does enhance performance. Fiberglass poles for vaulting, tennis racquets composed of composites, and the replacement of wooden golf shafts by steel ones are examples of technological innovations that enhance performance.[14] How does the introduction of performance-enhancing drugs differ? Second, changes in diet are widely believed to enhance performance. If runners can "load-up" on carbohydrates before a race to improve their times, why can't they take steroids as well? Third, steroids and other performance enhancers are not magic bullets that immediately produce results; they yield improvement only in conjunction with hard training and a demanding work ethic; they allow muscles to recover faster and so permit more intense and more frequent workouts than nonusers are able to manage. Finally, why isn't the decision to use steroids just as much a person's decision to make as the decision to use weight training? What reason have we to say that weight training reflects our status as persons and the use of steroids does not?

Let us consider the point about technological innovations in equipment first. Although I doubt there is any one principle that explains when an innovation in equipment is acceptable and when it isn't, some distinctions can be made. For example, some technological improvements in equipment remedy previous defects. Old wooden shafts in golf clubs twisted to varying degrees under the pressure of the golf swing, producing arbitrary results. The same player could make two equally good swings but get different results because of too much torque in the wooden shaft. This defect was remedied by introducing more consistent steel golf shafts. Similarly, improved athletic shoes remove defects of unnecessary weight and faulty structure. Although both innovations made it easier to perform better, neither changed the character of the game and both can be regarded as removing handicaps created by faulty equipment that were extraneous to the real challenges set by the sports in question.

Other changes in equipment that have been regarded as permissible cannot so easily be seen as simply removing defects in materials used earlier. In golf, the sand wedge, a club with a specially designed flange, invented by professional Gene Sarazen, made escaping from sand bunkers far easier than before. Many skilled professionals would rather have a missed shot land in the sand than in a difficult lie on grass because the sand wedge has made highly accurate recoveries likely for the advanced player. Similarly, fiberglass poles have made it possible for pole-vaulters to achieve heights previously considered unreachable. Graphite and other composite materials have contributed to advances in play in golf, tennis, and other sports. In other words, it does not appear true that all technological advances in sports equipment are simply remedies for defects in earlier materials. Why should such advances be allowed and steroids prohibited?

Not all advancements in equipment are allowed by sports authorities. Some technological advances are prohibited because they make the game too easy or reduce its challenges in some significant way. But other advancements can make the game more competitive or make its challenges more reasonable. Thus, the use of the sand wedge in golf can be defended on the grounds that without it, bunker shots were simply too difficult. The game was made better by allowing the equipment.

Although technological improvements in equipment do yield advances in achievement, the equipment must still be used by persons. Performance-enhancing drugs, it might be argued, change the nature of those who use the equipment and so undermine the challenge presented by sports. Instead of meeting the challenge of the test, we change the nature of the test takers to minimize the challenge they face. If steroids and other performance-enhancing drugs were permitted, the way athletes were affected by the drug would significantly affect outcomes. But this seems athletically irrelevant. Jones should not defeat Smith because Jones's body processes steroids more efficiently than Smith's. We want the winner to be the best athlete, not the individual whose body is best attuned to a performance-enhancing drug! Performance enhancers thus turn sport from a contest among persons into a contest among "designer" bodies that are manufactured through a technological fix.[15] The winners are the individuals whose bodies react best to the available drugs, which hardly seems to be what is meant by sports as a mutual quest of persons for excellence through challenge.

However, a proponent of the use of performance enhancers might ask whether the same thing isn't true of special diets. Thus, "carbohydrate loading," or consuming unusually large amounts of carbohydrates before competition, seems to be a common and accepted practice among long-distance runners; but clearly, some competitors may gain more from the practice than others. Is this an example of outcomes being unfairly affected by athletically irrelevant qualities? Or if it is permissible to adhere to a performance-enhancing diet, why isn't it also acceptable to use performance-enhancing drugs?

Even if this point is ignored, proponents of steroid use might charge that the argument against steroids is inconsistent in another way. Competition in sports has been defended here because it is expressive of our moral status as persons. But by prohibiting athletes from using performance-enhancing drugs, it can be argued that we show disrespect to them as persons. That is, we deny them the control over their own lives that ought to belong to any autonomous, intelligent, and competent individual. In other words, aren't athletes persons? If so, shouldn't their choices, including the choice of using drugs to enhance performance, be respected?[16]

The debate so far raises several key issues. Just when are changes in equipment allowable and when should they be prohibited? Why does steroid use "change the nature of persons" but training, diet, and vitamins do not? And why should our current conception of persons (assuming it is clear enough to be useful) be sacrosanct? It appears that both the proponents and the critics of the use of performance-enhancing drugs in sports have advanced points well worth considering, but that the arguments presented by both sides are still inconclusive.

A Presumptive Case Against Performance Enhancers

Our discussion about the ethics of using performance-enhancing drugs in sports suggests that, although critics and proponents have advanced important arguments, neither side has won conclusively. Perhaps the debate can be resolved through further critical inquiry.

In the meantime, sports authorities must promulgate rules about whether to permit the use of anabolic steroids. Policymakers often have to decide difficult issues over which reasonable persons of good will disagree. If we had to wait for the emergence of decisive arguments on controversial moral issues, we often would be paralyzed in circumstances demanding some action. In fact, we often have to draw lines between what is permissible and impermissible in areas where reasons for making the distinction do not apply in as sharp a fashion as we would like. For example, the democratic state must distinguish between those who are mature enough to vote and those who are not. Because the maturity of each person cannot be evaluated on the merits of individuals, we attempt to draw a line reasonably. So long as the process by which the line is drawn is itself consistent with democratic values, and the boundary is reasonable, there are good grounds for regarding it as justified. We need to avoid the fallacy of insisting that if we cannot find the perfect place to draw a line, we should draw no line at all.

Given the sharp division in sports over the morality of using performance-enhancing drugs, yet the majority involved are repelled by the practice, we may want to give sports authorities the discretion to prohibit performance enhancers if their best judgment supports such a policy. If sports authorities, such as the NCAA or the IOC, have *reasonable* grounds for making distinctions between impermissible performance-enhancing drugs and permissible diets, equipment changes, and the like, and if they are not acting in an autocratic or dogmatic fashion, then even if no conclusive argument can be given for drawing the line in one place, their decision still has normative force.

Several points emerge from our discussion to support such a conclusion:

1. Athletes who choose to use harmful performance enhancers create a situation in which nonusers must either subject themselves to serious health risks or cease to be competitive. It is far from clear that users have the right to impose this choice on others.

2. It is doubtful whether rational and impartial athletes concerned with regulating competition would support a universal rule allowing the use of potentially harmful performance enhancers.

3. More controversially, the use of harmful performance enhancers moves sport closer to transforming persons into tools for athletic success than do special diets, weight training, or vitamin supplements.

4. Finally, the use of harmful performance enhancers by elite athletes is likely to encourage by example the use of such harmful substances by aspiring young athletes who are beneath the age of consent, and so may be prohibited to avoid or minimize such dangerous consequences.

Thus, our discussion does suggest that although no conclusive argument or knock-down proof is available, good reasons can be given for prohibiting steroids as performance enhancers and that official governing bodies in sports can therefore prohibit their use. Unless it can be shown that such decisions are arbitrary, dogmatic, or authoritarian, they are given moral weight because they are promulgated by legitimate governing bodies.[17] Rather than assigning the burden of proof to those who find the use of performance enhancers to be immoral, why not maintain instead that where the sports community is in deep disagreement, the decisions of governing bodies are morally binding as long as they are not unreasonable, undemocratic, or arbitrary?

Moreover, the lines of argument we have considered for prohibiting the use of performance-enhancing drugs, although not determinative, might well be strengthened by extended discussion and debate. Although none of these arguments avoids serious objection, it is far from clear that the objections are decisive enough to justify their total rejection. Perhaps they even are sufficient to show that the policies of those governing bodies of organized sports that prohibit the use of performance enhancers in their competitions are sufficiently reasonable to support a policy of prohibition, at least until the ethical issues involved are more satisfactorily resolved.

Enforcement

If the rules prohibiting the use of performance-enhancing drugs are to be effective, they must be enforced. Enforcement, however, raises a host of ethical issues. For example, drug use often can be detected through urinalysis and other scientific tests, although elite athletes have made attempts at chemically disguising evidence of drug use. But assuming that tests are often effective, should athletes be required to take them? Does this amount to forcing users to incriminate themselves, violating constitutional guarantees against self-incrimination? Do drugs tests violate a right to privacy? Which methods of enforcement are ethical and which are not?

What is the principal ethical objection to requiring athletes to be tested for performance-enhancing substances? Clearly, it has to do with liberty and privacy. One of the most cherished principles of Anglo-American law, and of the liberal political theories from which it derives, is that the presumption is on the authorities to prove the guilt of an individual. Individuals are to be left free and undisturbed unless a reasonable case can be made to show that particular persons are guilty of some infraction.

To see why this principle is so important, consider the alternative. Under a presumption of guilt, individuals could be detained, their homes searched, and their lives disrupted simply because prosecutors decide they might find evidence of an infraction if they looked hard enough. Our liberty and our privacy would be minimal at best under such an arrangement. We would have them only to the extent that the authorities permitted us to keep them, which is to say we would not have them in any meaningful sense at all.

Requiring the individual to submit to drug tests seems to those concerned with our liberties similar to requiring individuals to open their homes to searches, or to detaining individuals against their will, without evidence that, if it existed, might justify such intrusions. Accordingly, it seems that those of us committed to respect for the freedom of the individual must reject the required testing of athletes for drug use.

But although this argument does have considerable force, it may also admit of exceptions. For example, shouldn't those persons directly responsible for the safety of others be required to show that they are not under the influence of alcohol or

other mind-altering drugs? Airline pilots, railroad engineers, surgeons, police officers, and firefighters are among those with special obligations to care for the safety
of others. Accordingly, requiring them to take drug tests seems to be an exception
permitted even by Mill's Harm Principle because its purpose is to prevent direct injury to others.

This argument can be gradually extended until it becomes dangerously broad.
Thus, although loss of worker efficiency due to drug use is a major national problem, could we justify required testing of all workers in an effort to prevent harm to
fellow workers and to consumers? What happens to our civil liberties then?

Although we cannot pursue this important question in depth here, we ought
not to be driven down the slippery slope too quickly. Although drug use on the job
by some workers may indirectly injure consumers, lines can be drawn. The greater
the threat of harm, the more serious the kind of harm at stake; and the more directly it is attendant upon drug use, then the greater the argument for required
testing. Usually, the threat of harm will be sufficiently indirect or weak, or other
methods of protection and detection will be available. It is therefore doubtful that
making exceptions to the general principle of noninterference in instances of direct
and serious harm to individuals will undermine civil liberties generally.

Is there another kind of exception that might apply to organized athletics?
After all, unlike airline pilots who use drugs, athletes who take steroids do not directly endanger the general public.

Perhaps the idea of a collection of individuals voluntarily taking part in a joint
activity requiring the mutual observance of common rules applies here. Thus, in
professional baseball, an umpire has the right to require a pitcher to empty his
pockets so the umpire can check that the player is not carrying special prohibited
substances that when applied to the baseball can alter its flight, making it more difficult to hit. Off the field, the umpire would have no right to search the player but
does have such a right in the special context of the game. This is because the game is
fair only if all players observe the same rules. The umpire, with the consent of the
competing teams, is charged with enforcing the rules, thereby insuring a fair contest. As a result, umpires acquire rights in virtue of their role that they do not have
as ordinary citizens. The civil rights of the players have in effect been limited in the
context of the game because the players accept its rules and enforcement procedures.

A similar argument can be applied to testing for the use of performance-enhancing drugs in organized athletics. Participants consent to playing by publicly acknowledged rules. No one is forced to participate, but once consent is given to

participation, players are owed protection from those who would intentionally violate the rules. Without enforcement, no protection would be provided. In particular, if effective means of detection were not used, athletes would suspect each other
of breaking the existing rules. Pressures would exist to use such performance-
enhancing drugs illegally in attempts to remain competitive.

Because participants voluntarily agree to participate and because they agree to
play under the assumption that the rules will be applied fairly to all, they are owed
protection against violators. Drug testing of athletes, in this view, seems not a violation of their civil rights but a reasonable protection against being unfairly disadvantaged. To the extent that requiring athletes to submit to drug tests can be defended,
it is because each participant is entitled to play under the public conditions specify-
ing the rules of the contest. If umpires in baseball can enforce such an entitlement
by requiring pitchers to reveal whether they are carrying illegal substances that can
alter the flight of the ball, why don't sports authorities have a similar justification
for drug testing to ensure that advantages prohibited by the rules are not obtained
through ingestion of illegal substances of a different kind?

Summary

Our discussion in this section has explored important lines of argument for and
against the view that the use of performance-enhancing drugs in sports is immoral.
Although arguments for different positions on these issues need to be defended further, our examination provides provisional but not conclusive support for a prohibition on the use of such drugs and supports drug testing as a principal means of
detection and enforcement in certain situations. Critics of the use of steroids and
other performance enhancers will no doubt wish for an even stronger verdict on
their behalf. Perhaps such a verdict will be justified by further critical reflection on
the issues we have discussed. As we have seen, however, there are important criticisms of the arguments for prohibiting steroid use, not all of which have yet been
answered satisfactorily. In the meantime, while debate continues, rules prohibiting
the use of steroids in organized sports can be defended as permissible because they
have not been shown to be arbitrary, unreasonable, or illegitimately imposed. To violate those rules covertly solely to gain a competitive advantage seems unjustifiable,
whether or not the rules themselves ultimately should be revised.

Violence in Sports

"On Lincoln's Birthday, 1982, . . . Benjamin Davis and Louis Wade walked into the
Civic Auditorium in Albuquerque to fight each other in the semi-finals of the New

Mexico Golden Gloves. . . . You could not hope to meet two nicer boys. One would help kill the other in the ring that night."[18]

Benjamin Davis, known as Benjii, and Louis Wade had never met before that tragic night in 1982. Although they came from different ethnic backgrounds—Benjii, twenty-two, was a Navaho, and Louis, only sixteen, was Anglo—they had much in common. Both loved sports, were hard-working students, were loved by their families, and were regarded as fine young men by those who knew them. They participated in boxing not because they wanted to become professionals but because they wanted to work out and because they enjoyed the competition.

The tragedy happened in the second round. Benjii received several hard blows and seemed dazed, but the referee did not stop the fight. After another series of hard blows, Benjii crumpled and fell in a heap on the canvas, never to recover. Apparently, no one in Benjii's family blames Louis. "To this day, they only have compassion for him and everyone keeps assuring Louis that it was not his fault. Sometimes he believes that."[19]

Surely Louis is not to blame for playing by the rules of an activity in which both he and Benjii were involved, an activity that carried elements of risk to both participants. But is the activity, boxing, itself acceptable? Should our society permit young men and boys to participate in boxing, let alone make wealthy heroes out of the most successful? Hundreds of boxers have been killed in the ring. Moreover, the risks are borne not only by seasoned professionals but by boys and young men such as Louis and Benjii. Even boxers who survive the ring frequently suffer various degrees of brain damage, as the stumbling walk, halting speech, and poor memory of the "punch drunk" fighter attest.

Proponents would argue that much is to be said in favor of boxing as a sport. The use of violence in boxing, as in other contact sports, is restricted by the rules. Moreover, boxers often demonstrate great physical courage, dedication in training, and willingness to overcome obstacles. Boxing has also been an avenue through which young athletes, often from minority backgrounds, could rise from poverty to fame and fortune.

The claim that problems raised by violence in sports are not restricted to boxing is well taken. Football is regarded as a violent sport, and neck injuries in football have led to paralysis and death. Moreover, violence, in the form of hard body contact, and even intimidation and physical attack, is hardly unknown in other sports. For example, the joke "I went to a fight the other night and a hockey game broke out" says something significant about the level of violence in professional hockey.

Violence in sports is an increasing problem in the United States and around the world. According to many observers of American sports, violence is on the rise not only on the field but among spectators as well. Indeed, the nation was shocked in 2001 when a fight between a parent and the coach of a youth hockey team in Massachusetts resulted in the death of the coach after what witnesses described as a severe beating. The nature of violence raises many questions about its place in sports. Is boxing immoral? Is fighting in hockey permissible ("boys will be boys"), or should it be more severely punished? Is football a violent and, therefore, a morally objectionable sport? What is violence anyway?

In this section, we will examine certain ethical questions about the role of violence in sports. As we will see, the issues raised apply not only to sports but also concern the meaning and scope of individual liberty, the relationship between society and the individual, and the significance of respect for persons.

Conceptions of Violence

Examples of violence are all too frequent. If one person assaults another, a violent act has taken place. But how is "violence" itself best characterized? Are brushback pitches or hard tackles just as much instances of violence as an assault?

Violence generally involves the use of force, but not every use of force is violent. For example, a tennis player uses force in serving, but few of us are even tempted to characterize the act of serving in tennis as violent. Perhaps some acts, such as intense verbal abuse, should be characterized as forms of (psychological) violence even though they do not involve the use of force. So violence and the use of force cannot be equated. Sometimes it is argued that there can be forms of institutional violence that, although not intended or carried out by any one person, are the effect of unjust institutions upon the oppressed.

Can violence be characterized as the wrongful use of force? Leaving aside possible cases of psychological violence, which might not involve the use of force, other difficulties arise.

In particular, the proposed account of violence is morally loaded. That is, before we can determine whether any act is one of violence, we must first determine whether the act was morally wrong. This means that what we characterize as violent depends upon our moral views. Thus, if we regard the use of force by the Allies against Hitler in World War II as justified, we would not be able to call that use of force violent, since it was not wrongful.

What the proposal ignores is that sometimes it is far clearer that behavior is violent than whether it is right or wrong. Indeed, we may regard behavior as wrong precisely because it is violent, which would be pointless if we first had to decide an act was wrong before we could properly describe it as violent. For example, we might decide an assault was wrong because of the violence inflicted on the victim rather than deciding it was violent because we thought it wrong on some other grounds.

It will be useful to keep our account of violence as morally neutral as possible. Although it is sometimes impossible or undesirable to disentangle the normative and nonnormative elements of a concept, for example, "heroism," doing so here will help us distinguish importantly different issues. One issue concerns which acts are properly characterized as violent. A second distinct issue concerns whether such acts are right or wrong. Nothing is gained in this context by blending the two issues together.

Rather than try to define "violence" formally, a task that, even if it can be satisfactorily carried out, would take up far too much space for our purposes, it seems more useful to provide a rough explication instead. An explication will fall short of supplying necessary and sufficient conditions for an act to be violent but will pick out the central features of clear examples of violence. It will be useful in allowing us to examine moral evaluations of behavior exhibiting the central or paradigmatic features of violence.

Typically or paradigmatically, violence involves the use of physical force with the intent to harm persons or property. Thus, assault, war, rape, fighting, and armed robbery clearly involve violence or the threat of violence. This is not to deny that it sometimes may be justifiable to speak of psychological violence or that unintentional violence is possible, but only to suggest that special argument is needed to establish those points. Sports, to the extent that they involve violence at all, generally involve the use or threat of use of physical force to harm opponents, so it is upon physical force intended to harm opponents that we will mainly focus.

Perhaps the most controversial use of violence in sports involves boxing. Should boxing be prohibited because of its apparently violent nature?

The Case Against Boxing

What is the case against boxing? Is boxing immoral? Should it be prohibited?

Actually, there are several arguments for the prohibition of boxing. One important reason frequently cited in favor of prohibiting boxing is the protection of the boxers themselves. The violence inherent in boxing may make it too dangerous for the participants. In this view, society ought to protect boxers from harm by banning the sport. But there is a broader issue that is also of concern. What of the social consequences of not only allowing but publicizing boxing and giving it public recognition as a major sport? Might we somehow become less civilized, or morally more insensitive, if boxing is permitted to continue? Does boxing as a social practice desensitize us to violence? The question concerning what civilized societies ought to permit implies that the practice of boxing may have social consequences that are harmful, not just to boxers, but to others as well. Do either of these lines of argument justify the prohibition of boxing?

Paternalism and Mill's Harm Principle

There is little question that boxing can be harmful to the participants. Every boxer who enters the ring faces the real possibility of serious injury. Doesn't society have the right as well as the duty to prohibit boxing legally so that boxers themselves will be protected from harm and even death?

Before we agree too quickly, we should consider the following examples. Should your friends prevent you from ordering ice cream and fatty meats when you go out because such foods contain too much cholesterol? Should your friends prevent you from trying out for the basketball or football team because other sports you might play, such as golf, are much safer? On a broader level, suppose the state passes legislation requiring that reasonably healthy adults who do not exercise for at least thirty minutes a day must pay substantial extra taxes. This legislation is justified as an attempt to save the sedentary from themselves by requiring participation in a healthy lifestyle.

The issue at stake here, as we have seen in our discussion of performance-enhancing drugs, is one of paternalism. Paternalism refers to interference with the liberty of agents for what is believed to be their own good. A major objection to paternalism is that it wrongly disregards the liberty and autonomy of those very agents who are interfered with for their own good.

As mentioned earlier in this chapter, perhaps the most influential argument against paternalistic interference with the liberty of competent agents was presented by John Stuart Mill in his *On Liberty*.[20] At first glance, utilitarianism does not seem to be particularly hostile to paternalism or especially protective of the freedom of the individual because it seems that paternalistic interference with liberty would be justified on utilitarian grounds whenever it produced better consequences than the available alternatives. Utilitarians might turn out to be interfering busybodies on the individual level and benevolent versions of Big Brother on the state level, interfering with freedom whenever necessary to bring about the best results.

However, in *On Liberty,* Mill advanced important arguments against applying utilitarianism so crudely. Even if, as many suspect, Mill was unable to remain consistently within the utilitarian framework, he did advance important arguments against paternalistic interference with the individual based on respect for the liberty and autonomy of the individual.

In one of the most widely discussed passages of *On Liberty,* Mill declared that "the sole end for which mankind are warranted individually or collectively in interfering with the liberty of action of any of their number is self protection" (see the passage quoted from *On Liberty* earlier in this chapter).

According to Mill, as long as another person's acts are self-regarding, so long as they do not harm or constitute a threat to the welfare of others, interference with them is unjustified.

Why did Mill reject what would seem to be the position most in harmony with utilitarianism, namely, that paternalistic interference with freedom is justified whenever it produces better consequences than alternatives? Perhaps the argument Mill advances that is most compatible with his official utilitarianism is one of efficiency. Paternalistic interference is likely to be inefficient. After all, agents generally know their own interests better than others. Moreover, paternalists may often be influenced by their own values and prejudices or by fear for the safety of others, and so are unlikely to calculate properly the consequences of interfering. As a result, allowing paternalism will create a society of busybodies who, in their efforts to do good, will interfere in the wrong place at the wrong time for the wrong reasons.

Although this argument is not implausible, it may not accomplish as much as Mill thought it would. After all, wouldn't paternalism still be justified in those few situations where we are convinced it would do more good than harm?[21]

Mill advanced a second line of argument, not easily reconciled with utilitarianism, which has perhaps been more influential than the approach sketched above. Even if paternalistic interference produces more good than harm, constant interference with our liberty will stunt our moral and intellectual growth and eventually make us incapable of thinking for ourselves. As Mill maintained, "The human faculties of perception, judgment, discrimination, feeling, mental activity, and even moral preference are exercised only in making a choice. . . . The mental and the moral, like the muscular powers, are improved only by being used. . . . He who lets the world . . . choose his plan of life for him, has no need of any other faculty than the ape-like one of imitation."[22]

Here, Mill seems to be appealing more to the value of the idea of autonomy than to social utility understood in the sense of a balance of pleasure or satisfaction over pain or frustrated desires. The appeal to autonomy is more fundamental than the appeal to utility because one must be autonomous to evaluate any moral argument at all, including utilitarian arguments. Autonomy is a fundamental value, it can be argued, precisely because it is presupposed by the practice of moral argument itself. (Mill himself might retort that autonomy itself is a component of utility, or promotes it, and so affirm that his argument is consistent with utilitarianism after all.)

Finally, one can reinforce Mill's case by arguing that paternalism interferes with the fundamental moral right of individuals to control their own lives. Although moral rights may sometimes be justified by the degree to which they promote utility, or as protections for autonomy, they can also be justified as basic moral commodities that protect individuals from being regarded as mere resources to be used for the good of the greater number. In a sense, rights function as political and social "trumps" that individuals can play to protect themselves from being swallowed up in the pursuit of the social good.[23] Individual rights to liberty protect the ability of persons to live their lives as they choose rather than as someone else, however benevolent, thinks such lives should be led.

Accordingly, supporters of boxing can appeal to the arguments suggested by *On Liberty* to reject the claim that boxing ought to be prohibited. In particular, they can maintain (a) that it is unclear whether prohibition really will promote the most utility; (b) even if it does, it prevents boxers and spectators alike from making the moral choice of whether to engage in and support the sport; and finally (c) it ignores the rights of the boxers and spectators to live their own lives as they themselves see fit. Are such arguments decisive?

Exceptions to the Harm Principle

Is it possible to accept the Harm Principle and still maintain that paternalistic interference with boxing is sometimes justified? For one thing, Mill himself acknowledges that the Harm Principle "is meant to apply only to human beings in the maturity of their faculties."[24] Thus, interference with children and the mentally incompetent for their own good would be allowed by the Harm Principle. This surely is a plausible restriction because such persons cannot evaluate their desires rationally so as to determine their real interests, and they are not (yet) capable of making rational and autonomous choices.

As we saw in our discussion of performance-enhancing drugs, such a restriction would not allow interference with the behavior of competent adults, some of whom can and do choose to box. One could argue that because some persons choose to box merely demonstrates their irrationality and incompetency and thus disqualifies them from protection by the Harm Principle; but if the only reason for thinking such people are irrational is that they make a choice others don't like, such an argument must be rejected. The very point of the Harm Principle is to protect individuals from having the values of others imposed upon them, so we must have independent reasoning to think that agents are incompetent or immature before we are justified in interfering with their behavior.

A second kind of exception to the Harm Principle might allow interference with the choice of competent adults to participate to protect their status as rational and autonomous agents. For example, suppose a person of sound mind and body is about to take a drug that, although creating pleasurable experiences, is highly addictive and will eventually destroy her capacity to reason. Aren't you justified in interfering to remove her supply of the drug, even against her will? After all, your goal is not to impose your conception of happiness upon her but to preserve her capacity to choose her own conception of the good life.

How does this argument apply to the prohibition of boxing? In particular, repeated blows to the head produce brain damage, leading to the symptoms associated with the behavior of the "punch drunk" fighter. Long before those symptoms become evident, however, irreversible brain damage, and gradual diminishment of rational capacities, might have taken place.[25]

Although this sort of argument does provide grounds for interference, whether these grounds are sufficiently strong or weighty to justify interference with liberty is controversial. In particular, unlike the example of a mind-destroying addictive drug, the effects of boxing on mental capacity are long term and uncertain. Moreover, the rewards that some professional fighters can obtain are potentially great. Why is it less justifiable to risk one's capacity for rational choice to secure a great gain than it is, say, to risk shortening one's life span by following an unhealthy but pleasurable diet, or putting oneself under unhealthy stress to succeed in business?

Perhaps a third ground for making exceptions to the Harm Principle provides a stronger justification for interference with boxing. We have been assuming that athletes freely and autonomously choose to engage in boxing; but there are grounds for doubting the truth of that assumption.

For one thing, many boxers may be ignorant of the risks of engaging in their sport. Hence, they no more freely consent to run those risks than the person who drives over an unsafe bridge in the mistaken belief that it is safe consents to being thrown into the raging river below. Of equal importance, many of the participants in professional boxing come from severely disadvantaged backgrounds. These men see boxing as their main chance of escape from the economic and social disadvantages of the ghetto. In this view, the athlete who chooses to box is not responding to an offer or opportunity, that is, "You can better yourself by becoming a boxer," but rather to a threat, that is, "If you don't become a boxer, you will continue to be a victim of social injustice and neglect." Therefore, because boxers are not autonomous freely choosing agents, but rather are forced to box, they are not covered by the Harm Principle in the first place.

Proponents of individual liberty will regard such a view as too extreme, for reasons similar to those advanced against the coercion argument in our discussion of performance-enhancing drugs. Carried to its logical limits, they will point out, it implies that victims of injustice as well as the very poor and deprived should have less liberty to direct their own lives than the rest of us because they are not "truly free" to begin with. In the name of protecting them from themselves, we would be depriving the disadvantaged of one of the most basic elements of human dignity, the ability to have some control of their own lives. By viewing them only as victims, we would no longer see them as persons in their own right.

This point does have force, but it must also be remembered that poverty and deprivation can lead people to take risks that no one would take unless desperate. The justice of a system that presents people with such cruel choices can be called into question. Thus, a proponent of prohibition might agree that the poor and deprived are not mere victims and can make choices, but might regard the choice between becoming a boxer and living a life of deprivation as itself unjust. Perhaps a prohibition on boxing could be justified to prevent the imposition of such unjust choices upon the disadvantaged.

The evaluation of this point will depend upon whether one regards the athlete from a disadvantaged and perhaps minority background as having a reasonable set of available choices in our society. If one believes that the alternative to boxing is not starvation, or even welfare, but that educational opportunities are available for those who want them, then one will view the chance to become a boxer as an opportunity. If one regards alternate opportunities as shams, one will be inclined to see boxers as the victims of societal coercion. In any event, to the extent that alternate opportunities are available, coaches and parents are responsible for informing young athletes about them and the relatively infinitesimal chances of being successful in professional sports.

Be that as it may, it is doubtful whether the current argument supports an across-the-board ban on participation in boxing, even if one makes highly pessimistic assumptions about the range of opportunities available to disadvantaged youth in our society. This is because not everyone who chooses to participate in boxing need be from a disadvantaged background. At most, the argument justifies closing boxing only to certain classes of people; namely, (a) those for whom it is a last resort and who may be "forced" into it because of social or economic pressure, and (b) those who lack the education or have not had the opportunity to understand fully the risks of participation.

We can conclude, then, that although paternalistic arguments in favor of prohibition of boxing are not without force, they are not conclusive, either; concern for individual liberty and autonomy justifies us in placing the burden of proof on the paternalist. Although further discussion might warrant us in revising our opinion, it appears that the burden has not yet been met where participation in boxing (and other risky activities) is at issue.

Boxing and the Protection of Society

So far, we have been assuming that the only grounds for prohibition of boxing are paternalistic. But what if participation in boxing is not simply self-regarding but has harmful effects on others? The Harm Principle permits interference with the individual liberty of some to prevent them from harming others.

But how can boxing harm others? At first glance, it may appear that the only ones boxers can harm are themselves. However, first glances can be deceiving. To see how boxing can harm society, consider the imaginary sport of Mayhem.[26] The rules of Mayhem are simple. Adult volunteers, who have given their informed consent to participate, are armed with swords and spears, placed in an arena, and divided into two teams. They fight until only members of one team are left alive. Those on the winning, that is, surviving, team then share $10 million.

Does it follow that if there are no paternalistic reasons strong enough to justify prohibiting Mayhem, there are no reasons at all to justify prohibition? Isn't it plausible to think that even though there is no direct harm to spectators—the gladiators refrain even from attacking those fans who boo—the indirect harm is substantial. Children might come to idolize (and imitate) trained killers. (Would youngsters collect gladiator bubble gum cards with kill ratio statistics on the back side?) Violence would be glorified and the value of human life inevitably would be cheapened. Such effects may not be inevitable, but the likelihood of eventual harm to others seems sufficient to justify a civilized society in banning Mayhem.

Can't a similar argument be applied to boxing, for as one newspaper editorial exclaimed, "The public celebration of violence cannot be a private matter."[27] After all, although many sports involve the use of force and risk of injury, only boxing has violence in the sense of intentional attempts to injure opponents at its core. Do we want our society to glorify such an activity in the name of sports?

How powerful are these considerations? In fact, they can be understood as supporting two distinct arguments. According to the first, public exposure to boxing causes spectators (and perhaps indirectly those with whom they come in contact) to be influenced adversely and as a result they become more violent or tolerant of violence themselves. In this way, exposure to boxing contributes to the rise of violence throughout society. According to the second argument, public adulation of the violence inherent in boxing undermines community standards and generally debases society.

The difference between these two arguments is that the first is more individualistic, the second more communitarian. The first argument needs to be supported by empirical evidence, which is likely to be inconclusive. Psychologists have maintained for some time that we can be, and often are, influenced by models, and, accordingly, if society presents persons engaging in violence as its heroes, toleration of violence and the tendency to commit it will increase. On the other hand, it is unlikely that the normal boxing fan is going to act violently after watching a match. Thus, it is unlikely that any direct and immediate tie between boxing and broader social violence exists.

For communitarians, the role of individual liberty has been misrepresented in our entire discussion. We have proceeded as if the individual is an autonomous atom who can step back from social institutions and make choices in isolation. It is this individualistic choosing self who is seen as the locus of value, yet, according to the communitarian, such a self is in many ways a fiction. Rather, selves are formed within communities and are constituted or defined by their relationships with others in their social settings. Thus, one is a parent, teacher, coach, member of a religious group, and citizen rather than an isolated individualistic pure agent, allegedly capable of stepping aside from all roles and autonomously evaluating them. What would such an abstract individual be but a mysterious "0" stripped of all distinguishing human characteristics?[28]

What has this roughly sketched communitarian picture of the self have to do with the critique of boxing and with violence in sports? Although the specific implications for policy of theoretical communitarianism are not always clear, the communitarian approach at least emphasizes the need to preserve the common values that bind society. Boxing and the public celebration of violence undermine the standards of the community and hence transform the kind of individuals it produces. There is no asocial individual who can stand outside his or her community to evaluate boxing. If we tolerate boxing, and violence in other areas, we will end up with individuals who no longer share the standards and traditions that lead to the condemnation of violence. Our community will gradually be replaced by one that tolerates and may even welcome behavior that the previous community would have regarded as degrading, threatening, and immoral.

Although all aspects of the debate between communitarians and what they regard as their liberal individualistic opponents cannot be touched on here, two important points should be kept in mind.[29] First, if the communitarian's major point is that we are so tightly situated within specific communities and traditions that free, rational, and autonomous choice is impossible, we cannot freely, rationally, and autonomously choose to believe communitarianism. That some of us accept a communitarian approach would be just another social fact, to be explained by reference to our social situation, rather than by the truth of communitarianism or the strength of the rational justification for it.

Presumably, the communitarian would not want to accept such a conclusion. But, then, some weight must be given to free, rational, and autonomous choice within communitarianism, even if the account of such choice differs from that of more individualistic approaches to political theory.

But what weight should communitarians give to liberty? If they reply, "Its up to the standards of one's community," then they must be reminded that many communities are oppressive, racist, intolerant, and fanatical. But if they are to avoid giving weight to the standards implicit in the practices of immoral communities, they seem to be committed to some standard, such as Mill's Harm Principle, or liberal rights to free choice, which is relatively independent of the standards of particular societies. Thus, they cannot settle the issue of whether boxing ought to be prohibited by appealing to the standards of the community, for even assuming there is just one community in our society, the moral question of why its standards ought to be obeyed still remains to be answered. (It can be argued that many communities in the United States do find the violence in boxing acceptable. Does that settle the moral question of whether it is acceptable?)

Boxing, Morality, and Legality

Our discussion has not provided conclusive reason for thinking boxing ought to be legally prohibited. Paternalistic arguments do not seem strong enough to justify a general prohibition, the link between boxing and individual violence is too tenuous and indirect to support such a general prohibition, and the standards of the community are an insufficient guide to action. Boxers exhibit important virtues such as physical courage and determination to succeed; in these respects, they may be good examples for others.

Yet, although most of us regard individual liberty as of the greatest value, we would probably agree that society does have the right to prohibit professional gladiatorial contests (such as Mayhem), perhaps on communitarian grounds or perhaps because we doubt that the choice to participate can be truly free or informed. The trouble is that boxing seems to be a less clear case than Mayhem. It is not nearly as dangerous as Mayhem, the harm is not as certain or direct, it is governed by strict rules limiting how contact can be made, and we can at least begin to understand how a participant can voluntarily accept the risks involved. As one critic of the Mayhem example has pointed out, "The stringent rules, the delimiting of time, the quality of medical supervision, and the skill of the participants, serve to distinguish boxing from Mayhem and from all forms of untrammeled physical aggression."[30] Thus, the arguments both for and against prohibition seem to be at something of a standoff. Given the dangers of interfering with liberty, perhaps the best policy would be one not of legal interference but moral sanction and reform.

Thus, whether or not the argument for legal prohibition is determinative, many reasons have been given for moral concern about boxing. In particular, boxing allows the infliction of physical harm upon an opponent as a legitimate means to victory. It is appropriate for those who share such moral concerns to refuse to support boxing, to urge others to refrain from supporting it, and to advocate strong reforms in its practice. Reformers may want boxing to become an example of the constrained use of force rather than of violence. This view sees boxing as a sport that should be distinguished from boxing as a form of violence, just as we now distinguish fencing from actual dueling. Reforms that work in this direction include the mandatory use of helmets by fighters and emphasis on scoring points through skill rather than on inflicting damage to opponents. Although boxing will probably never be sedate, it can be modified so that it bears a closer resemblance to fencing than to Mayhem.

To conclude, even if boxing should be immune to legal prohibition on grounds of respect for individual liberty, reform of the sport seems to be morally justified. Boxing has the goal of inflicting harm at its core, and so makes violence central. No other sport requires the intentional infliction of harm upon opponents as a clear and approved means of victory.

Violence and Contact Sports

Can arguments concerning violence in boxing be carried over to contact sports? For example, if it can be successfully argued that boxing morally (if not legally) ought to be eliminated or at least reformed in part because it is inherently violent, shouldn't the same conclusion(s) be drawn about football?

Critics of football maintain that it is a violent sport. Coaches and fans some-times urge players to "smash," "smear," or "bury" the opposition. This view sees foot-ball as a miniaturized version of war. Even players who claim to compete within the rules acknowledge that physical intimidation is part of the game. As former Oak-land Raider safety Jack Tatum puts it in his perhaps aptly named book, *They Call Me Assassin*, "My idea of a good hit is when the victim wakes up on the sidelines with the train whistles blowing in his head and wondering who he is and what ran him over."[31] Unfortunately, one of Tatum's hits in a game against the New England Patri-ots resulted in what appears to be the permanent paralysis of the Patriots' receiver, Darryl Stingley.

Tatum claimed that although he hit hard when he tackled, he played within the rules and did not take illegal "cheap shots" at opponents. His view is he is paid to make sure that pass receivers don't make catches in his territory. A good way to achieve this goal is to make receivers aware that they will get hit hard when running pass patterns. Then, the next time a pass in thrown, the receivers may think more about getting hit and concentrate less on doing their job and catching the ball. As Tatum put it, "Do I let the receiver have the edge and give him the chance to make catches around me be-cause I'm a sensitive guy or do I do what I am paid to do?"[32]

It is understandable why, to its critics, football glorifies violence, encourages militaristic attitudes, and amounts to a public celebration of many of our worst val-ues. In effect, these critics claim that football is to our society what bloody gladiato-rial contests were to Rome: distraction for the masses through the presentation of violence as entertainment.

Paul Hoch, author of *Rip Off the Big Game*, a highly ideological critique of American sports but one that raises many serious issues for consideration, sees football as an expression of suppressed violence in the American psyche. He sug-gests that because violence in football is rule governed, it "provides powerful ideo-logical support for the officially sanctioned, rule-governed violence in society, in which judges have the final say. In short, the fans are supposed to identify with the distorted framework of law and order, both on the football field and in society, irre-spective of what that law and order is supposed to protect."[33]

Ethics, Football, and Violence

The charges against football suggested in the comments above can be understood in diverse ways, but two sorts of claims seem especially worth discussing. First, foot-ball is held to be a violent sport. Second, football is thought to express or encour-age acceptance of officially sanctioned violence while discouraging external criticism or struggle against the official rules themselves. Thus, football, in our society at least, is not ideologically neutral but expresses a conservative bias against social change.

Are these charges justified? In considering them, we need to keep some distinctions in mind. The first concerns whether violence is necessary to football or merely contingently attached to it. The second is between violence and the use of force.

Violence in the sense of force aimed at harming an opponent is normally as indefensible in sports as it is elsewhere. Such violence treats the opponent as a mere thing to be used for one's satisfaction or gratification; thus, it violates the morality of respect for persons, expressed in the ethic of competition as a mutual quest for excellence. But is violence in this strong sense necessarily part of football in the first place?

Football is a contact sport requiring the use of bodily force against opponents; but it does not follow that football is necessarily violent. As we have seen, the use of force is quite distinct from violence because only the latter covers the intent to harm others. In particular games, or on particular teams, players may indeed act violently towards opponents, but it does not follow that football itself is a violent game.

How is the line between violence and the use of force to be drawn? When Jack Tatum attempts to intimidate an opponent through hard hits, is he being violent or is he merely using force efficiently? Tatum would say that because it is not his intent to injure his opponent, he is using force but not ethically indefensible violence. How is this claim to be evaluated?

To begin with, it is clear that many sports often involve the use of physical force applied to opponents to achieve strategic goals. The use of the brushback pitch in baseball, the hard smash directly at the opponent in tennis, and the hard drive to the hoop in basketball, can all involve the use of force against opponents. Not infrequently, this use of force carries some risk of injury. Presumably, participation requires that players willingly bear the risk. The key ethical question in fair competition may be whether the use of force takes advantage of an opponent's physical vulnerability. Thus, major league batters are supposed to have the reflexes that can enable them to avoid a brushback pitch.[34] The same pitch may be indefensible when thrown against an out-of-shape older businessman who hasn't played ball in years.

If this suggestion has force, it supports what might be called the Vulnerability Principle, or VP. According to the VP, for the use of force against an opponent in an athletic contest to be ethically defensible, the opponent must be in a position and condition such that a strategic response is possible and it is unlikely that injury will ensue. Thus, attempting to block a shot from the front of an opponent in basketball conforms to the VP, but "undercutting" an opponent already in the air from behind does not.

Normal play in football does conform to the VP as long as opponents are able to respond with strategic countermoves reflecting the basic skills of the players. A tackle from the receiver's blind side when the receiver is in a position of vulnerability is ethically dubious. Indeed, defensive backs such as Jack Tatum have argued that the rules be redesigned to give more protection to receivers.

Our discussion so far suggests that football can be (although not always is) played without players intending to harm opponents. It is often difficult to draw the line between the defensible and indefensible uses of force in contact sports, although the VP may represent a useful first step in that direction. Perhaps football can be criticized because violence is too prevalent in the sport or because the use of force creates too much risk for the players, but it does not seem that football by its very nature must be violent.

Sports and Ideology

If football is not necessarily violent in a pejorative sense, the charge that football functions as an ideological defense of officially sanctioned violence is open to serious question. This is because not all instances of football are violent to begin with; however, the thesis that football (and perhaps other sports) are ideologically biased deserves fuller consideration. Just what does such a charge amount to?

Perhaps it means that the attention given to big-time football causes people to tolerate unjust situations and oppose disruptive protest, possibly because sports create identification with the values of those in power. Alternately, perhaps it means that the values expressed by a sport such as football are inherently objectionable; football is warlike or football requires unquestioning acceptance of officially sanctioned violence.

The causal thesis must ultimately be confirmed or disconfirmed by empirical data. The existing data, although sketchy and difficult to interpret, can perhaps be read to provide for a modest association of interest in sports with adherence to conservative values.[35] Nevertheless, key philosophical points must be kept in mind in interpreting empirical studies.

Suppose, for example, empirical evidence shows that football players and coaches adhere more to traditional values than a control group not associated with or interested in football. Can we conclude that football produces such value commitments? We cannot. As noted in Chapter 2, it is entirely possible that people with certain values tend to become football players and coaches, not that participation in football generates specific values among participants. Even more likely, some third factor, such as socioeconomic background, may tend to promote participation in football and adherence to certain values. Or it may be true that participation in football tends to reinforce values already accepted by those who play. Whatever the relationship, the mere existence of a correlation, if one does exist, does not establish why the correlation holds.

Even leaving this point aside, there is a deeper philosophical point also at issue. If what we are looking for is whether football and other major sports promote such traits as "unquestioning obedience to authority," "acceptance of official violence," "uncritical toleration of injustice," and "unwillingness to challenge the system," we need to be careful that we do not beg the question in favor of certain values over others. What one investigator may see as blind obedience, another may regard as admirable loyalty and discipline. What appears to some as "unwillingness to challenge the system" or "toleration of injustice" may be considered by others as rational allegiance to a defensible set of rules. Accordingly, although critics of football are quite right to raise the issue of the social significance of sports, they may smuggle in assumptions that have not been adequately defended. For example, they may assume that violence rather than the controlled use of force is a necessary element of football or that the relationship of players to coaches is more like one of robots to programmers rather than pupils to teachers. Thus, in assessing the effects of sports such as football on participants and spectators alike, we need to be careful to specify just which effects are being looked for rather than jumping to interpret the data so as to confirm our own biases.

What about the idea that, regardless of its effects, football expresses or illustrates such values as conformity, toleration of violence, and blind obedience to authority? Again, although it is probably true that some players, coaches, and teams accept or attempt to promote such values, they do not seem to be necessary constituents of the game.

Consider, for example, the claim that excellence in football requires blind submission to the dictates of the coach, and therefore teaches a hidden agenda of uncritical acceptance of the dictates of those in power. Although some coaches might well encourage such blind loyalty, nothing in the profession of coaching requires such a conception of the role and much goes against it. A good coach, it can be argued, prepares his or her players to think for themselves in the context of the game.

Such a conception of the coach as teacher seems not only possible but required if players are to reach their full potential in the quest for athletic excellence. A good coach may insist on discipline and hard work, but it is hard to see why this makes the coach any more of an authoritarian or any more conservative than the philosophy professor who insists that her students work to their best potential. (More in later chapters about the ethics of coaching.)

Thus, our discussion undermines the view that football is necessarily violent, as well as the claim that football expresses a bias in favor of conservative political values. Of course, in practice, football and other major sports sometimes may do all of the above. But as properly practiced, football and other contact sports should express the values of a mutual quest for athletic excellence, which include respect for opponents, a sense of fair play, and intelligent and critical application of the skills of the game. Even though football in particular involves the use of a good deal of physical force, and therefore may be criticized because of danger to the participants, it need not involve the intention to harm opponents or the support of a particular partisan political ideology.

The Actual and the Ideal in Philosophy of Sports

At this point, some critics of violence in sports may be exceedingly impatient with the course of the discussion. They see the exercise as an example of the philosopher's futile interest in the ideal, a focus that allows the theorist to ignore real abuses. "It is all too easy to say football is not *necessarily* violent," such a critic might exclaim, "when the important task is to show what actually is wrong with sports, and then change it."

Although much of our discussion has been concerned with standards that should apply to sports, that hardly makes it impractical. It is difficult to understand how we could even identify abuses in sports unless we had some grasp of the ethical principles that were being violated in the first place. Besides, without some standards at which to aim, we would not know the proper recommendations to make for moral change.

Moreover, moral reform involves more than simply adopting ethical principles whatever the cost. At a minimum, ethical principles must be adopted and applied in a fair and just way. For example, even if boxing ought to be prohibited or reformed, it doesn't follow that we should simply make sudden changes without consideration for the fate of those boxers who might suddenly find themselves unemployed. Sometimes, the moral and political costs of some principles may be so great that considerations of justice or utility require us to adopt a "second best" solution. Be that as it may, unless we know what ideals should apply in sports, how can we tell what reforms are needed in current practice?

In any event, the views developed in this chapter do have implications for policy. They indicate that although it is difficult always to draw the line between what sportsmanship and fair play permit and what they forbid, those values are not vacuous and do apply to the behavior of competitors in sports. And although our discussion does not indicate that the argument for legal prohibition of boxing is compelling, it does provide ground for the condemnation of many forms of violence in sports. For example, those who defend the constant fighting in professional hockey as "part of the game" make the very same error as those who see football as essentially violent; namely, confusing violence with the use of force. Some uses of force, such as body checking, may be part of the game of hockey, but fighting involves the use of force with intent to harm and therefore is in a different ethical category entirely. If such violence is truly part of the game, the game is not morally defensible to begin with.

If competition in sports is thought of as a mutual quest for excellence, then violence, cheating, and bad sportsmanship are in different ways violations of the ethic that should apply to athletic competition. A defensible sports ethic, one that respects participants as persons, should avoid the twin errors of, on one hand, leaving no room for the clever strategic foul or the intelligent use of force, and, on the other, assuming that players in the pursuit of victory can do no wrong.

5

Girls and Boys, Men and Women

In all cases, excepting those of the bear and the leopard, the female is less spirited than the male . . . more shrinking, more difficult to rouse to action, and requires a smaller quantity of nutriment. . . . The fact is, the nature of man is the most rounded off and complete.

Aristotle, *History of Animals,* Book IX

Games and recreation for all types of girls, by all means, which develop charm and social health, but athletic competition in basketball, track and field sports, and baseball? No!

Frederick R. Rodgers, *School and Society,* 1929

The passages quoted above express attitudes that have probably been dominant in most periods of Western civilization. For example, the belief that women are naturally sedentary was reinforced by the customs of Aristotle's culture, which kept women largely confined to the home. But the view that women are neither fit for nor interested in sport, or that it is somehow not appropriate for women to participate in serious athletic competition, was a dominant one even in our own society well into the late twentieth century, and still influences policy in many parts of the world.

These attitudes have sometimes been challenged, although the challengers frequently shared more with proponents of the dominant outlook than they might have acknowledged. For example, a Women's Division of the National Amateur Athletic Federation was formed in 1923 to stress "sports opportunities for all girls, protection from exploitation, enjoyment of sports, female leadership [and] medical examinations."[1]

The purpose of this "creed," as it was sometimes called, was to promote greater participation in sports for all women rather than promote intense competition for highly skilled female athletes. "Soon female competitive athletics began to decrease. . . . In place of competition, play days and sports days were organized. This philosophy of athletics for women and girls continued into the early 1960s."[2]

As a result, women and girls who really did want to participate in competition were usually made to feel strange or unfeminine. Former tennis star Althea Gibson described what it was like to be a female athlete in high school in the south in the 1940s: "The problem I had in Wilmington was the girls in school. . . . 'Look at her throw in that ball just like a man,' they would say, and they looked at me just like I was a freak. . . . I felt as though they ought to see that I didn't do the things they did because I didn't know how to and that I showed off on the football field . . . to show there was something I was good at.'"[3]

Although the attitudes that troubled Gibson have not been eliminated, the role of women in competitive sport has changed drastically. The growth of women's and girls' sports and the intensity and quality of their performances in the 1970s and 1980s is unprecedented. For example, in 1970–1971, 3.7 million boys and only 300,000 girls participated in interscholastic sports. By 1978–1979, after the passage of Title IX, an important law with significant implications for gender equity in athletics, 4.2 million boys and 2 million girls were participants in interscholastic athletics. A similar rate of increase in the participation of women in intercollegiate athletics took place during the same period.[4] Today, in the United States, women and girls continue to participate in organized athletics in significant numbers. By the late 1990s, over 3.7 boys million and nearly 2.6 million girls participated in high school sports.[5]

However, controversy continues over just how gender equity in athletics is to be understood and over what principles should be employed in its enforcement. In particular, debate about how Title IX should be interpreted and applied to intercollegiate sports remains intense and reflects, if not different conceptions of gender equity, at least different explanations for and responses to the continuing gap between participation rates of males and females in sports.

Sorting Out the Issues
Title IX and Gender Equity

The changes described above were not easily achieved. *Sports Illustrated,* in a 1973 article, reported widespread indifference, even among educators, to women's athletics.[6] There is no doubt that before the recent increase in interest in women's athletics and broader feminist concerns about sex equality, women's sports were separate and unequal. Only a tiny fraction of athletic budgets was devoted to the needs of women students, who were excluded from participation in most varsity and intramural programs.

Such inequalities were sometimes defended on the grounds that relevant differences between men and women justified the differences in treatment. Women were held to be less interested in participating than men, or less aggressive and therefore less in need of the outlet of intense athletic competition.

Perhaps more often, inequalities in sport between men and women were not explicitly defended but just taken for granted as part of the then normal cultural and social context.

Although, as we will see, sex differences may be relevant to the form sex equality takes in sports, they hardly justify the exclusion of women from sports or the relegation of women's sports to second-class status. First, the increased participation of girls and women in organized competitive sports is a most convincing refutation of the claim that they have little interest in taking part. (We will see that whether the interest in participation is substantially the same for men and women as groups is still debated.) Second, the claim that women are naturally less aggressive than men, even if it were true, is irrelevant to the right to participate and compete. After all, males who have less need to discharge aggression against other males are not excluded from participation.

In any event, whether or not competitive sports are instrumental in helping some of us discharge aggression (a controversial empirical claim at best), they are also of value in part because they are an important source of fascination, challenge, recreation, and fun. Much of the intrinsic value, ethical importance, and interest of competitive sports lies in the pursuit of challenges set by opponents. Opponents respond to each other as persons within the rules of the sports contest. Males and females have an equal claim to participation. Members of both sexes may seek the challenges presented by competitive sports. Whether or not sports fulfill other social functions, such as allowing for the harmless discharge of aggressive impulses, their value does not lie primarily in such consequences.

What are the requirements of gender equity in athletic programs at the inter-collegiate and interscholastic levels? Does sex equity simply require lack of discrimination? Should the coaches pick the best players, regardless of sex? Does sex equality require separate teams for women? If so, are such teams required in all sports or just those in which women are physiologically disadvantaged with respect to men? Are separate teams for physiologically disadvantaged men also required? Does sex equality require greater emphasis on competition in sports, such as gymnastics, where women may have physical advantages, or the introduction of new sports in which the sexes can compete equally?

We will begin our examination of these and related questions by considering the most important federal legislation addressing sex equality in sports. Title IX of the Education Amendments of 1972 prohibits sex discrimination in federally assisted education programs. The section of Title IX dealing with athletics states that "no person shall, on the basis of sex, be excluded from participation in, be denied the benefits of, be treated differently from another person or otherwise be discriminated against in any interscholastic, intercollegiate, club, or intramural athletic program offered by a recipient" (Section 86:41a). One interpretation of this section requires that athletic programs not make distinctions on the basis of sex. As long as no discrimination takes place, men and women have been treated by the same standards and so have no grounds to complain of inequity. In this view, sex equality in sports requires that we pay no attention to the sex of participants.

The problem with this is that, if it were applied, far fewer women than at present would be competing in interscholastic or intercollegiate varsity contests in such sports as basketball, soccer, lacrosse, track-and-field, tennis, and golf. Although many women athletes in such sports have more ability than most men, it does appear that males have important physiological advantages, for example, in size and upper body strength, that make a crucial difference at top levels of competition in most sports.

To avoid the virtual exclusion of women from varsity competition in many sports, particularly the so-called contact sports, Title IX departs from simple nondiscrimination by allowing institutions to sponsor separate teams for men and women. Title IX does not require that there be separate teams for each sex in each sport an institution offers, but it does stipulate that through an appropriate combination of mixed and single-sex teams, the opportunities for each sex be equivalent.

As described above, Title IX seems to represent a combination of two approaches to sex equality. According to the first, sex equality is equated with blindness to sex. Thus, a coeducational college that pays no attention to the sex of applicants in deciding whom to admit has adopted the first approach. A second approach is to acknowledge sex differences in an attempt to insure that members of each sex receive equivalent benefits.

The two approaches are, at best, not easily reconciled and, at worst, plainly inconsistent. The first requires that we ignore sex and assign no special significance to it; the second requires that we recognize sex differences when they are relevant to our practices. Title IX combines elements of each approach. The policy of instituting separate sports programs for each sex requires viewing sex as a relevant ground for making distinctions, but the requirement that no one be treated differently with regard to sex seems to require that sex not be viewed as a relevant ground for making distinctions.

But although a policy combining these two approaches to sex equality might appear to be inconsistent, the two apparently conflicting approaches may be combined coherently, for example, by distinguishing different levels of analysis. Thus, perhaps sex is relevant in sports where one sex has a physiological advantage over the other, but not in sports where such advantages are either minimal or nonexistent, such as riflery. Also, it is important to distinguish levels of analysis. At the most general level, Title IX does call for sex blindness. Men and women in educational institutions are to have equivalent opportunities for participation regardless of sex. To achieve this goal, institutions need to take physiological differences between the sexes into account; therefore, separate sports for each gender are needed when physiological differences make gender-blind competition inequitable.

Before turning to current controversies over the meaning and application of Title IX, let us examine the two approaches to equality between the sexes, sex blindness and sex pluralism, to find the degree to which each approach is defensible before applying it to sports and athletics.

What is the relationship between sex equality and gender equity? To many scholars, "sex" refers to the biological components of our identities and gender deals with socially constructed differences between males and females within a cultural context. This dichotomy, although sometimes useful, may be too simplistic since biological differences arguably influence cultural contexts in various ways; therefore, the line between what is natural and what is social may be difficult to draw. In any event, in the next section, the ideals of sex equality will have to do with broad social visions of what equality between men and women entails. Equity will have to do with fairness between men and women in athletics.

Ideals of Sex Equality

Like virtue, honesty, and truth, sex equality has few contemporary opponents, at least in public. Even those who opposed the Equal Rights Amendment, including former President Ronald Reagan, claimed to support equal rights, properly under-stood, for men and women.

Not so often noticed is that sex equality is open to diverse interpretations. Just as equal opportunity can be understood in a variety of ways—as requiring simple nondiscrimination, as requiring conditions of background fairness, as requiring equal life chances for representative persons from all major social groups—so, too, there are diverse and competing conceptions of sex equality. Thus, abstract support for a general ideal of sex equality from a variety of perspectives can obscure deep divisions on just how sex equality is to be understood, what it implies in concrete contexts, and how it might best be achieved.

To those who identify sex equality with assimilation, a society has achieved sex equality when, as one writer put it, no more significance is attached to the sex of persons than is attached to eye color.[7] In this view, sex equality is equated with al-most total blindness to sex. In the assimilationist society, at least in its most uncom-promising form, one's sex would play no role in the distribution of civil rights or economic benefits and, at most, would play a minimal role in personal and social relations. This assimilationist model of sex equality strongly resembles the integra-tionist ideal of racial equality. In particular, it implies that "separate but equal" is as unacceptable in sex equality as it is in race. The implication for sports is that sepa-rate teams for each sex is a violation of what sex equality ideally requires.

Perhaps the principal argument for the assimilationist ideal is that it is required by the value of personal autonomy. Although "autonomy" is far from the clearest notion employed by moral philosophers, it refers to our capacity to choose our ac-tions and determine the course of our own lives. It has to do with self-determination rather than determination by others.

Defenders of the assimilationist ideal argue that it is justified by the moral re-quirement of respect for the autonomy of women because autonomy requires the withering away of sex roles. As Richard Wasserstrom, a distinguished advocate of the assimilationist ideal, argued, "Sex roles, and all that accompany them, necessar-ily impose limits—restrictions on what one can do or become. As such, they are . . . at least prima facie wrong."[8] Perhaps what Wasserstrom had in mind is that roles set up proper norms of behavior for those who fill them. Deviation from the norm exposes one to criticism from others. Conformity is enforced by social pressure. The effects of sex roles in sports was seen in a 1975 study, which reported that 90 percent of the respondents, selected from the general population, believed that par-ticipation in track and field would detract from a female's femininity; only 2 percent thought participation in swimming, a more traditional sport for girls and women, would have the same effect.[9]

No society can exist without roles of any kind. But according to proponents of the assimilationist model of sex equality, sex roles are especially objectionable. Whether they arise from biological differences between men and women or from socialization and learning, they are unchosen. As Wasserstrom maintained, "Involuntarily imposed restraints have been imposed on some of the most central factors concerning the way one will shape and live one's life."[10]

The sex-blind conception of equality favored by the assimilationist does seem particularly appropriate to many significant areas of life in our society. For example, in basic civil rights and liberties, justice and equity surely are sex blind. Freedom of assembly, religion, or speech are rights of all persons equally regardless of their sex. Similarly, in employment or the distribution of important social benefits, the making of distinctions by sex is arbitrary and unfair.[11]

But should sex equality be identified across the board with blindness to sex, as the assimilationist model requires? What, for example, are we to say of sexual attraction? If sex equality requires blindness to the sex of others, does it follow that people with relatively fixed sexual preferences, whether for members of the opposite sex or their own, are engaged in the social counterpart of invidious sex discrimination?[12] Might there not be other areas, such as athletic competition, where the assimilationist model also breaks down? Accordingly, we might want to consider ideals of sex equality other than assimilationism, for the identification of sex equality with sex blindness may not always capture our sense of what is just or reasonable.

In particular, as we have seen earlier, equal treatment in the sense of identical treatment is not always a requirement of justice or fairness. Sometimes, equality is to be understood as requiring equal respect and concern, which in turn requires us to acknowledge the significance of relevant differences among persons. For example, equal respect for persons may require us to respect their choice to participate in athletic competition, leading us to evaluate their performance according to how well they meet the opponent's challenge.

A second ideal of sex equality, which recognizes the significance of difference, might be called the pluralistic model. As Wasserstrom pointed out, the pluralistic conception of equality is best illustrated by the tradition of religious tolerance in the United States. According to this tradition, religious equality does not require that we accord to religious differences only the significance presently attached to

eye color. Rather, a defensible conception of religious equality stipulates that no religion be placed in a position of dominance over others.[13]

Unlike assimilationism, pluralism does not reject the ideal of "separate but
equal" out of hand if separation is not coercively imposed by the dominant group
and is justified by equal respect for all. Thus, it might allow separate but equal athletic programs for women. Although pluralists reject rigid sex roles, they concur
that important sex differences may exist and should be taken into account in an equitable manner in public policy.

Can the pluralist respond satisfactorily to the charge of the assimilationist that
any tolerance of sex roles violates personal autonomy by forcing women (and men)
into the straightjacket of fixed social expectations? Is pluralism or assimilationism
the more defensible model of sex equality? Which approach has the most acceptable
implications for sex equality in sports? We will consider these questions in the next
section.

Gender Equity in Athletic Competition
Pluralism and Sports

Much of the controversy over sex equality in sports concerns whether men's and
women's athletic programs are being treated equally in our schools, colleges,
and universities. Is the women's program receiving its fair share of the budget?
Does the women's basketball team enjoy the same kind of publicity as the men's
team? Are there equivalent opportunities for men and women to play intramural
sports? What does it mean for opportunities to be equivalent?

Such questions presuppose that separate sports programs for men and women
are requirements of sex equality in sport, or are at least permissible ways of achieving equality. But there are different and competing conceptions of sex equality, not
all of which would endorse separate athletic programs for men and women. Which
of the ideals we have considered, assimilationism or pluralism, is more defensible in
sports?

The problem with assimilationism in sports is that sex blindness requires us to
ignore what seem to be relevant sex-related differences in the average athletic ability of men and women. Generally, women are not as big, as strong, or as fast as
men, although there is some evidence that, over long distances, females may show
as much or more stamina than males. It does appear that in the popular contact
sports, such as football, lacrosse, and basketball, as well as in baseball, soccer, tennis, and golf, the greater size, speed, and strength of men give them a significant
physiological advantage over women. In short, if athletic competition were

completely sex-blind, women might be virtually absent from sports competition at the highest levels.[14]

This picture may be changing somewhat as women and men's times edge closer together in some track-and-field events. Annika Sorenstam, the best female golfer now actively competing and possibly the best ever, and Suzy Whaley, a club professional from Connecticut, will compete on the (male) PGA Tour in the summer of 2003, although it is unclear how well even top women golfers will be able to do on the longer courses and firmer greens found on the men's tour. Still, it seems difficult to deny that men have physiological advantages over women in most major sports and, at least for the immediate future, separate competitions for each gender seem the best way of insuring that women participate in athletics at elite levels of competition.

Before we consider responses to this argument, we need to be clear about its scope. For one thing, the argument seems most fully applicable to sports played at high levels of skill and intensity. Thus, even if the argument does justify separate teams for males and females in intercollegiate or interscholastic competition, it may not do so in a less intense recreational league or intramural program. Moreover, in sports where one sex does not have significant physiological advantages over the other, sex-blind competition may well be desirable or even required.

It is therefore largely an empirical issue as to which sports the argument about physiological differences applies. But is the argument acceptable even in sports played at high levels of competition and in which there are significant physiological differences between the sexes? We will consider two objections to the defense of pluralism based on physiological sex differences. The first is based on appeal to assimilationism. The second maintains that separate sports programs provide women with the illusion of equality rather than the reality.

Evaluating Pluralism in Sports

To an advocate of the assimilationist ideal, sexual pluralism in sports may seem morally pernicious because pluralism may only express and reinforce the traditional system of sex roles.

Such a rejoinder is implausible for a variety of reasons. For one thing, the point of having separate athletic programs for women is to expand the options available to them. The opportunities that pluralism provides women are in sports like basketball and lacrosse, which, until recently, have been the preserve of males.[15] A proponent of pluralism in athletics, then, can argue that separate athletic programs for men and women in sports where performance is affected by physiological sex differences not only increase opportunities for women but also help break down stereotypes about what sports are appropriate for women.

A proponent of assimilationism might respond that if the ideal of sex blindness was adopted throughout society, it would not matter that few, if any, women played at the higher levels of athletic competition. This is because in the assimilationist society, when an individual's sex would be regarded as no more important than eye color is regarded in our society, it would not be important that nearly all the top athletes were male. At least, it would not be regarded as any more important than the widely acknowledged fact that virtually no individuals under five feet ten inches have a chance to play professional basketball.

This rejoinder is open to two strong objections. The first is that because we are not yet in the assimilationist society, it would be unfair to apply the assimilationist ideal only to sports, an area where it would particularly disadvantage women. It is one thing to say pluralism in sports is unnecessary in the assimilationist society but quite another to say it is unnecessary in ours.

This distinction between the ideal and the actual raises a fundamental point. Sometimes, theorists believe they have succeeded when they present a defensible ideal conception of justice, equality, or liberty, and that practical choices will attain the ideal. But this ignores the issue of whether and of how it is morally permissible to reach the ideal.[16]

For example, suppose a defensible ideal of equal opportunity required that we abolish the family. It doesn't follow that individuals presently part of families can just ignore their duties to other family members on the grounds that in an ideal society the family might not exist. Indeed, if there were no way to adopt the ideal without seriously violating duties to members of presently existing families, that ideal may be morally impermissible for us.

A similar point may apply to the assimilationist ideal of sexual equality. Even if assimilationism is superior to pluralism as an ideal, it seems morally impermissible to introduce assimilationism in sport, where it would disadvantage women, before it is implemented elsewhere in society.

But even leaving aside implementation, it is far from clear that assimilationism is the best ideal of gender equality, or is fair, just, and equitable in all contexts. In particular, competitive sports stand as a counterexample to the thesis that recognition of sex differences always involves coercive sex roles. On the contrary, the recognition of sex differences in sports frees women from traditional restrictions and makes it possible for them to engage in highly competitive forms of athletics in a variety of major, traditionally male, sports. In sports, it seems to be assimilationism rather than pluralism that limits opportunities for women.

Similarly, if there are other significant physiological or psychological sex differences between men and women, equality might involve equal respect for such differences rather than denial of their importance. Socializing men and women to ignore such differences or to inhibit gender-linked forms of behavior may be just as subversive of autonomy as the socializing of women to conform to traditional sex roles. Although a conception of sex equality required by justice surely rules out a rigid system of sex roles, it is doubtful that sex equality requires us to forget about one another's sex.[17]

Unfair to Females?

Does pluralism in sports really work to the advantage of women? A critic might respond that if men really are better in certain sports, the women's teams in those sports necessarily will be thought of as inferior. Rather than liberate women, such teams will stigmatize women. As philosopher Betsy Postow maintains, "The number and prestige of sports in which men are naturally superior help perpetuate an image of general female inferiority which we have moral reason to undermine."[18] This perception of inferiority might be thought to account for the generally lower attendance at contests between women's teams as well as generally lower public recognition of the achievements of top women athletes than of top male athletes.

However, as we have already pointed out, if competitive sports were organized according to the assimilationist model, females would be almost absent at the top levels of competition. Is that preferable to pluralism? Is it fairer?

More important, we need to scrutinize the perception that women's sports are inferior versions of male sports. Perhaps, in spite of achievements of such female stars as Chamique Holdsclaw, Annika Sorenstam, Sue Bird, and Venus and Serena Williams, much of the public still does perceive such sports as inferior; but is that perception justified?

The claim that in the traditional major sports women's competition is inferior to that of men at similar levels could mean one or more of the following:

1. Women's programs receive less financial and coaching support than men's programs.
2. Contests between women or women's teams are less interesting and less exciting than are contests between men or men's teams.

3. Men's teams will always beat women's teams in a particular sport if both play at roughly the same level of competition, e.g., intercollegiate athletics.

What are the implications for our discussion of sex equality of these different interpretations of the claim that women's sports are inferior? If claim one is true, and women's programs receive less financial and coaching support than men's programs, this shows only that pluralism has not been fully implemented, not that it should be abandoned. The obvious remedy is to provide equivalent support for the women's program.

Claim three, however, is likely to be true. It is hardly likely that even a top women's intercollegiate basketball team will be able to beat an average male intercollegiate team. In fact, if claim three were not true, there would be no need for separate women's sports teams in the first place. What does claim three imply about pluralism in sports?

Many would argue that claim three justifies claim two. It is precisely because men's teams can beat women's teams at similar levels of competition that women's sports allegedly are inferior and uninteresting. Although much of the sporting public may accept such an inference, it is fallacious. Simply because the men's team would beat the women's team, it doesn't follow that the men's contest is more exciting, more interesting, or of greater competitive intensity. It would be just as fallacious to argue that simply because the worst men's professional basketball team could beat the best boy's high school team, a contest between two mediocre professional teams will be more exciting, more interesting, and more competitively intense than a championship game between two top high school teams.

If what is of major interest in a competitive sports contest is the challenge each competitor or team poses to the other, and the skill, intensity, and character with which the participants meet the challenge, there is no reason why women's contests should be less exciting or less interesting than men's contests. This has long been known in Iowa, where girls' high school basketball is a state mania, and at the University of Connecticut and the University of Tennessee, where the championship women's teams have huge followings. It surely is accepted by tennis fans that top women stars such as the Williams sisters get as much attention as their male counterparts.

Indeed, in sports such as tennis and golf, and perhaps team sports such as basketball, one can plausibly argue that the women's game differs from the men's in ways that make it at least as good as a spectator sport. In tennis, the power of male players' serves limits the extent of volleying, but the women's game is characterized more by clever use of ground strokes. In fact, fan interest in women's professional tennis is at least as high as in the men's game. Similarly, in golf, women must have superb timing and coordination to compensate for their lack of strength in comparison to males. Why shouldn't it be just as exciting and interesting to watch the timing and tempo of a top female player, such as Annika Sorenstam, as it is to watch the force applied by a male player? In women's basketball, the dunk or jam is virtually absent, and one-on-one moves may be somewhat less spectacular than in the men's game, but the intelligent use of screens to get open shots, movement without the ball, and brilliant individual play are all there. It is simply a matter of appreciating different aspects of the game as well as the competitive intensity and character of the women playing it.

If women's sports can be as exciting and interesting as men's sports, in part because they are equally competitive and in part because subtly different qualities are being tested, it is hard to see why pluralism in sports necessarily stigmatizes women. Full appreciation of these sports may require better education of the general public, but it is hard to see why women should be denied the opportunity to compete simply because many fans are fascinated, perhaps unjustifiably so, by the power game played by males. Although spectators may in the long run favor aspects of the men's game over the women's game, there is no reason why this *must* happen, and much reason to believe that, in some sports, the women's and men's games may turn out to be equally appealing. If such a suggestion has force, it is not that women's sports are inferior, but rather that more of us need to make the effort to appreciate the diverse qualities that are exhibited in athletic competition.

Such considerations may have some appeal even to those feminists who have been suspicious of "separate but equal" as a model of sex equality. Why not place more emphasis on sports in which "female" abilities or qualities are especially advantageous? The suggestion here is that we redefine our catalog of major sports. The intuitive idea is that equal opportunity, even on the pluralist model, requires more than equal recognition of or appreciation for women's athletics. It also requires equal emphasis on sports in which women can be the top athletes, and not merely the top "women athletes."

Thus, Postow has recommended that we "increase the number and prestige of sports in which women have a natural statistical superiority to men or at least are not naturally inferior."[19] Jane English has given a concrete example of what Postow may have had in mind: "Perhaps the most extreme example of a sport favoring women's natural skills is the balance beam. Here, small size and flexibility and low center of gravity combine to give women the kind of natural hegemony that men enjoy in football."[20] In other words, our traditional catalog of major sports has a built-in bias towards athletic activities favoring men. The way to remedy this bias is not simply to introduce athletic programs that institutionalize female inferiority; rather, we should radically revise our conception of which sports are most worthy of support and attention.

The suggestion that we should learn to appreciate and develop sports that reward the physiological assets of women, just as we now tend to appreciate those that reward the physiological assets of men, does have merit. Properly understood, it does not require the abolition of women's programs in basketball, volleyball, soccer, tennis, and other traditional sports, but the addition and increased support of other sports, such as gymnastics, in which women are physiologically advantaged (or at least physiologically equal).

This suggestion is supported by considerations of fairness and equity, but two competing considerations have to be kept in mind. First, individuals may continue to prefer traditional or currently more popular sports, even after they are introduced to alternatives. The general public may continue to prefer watching and playing basketball and football to watching or participating in gymnastics and high diving. This may be as true for the majority of female athletes as much as anybody else, especially since traditional sports seem open to a wider variety of age groups and body types than gymnastics.

Moreover, to require or compel individuals to attend or participate in certain kinds of sports and prohibit them from playing others would be a serious violation of individual liberty. It is one thing, for example, to require that schools introduce students in physical education classes to a wide variety of sports and athletic activities, many of which are not biased in favor of male physiology; it is quite another to require that female athletes compete in such activities, even if they are more interested in playing basketball, soccer, lacrosse, tennis, or golf. It is possible that a broad program of public education could change individual preferences; however, such a program, if morally permissible, must appeal to people as autonomous moral agents and not dictate in advance which sports people are required to find more interesting or of greater worth.

Does Sex Equality Require Forgetting Sex?

The conception of sex equality as blindness to sex is most plausible in the realm of civil and political rights and in the economic marketplace. The right to vote, the right to freedom of speech, and the right to be free of discrimination in the market-place normally should not be dependent upon one's sex.

But whereas assimilationism, or blindness to sex and gender differences, may be the favored conception of sex equality in many areas, such as civil rights, it is doubtful if it is acceptable across the board, in all areas of human concern. As our discussion of sports suggests, the assignment of significance to sex is not always a form of sexism.

We have not been shown, then, that separate athletic programs for men and women in those sports where one sex is at a physiological disadvantage are morally suspect or illegitimate. Unlike the doctrine of "separate but equal" in the context of racial segregation, separate athletic programs do not stigmatize one group or the other, are not imposed against the will of either sex, and actually enhance the freedom and opportunity of the previously disadvantaged group. Sports seem to provide a model of a defensible pluralistic approach to sex equality. In sports and perhaps in other areas as well, sex equality does not require blindness to sex.

Legislating Equality

What are the implications of the preceding discussion for policy? Much discussion focuses on Title IX of the Educational Amendments of 1972, the federal legislation that applies to gender equity in athletics in educational programs. Let us examine the interpretation of Title IX advanced by the Office of Civil Rights in 1996 to see why this legislation, which has done so much to promote greater equality in athletics, is also the center of a controversy over how best to achieve gender equity in athletics.

The Development of Title IX

As we already have noted, women's participation in competitive athletics was significantly limited before the civil rights movement, the rise of feminism, and the passage of Title IX itself. In the early 1970s, we pointed out that over 4 million boys participated in high school athletics compared to approximately 300,000 girls. Gross disparities in participation and expenditures on males and females also were the rule in intercollegiate athletics. James Michener, writing about the period before promulgation of Title IX, reported that "one day I saw the budget of . . . a state institution (a university), supported by tax funds, with a student body divided fifty-fifty between men and women. The athletic department had $3,900,000 to spend, and of this, women received exactly $31,000, a little less than eight-tenths of one percent. On the face of it, this was outrageous."[21]

The passage of Title IX, along with other concurrent social trends, including the emphasis of the early feminist movement on equality for women, resulted in almost immediate jumps in participation by females in athletics and increases in expenditures by educational institutions on athletic programs for women and girls. By 1979, 2 million girls were participating in high school athletics, compared to about 300,000 before 1972.

Although much progress has been made towards gender equity in athletics since the 1970s, it still seems that equity has not been achieved. Proponents of such a view argue, for example, that educational institutions still spend more on programs for males than females, rates of participation by males are higher, and that male athletes receive far more fan support and attention by the media than their female counterparts. Many observers wonder why, so many years after the passage of Title IX.

Perhaps part of the reason is the history of Title IX. Although passed by Congress in 1972, it was only in the late 1990s that a consistent and relatively clear interpretation of the legislation has emerged and been applied by the courts, although, as we will see, this interpretation is the subject of bitter controversy. Two court cases explain much of the confusion and delay about implementation. In *Grove City v. Bell,* decided in 1984, the Supreme Court ruled that Title IX applied only to programs directly receiving federal funds.[22] On this interpretation, if College X's physics department received a federal grant, Title IX would apply only to the physics department, and not to its athletics program. Since few, if any, athletic programs at high schools or colleges and universities receive federal grants, the Grove City case exempted them from legislative review under Title IX. This led Congress to pass the Civil Rights Restoration Act in 1988, which responded to the decision in *Grove City,* making Title IX apply to an entire institution that received either direct or indirect federal aid. In the second case, *Franklin v. Gwinnett County Public Schools,* decided in 1992, a unanimous Supreme Court ruled that plaintiffs' filing Title IX law suits are entitled to punitive damages if it has been found that the institution being sued intentionally took steps to avoid compliance with Title IX.[23] So disagreements about the scope and enforcement of Title IX help explain delays in implementation, since, even assuming good will on the part of educational institutions, it was unclear how to apply the legislation and what the remedy for failure to comply might be in different kinds of cases.

Moreover, in 1990, the Office of Civil Rights (OCR) issued a manual for interpreting Title IX that, along with clarifications made in 1996, has become authoritative. The OCR interpretation included what has been called the "three part test" that has become the center of controversy. Let us consider what Title IX, as it has evolved and been interpreted by the Office of Civil Rights, actually requires.

What Does Title IX Require

The OCR identifies three major areas of compliance with Title IX; athletic scholarships, accommodation of athletic interests and abilities, and other athletic benefits and awards. The first applies only to those institutions in Divisions I and II of the NCAA that award athletic scholarships. It requires roughly that male and female athletes receive proportional shares of available scholarships. The third requires that educational institutions treat male and female athletes equitably in the distribution of fields for practice, equipment, access to trainers, expense allowances, and the like. We will be concerned with the second area, accommodation of athletic abilities and interests, since it clearly is most fundamental. Before turning to that, it will be useful to consider the general understanding of equity that seems to underlie Title IX.

It might be natural to assume that Title IX requires identical treatment for men's and women's intercollegiate sports in the sense, say, of requiring identical expenditures on each; however, Title IX is better understood as requiring equivalent treatment rather than identical treatment.

Consider an example from another area. Suppose that half the students in a particular school want to develop their musical abilities and half want to learn computer science. The school buys musical instruments adequate for instruction and provides for sufficient computers and faculty to allow the formation of a computer science program. But because computers cost more than musical instruments, the school spends several times more money on the students in the computer program than on the musicians. Even so, the opportunities are equal for both groups in the sense of being equivalent. All the students have an equal chance to pursue their interests. Another way of putting it, following the legal philosopher Ronald Dworkin, is to say that both groups of students have been treated with equal respect and concern.[24]

This example suggests that "equal expenditures" and "equal opportunities" are two distinct notions. The examples have clear analogies in the world of sports. For example, suppose equipment for men's teams in a particular sport is more expensive than equipment for the parallel women's team, or that referees for one gender's games are paid on a higher scale than referees for the games of the other gender. Such differences are allowable. Thus, the set of principles underlying Title IX seem to require equal respect and concern for each gender, understood as provision of equivalent opportunities, rather than identical treatment.

Keeping the distinction between identical and equivalent opportunities in mind, let us turn to the OCR's three-part test for compliance. In particular, the OCR proposes that institutions can comply with Title IX in accommodating athletic abilities and interests by meeting any one requirement of the following three:

A. By providing opportunities for participation in the intercollegiate athletics program for students of each sex that are substantially proportionate to their respective enrollments in the student body as a whole.

B. If not, the institution can comply by showing a history and continuing practice of expansion of the intercollegiate athletics program responsive to developing interests and abilities of members of the underrepresented sex.

C. If not, the institution still can comply by showing that the interests and abilities of the underrepresented sex are "fully and effectively accommodated" by the existing program.

Legal compliance is established by satisfying any one of the three tests. An intercollegiate athletic program that fails an earlier element might still be in compliance with Title IX by satisfying one of the later prongs. The first is regarded as a "safe harbor" in the sense that a finding of proportionality will at the very least establish a strong and virtually overwhelming presumption of compliance. Failure to show proportionality (it is doubtful whether many institutions of higher education in the country now satisfy this requirement as strictly construed) is not sufficient to establish noncompliance if the other criteria still might be met.

The three-part OCR test has some important similarities to what might be called a presumptive approach to gender equity. It presumes that both genders will be treated equally, but acknowledges the possibility of there being allowable reasons for inequality. Representation of gender in proportion to its share of the overall student body will normally be taken as virtually conclusive evidence of equal treatment. If proportionality cannot be satisfied, inequality can be justified by showing compliance with one of the other two prongs of the test. Moreover, in assessing whether the interests of the underrepresented gender have been "fully and effectively accommodated," the assumption is that each gender will be treated equally in the absence of justifying reasons for inequality. But justifying reasons are possible. For example, sometimes where there is interest in developing a new women's sport at an institution that does not satisfy the first two prongs, it may be reasonable for the institution to expect that interest to continue for a reasonable time and for sufficient ability to be demonstrated by the prospective participants before taking steps to support the new sports team.

What counts as a justifiable reason for inequality often will be controversial. Does the past success of the men's basketball team at a Division I institution justify their playing a more nationally prominent schedule than the less successful women's team? What if the athletic director promises to upgrade the women's schedule as soon as the team develops sufficiently to compete successfully at that level? Should a 98-pound female gymnast receive the same daily meal allowance as a 275-pound male lineman on the football team when the teams are on the road? Is it an inequity if the lineman is given a greater allowance because he needs more food?

Rather than pursue the numerous questions that can be raised about what counts as justifiable reasons for inequality, which cannot all be explored here, it seems more useful to focus on fundamental issues raised by the OCR three-pronged test, particularly those concerning proportionality and the effective accommodation of interests. Because these areas are fundamental, exploring them may help shed some light on other important issues of gender equity that are likely to arise.

Proportionality

The idea that men and women should be represented in an educational institution's athletic program in proportion to their representation in the student body initially sounds plausible. After all, if participation in athletics provides significant benefits and opportunities, and if there is no reason to favor one gender in the distribution of these benefits and opportunities, then one would expect them to be made available to both genders equally. So if 60 percent of the student body is male and 40 percent female, in the absence of discrimination one would expect to find that about 60 percent of the institution's athletes were male and about 40 percent female.

But there are problems with this initial expectation. According to the 1993 NCAA Gender Equity Task Force, there were 3.4 million male and 1.9 million female participants in interscholastic sports at the high school level in the United States.[25] Moreover, the gender gap in high school participation did not change drastically during the second half of the decade, although there may have been some reductions in the gap during that period.[26] Given that there remains a disproportion in the representation of each gender in sports at the pre-college level, is it reasonable to expect the proportion of women participating at the college level, which is significantly more demanding than at the high school level, suddenly to jump significantly? If not, it seems unreasonable to place so much stress on proportional representation in the first place. Where will the additional female athletes needed to achieve proportionality come from?

This leads critics to raise a major objection to the proportionality require-ment; namely, that regardless of the intentions of its proponents, proportionality functions to decrease opportunities for male athletes rather than increase them for female athletes. That is because there are two ways to remedy the perceived under-representation of women. The first is to raise the proportion of women participat-ing; the second is to reduce the proportion of men participating.

Suppose an institution is 60 percent male and 40 percent female. Suppose fur-ther that 70 percent of its 1,000 intercollegiate athletes are male and only 30 per-cent of its intercollegiate athletes are female. The school could try to raise the percentage of female athletes to around 40 percent, but it may find it very difficult to do so, perhaps largely because of the expense involved and also because of the difficulty of finding interested female athletes. Instead, it can cut male teams and reduce the percentage of men playing to, say, under 60 percent of all athletes. That is, by cutting sports involving 300 male athletes, the school would be left with 700 athletes, 400 of whom would be male and 300 female. Males would now only con-stitute 57 percent of all athletes and women would constitute 43 percent. In other words, by cutting men's sports, the institution could achieve proportionality and a "safe harbor" from further legal action without adding an additional opportunity for even one female athlete to participate.

Although this hypothetical is undoubtedly an extreme example, the provision that proportionality is a safe harbor from legal action can act as an incentive to trim men's programs and appear to provide equal access to underrepresented women athletes without increasing opportunities for women. In fact, critics of the propor-tionality requirement charge that numerous less-visible men's sports teams seem to have been cut at various institutions, quite possibly in part to achieve a more re-spectable-looking ratio of female to male athletes, including well over 150 wrestling programs and many men's tennis, gymnastics, swimming, and golf teams.[27] Accordingly, the requirement of proportionality may have the unintended consequence in American colleges and universities of decreasing the number of slots on athletic teams, possibly without significantly increasing opportunities to participate for women, but mainly through decreasing them for men.

There are two important responses to this kind of criticism. The first is that Title IX does not require satisfaction of the proportionality requirement. Insti-tutions can comply by satisfying one of the other two prongs of the OCR three-part test. The second is that Title IX does not require institutions to eliminate less-visible men's programs, but rather allows them to shift resources from high-visibility and arguably bloated men's sports, particularly college football. Whereas these responses may blunt some of the force of the criticism that proportionality reduces opportunities for men without raising them for women, each also faces difficulties.

The first response is that colleges and universities need not achieve proportionality but can satisfy one of the other two requirements laid down by OCR. This point is correct, but in assessing its significance, practical difficulties also need to be considered. Thus, an institution could continue to expand its athletic program for the underrepresented gender (although at some point of expansion it would achieve proportionality and both requirements would be satisfied). This approach surely is acceptable and is perhaps the fairest method of compliance, but it also raises some difficult questions. In particular, it is important to remember that questions of distributive justice in intercollegiate athletics arise at least at two levels; distribution of resources within the athletic program and distribution within the university generally. Thus, should colleges and universities be required to increase expenditure on athletics at a time when many academic needs are unmet because of lack of funding? Is it more important to add a women's team than to support faculty, provide financial aid to needy students, or make computer facilities more accessible to everyone in the institution? Expansion, then, may be an ideal solution in some contexts but may not be affordable or educationally warranted in others.

Second, although it is plausible to think some resources might be shifted from football, particularly at the large Division I football powers, the implications are quite different at nonscholarship schools or those at the Division III level. In Division III, transferring support to football from other sports might result in smaller rosters, which means those young men at the bottom of the team's ability level could lose the opportunity to play. Since such athletes are playing primarily for love of the game, it is at best unfortunate that they would bear the brunt of compliance (although it is true that some funds might be freed up that could be diverted to the women's program).

If this point has force, the move to achieve proportionality by shifting resources from football does not entirely avoid the difficulty of imposition of costs to men; however, it might sometimes be an appropriate way of achieving proportionality in some specific contexts. Major college football teams could continue to play at an elite level after, say, a 5 to 10 percent cut in the athletic scholarships they offer, with consequent increased participation by walk-on football players who compete for love of the game. Nevertheless, the slogan "Cut big football budgets" is not necessarily an across-the-board solution to the problems raised by proportionality, particularly at the schools that play football, do not offer athletic scholarships, do not have bloated budgets, and where cuts in rosters would affect walk-on players without necessarily adding opportunities for females.

What of the point that women may not be as interested as men in participating in intercollegiate athletics? In other words, the argument that each gender should be proportionately represented in the university's intercollegiate athletic program presupposes that the members of each gender have an equal interest in participating. It is that very presupposition that critics of proportionality call into question.

In particular, proponents of proportionality reply that females in America have traditionally been discouraged from participating in athletics, and are only now beginning to overcome the socialization that has inhibited participation. Therefore, rates of participation are not adequate indicators of true interest. If colleges and universities provide additional women's sports, the participants will eventually come.

But are colleges and universities required to respond to purely hypothetical interests that some women would have had or might have had if they had been socialized differently?

Many observers would say yes. After all, if participation in athletics does have important educational, personal, and recreational benefits, why shouldn't women be especially encouraged to participate? Similarly, shouldn't the university take it as part of its mission to expose students to great literature even though they have no interest in it (or even a desire to avoid it!)?

Proponents of proportionality add that many more women than those who try out for teams may have an interest in athletics but do not express it for lack of encouragement. What counts as an expression of interest in athletics? At the very least, there is an obligation to go beyond crude measures, such as how many women try out for teams, before we conclude that women have less interest in athletics than men.

What should we conclude about this debate? First, both sides have points of some intellectual merit. The proponents of proportionality argue with plausibility that expressed preferences cannot simply be taken for granted when such preferences have been formed in a social climate that may reflect negative stereotypes about women in sports. Critics of proportionality have a point when they argue that however well intentioned the proponents may be, proportionality in practice is likely to result in further cuts in men's sports, possibly without the compensatory addition of sports for women. It is also far from certain that women's interest in participation is exactly the same as men's. Some scholars have argued that women and men differ in the moral reasoning they typically employ and in the way they socialize.[28] Although such scholarship must be assessed critically, it does suggest that not all gender differences are superficial. Could sex and gender differences also affect preferences for recreation?

In view of these conflicting arguments, it is natural to wonder whether compromise is possible. Although I doubt that any compromise will be fully satisfactory, the following suggestions may help carry the debate between proponents and critics of proportionality closer to a common ground.

First, more emphasis should be placed on fully accommodating the interests of the underrepresented gender, usually women, as required by one of the prongs of the three-part test. The usual objection to this is that simply continuing to add varsity sports for women is too expensive, diverting scarce resources from more basic educational purposes.

This rejoinder is not necessarily decisive. First, funds sometimes could be diverted from expensive men's programs without necessarily cutting sports or even slots on team rosters. For example, many teams could schedule more games locally and cut back on regional and national travel. Similarly, recruiting restrictions could be tightened by cutting back the often highly expensive budgets devoted to attracting student-athletes to the institution, most often for high-profile men's sports. (This might require the adoption of common guidelines by all institutions in a conference so that no one institution would be placed at a competitive disadvantage.)

Second, expansion of opportunities for women need not always mean the addition of varsity sports. In fact, in view of the nationwide disproportion of males to females in interscholastic varsity sports in the United States, the addition of developmental programs for women might promote the lifetime involvement of women in athletics without necessarily leading to the addition of full-fledged varsities. Perhaps what would be more appropriate in some circumstances than the addition of varsity sports are more general lower-level recreational programs designed to involve large numbers of women in sports. The addition of a varsity team or two hardly fulfills such a role and surely is better justified for individuals already strongly interested in participating. Varsity sports demand commitment and competitive intensity and seem most appropriate for those who are already interested in athletic competition.

This does not mean that institutions should be able to satisfy Title IX "on the cheap," say by adding disorganized and underfunded intramural leagues. The suggestion is that genuine developmental opportunities, including expert coaching and opportunities to develop skills through training, be made available to significant numbers of women. Although significant expense would be required, it should be less than continual addition of varsity sports and may eventually increase the overall interest of women in athletics.

Third, compliance with the proportionality requirement should be regarded as a last resort when it is achieved only by cutting men's sports. Institutions that attempted to comply by such means should have the burden of proof on them to show that less drastic means of compliance could not reasonably have been expected to work. Could travel schedules for men's teams have been reduced, recruiting budgets cut, even slots trimmed from some rosters, rather than actually eliminate a whole sport? Simply cutting men's sports does not result in increasing opportunities for women and should be an acceptable form of compliance only when it is a last resort to satisfy the law.

Finally, in the competition for scarce resources, it should not be forgotten that athletics help participants in meeting challenges, in developing dedication and commitment, in finding self-esteem, and in working for a common goal with people from different cultural, religious, and socioeconomic backgrounds, benefits that should be as available to women as to men. In short, athletics can have a significant educational component for all participants. We will explore this point more fully in later chapters, but it is important to insure that sports are not assigned too low a priority when the allocation of resources are considered. Although fundamental academic needs normally should take priority over athletic needs, it is not so clear that less fundamental concerns also should always come first. For example, is the addition of significant athletic opportunities for women always less important than the addition of administrative positions or renovation projects?

The Bush administration will be considering the work of a special advisory commission that issued a report in February 2003 containing a divided assessment of the proportionality requirement without recommending major changes in it.[29] Our discussion, while raising questions about proportionality, has attempted to find some common ground between the critics and the proponents of proportionality. Our proposals for compromise are simply a first attempt to reach a common ground between sides on the proportionality debate. Perhaps they suggest, however, that turning gender equity in sport into a zero-sum contest between men and women is far from the best strategy to pursue. Although some transfer of resources from men's to women's athletics may well be called for, particularly in large Division I institutions where budgets for high-profile men's sports may be out of line, the cutting of less visible men's sports without the addition of new opportunities for women is at best a last resort for achieving gender equity in intercollegiate sport.

Equivalent Opportunity

Although the public debate about proportionality has made Title IX seem more about the quantitative aspect of compliance, when seen as a whole, the legislation is best understood as requiring *equivalent* rather than identical opportunities for each gender. Thus, Title IX does not require that total expenditures on men's and women's sports be identical, and even allows for different expenditures in parallel sports if differences arise from such allowable factors as differences in costs of equipment for each group. Moreover, as argued below, the notion of equivalent treatment seems more appropriate a standard for a broad theory of gender equity in athletics than does, say, an identical distribution of resources to each gender.

But what makes opportunities equivalent? There is no easy answer to this question. Once the shift is made away from quantitative criteria that can be measured in dollars and cents, greater weight must be put on qualitative judgments, which, although they may not be "subjective," may well involve controversial and complex value judgments. A full examination of the issues that arise in evaluating whether opportunities are equivalent is not possible here. Factors that would clearly be relevant include the availability and quality of coaching, the availability of practice facilities, equal good-faith efforts in encouraging participation by members of each sex, and promoting women's sports as well as major men's sports.

As our previous discussion indicates, equivalent opportunity for men and women should not be confused with identical results in all areas of concern. At many institutions, women's teams may not generate the same sort of fan support or attention from the media as men's teams. Sometimes, this may be due to inequitable behavior by the institution and should be corrected. Educational institutions committed to equality should make good-faith efforts to provide equal media coverage for all teams. However, the games fans choose to attend or the publicity the external media decide to devote to particular teams and sports will often be beyond the control of the school or university.

On the other hand, superior performance and a supportive institution can generate large, enthusiastic crowds and frequent appearances on national television, as attested by the recent successes of the women's basketball teams at the University of Connecticut and the University of Tennessee. The players on the University of Connecticut women's team have attracted wide attention throughout the nation as well as in New England and have been excellent role models both academically and athletically. Star players in the college games such as Sue Bird, who played at Connecticut, and Chamique Holdsclaw, who starred at Tennessee, not only have demonstrated excellence on the court but also have attracted fans to the women's game from all around the United States. Yet, in spite of the presence of such prominent players, the Women's National Basketball Association (WNBA), the professional league for women, has not yet attracted nearly the national attention and fan support of the older men's professional league, the NBA (National Basketball Association).

Are there instances where the support provided for men's and women's programs should not be equivalent? One kind of case might involve nationally recognized men's intercollegiate teams in such major sports as basketball and football. These sports are alleged to generate huge amounts of revenues and support for their home universities—income that supposedly supports men's teams in sports that do not produce revenue, and much of the women's athletic programs besides. Thus, national television networks pay prices of over \$1 billion for multiyear rights to televise the NCAA Men's Basketball Championship, the sum to be distributed among NCAA member institutions. When men's teams can generate significant income and support, is it legitimate to provide them with such extras as national scheduling, a greater number of coaches, advantageous practice times, and extensive support in the area of public relations?

In considering this issue, it should be noted that men's football and basketball often not only fail to produce profits, they frequently operate deep in the red. Although figuring out just what revenues intercollegiate sports bring in can be complicated, and we will explore this in Chapter 6, recent data strongly suggests that the idea of a revenue-producing sport is more often myth than reality. Thus, "the most recent NCAA report informs us that in 1997, fewer than half of the Division I programs (43 percent) reported 'profits' and that the average 'deficit' reported at the other programs was \$2.8 million."[30] Although the major men's teams of several major colleges and universities do bring in enormous income, the argument for the special treatment of men's programs in major sports, based on their capacity to generate income, applies to fewer institutions than is often thought.[31]

What about institutions where the men's programs in high visibility sports do generate large amount of revenue? Even though the argument for special treatment may have some force in such contexts, it should be implemented only when certain other conditions are also satisfied. These conditions should be based upon justifiable requirements designed to insure that the assignment of special status to men's teams in major sports does not block the emergence of women's athletics or deny them the chance to achieve "showcase" status of their own. If we do not accept such conditions of equity, we concede that the utility produced by major sports justifies us in overriding the claims of each person to equal respect and equal consideration. The result of such a view is that the individual is reduced to a mere resource for use by others. If we want to respect individuals and their rights, we cannot allow a concern for efficiency alone to override concern for persons and their entitlements.

What moral limitations might apply to institutions where large revenue-producing sports warrant special consideration? It is difficult to formulate an exhaustive list, but perhaps these guidelines can serve as a basis for discussion:

1. The revenues generated, over and above those covering expenses, either must go into the general university budget for the benefit of the entire university community or must be distributed within the athletic program, so that the women's sports program (or perhaps men's and women's lower profile sports) receives the greatest benefit.
2. The university must be making significant efforts to insure that some women's sports have a reasonable opportunity to achieve the status of the showcase men's sports.

These criteria ensure that broad segments of the university community can benefit from the revenues generated by the men's program, with emphasis on providing greater funding of the lesser-funded sports programs (or to support general academic concerns, such as providing financial aid for needy students), so arguably they could be accepted by all members of the university from a position of impartial choice. That is, following the suggestion made in John Rawls's monumental work, *A Theory of Justice,* inequalities can be just when they operate to improve the situation of the less advantaged.[32] Impartial members of the university community, for example, those who reason as if they did not know their position in the athletic program, would have every reason to favor a solution that would work to their benefit whether they participated on a high-profile men's sport or in the women's program.[33] The same principles should also apply to high-profile women's programs, such as the Connecticut women's basketball team, when they generate significant revenues.

So far, we have been considering what the standard of equivalent treatment for men's and women's athletics implies for funding; however, problems with equivalency arise in other areas as well. Are the coaches in the men's and women's program similarly qualified? Are practice times allotted equitably? Are facilities shared? Are women's teams relegated to inferior fields or gyms?

There probably will be no precise or exhaustive formula for determining what counts as equivalent support. The trick is to strike a balance between blind adherence to a frequently inequitable *status quo* and too rigid a commitment to inflexible requirements of absolutely identical treatment. For better or worse, the attainment of equity is likely to rest far more on the sound judgment of men and women of good will than on quantitative formulas or rigid principles applied in ignorance of the particular context. Accordingly, even though the formula of equivalent support and respect is vague and raises problems that cannot be dealt with here, it seems far more acceptable than requiring rigid identity of outcomes regardless of differences between the men's and women's athletic programs in specific contexts.

Conclusions

This chapter has argued for two main conclusions. First, it has maintained that sex equality is not always to be equated with blindness to sex. In particular, the ideal of sex equality as sexual assimilation (sex blindness) seems inappropriate to the realm of sports. Second, it has been argued that the general emphasis of Title IX on equivalent opportunities for each sex in sports is more justifiable than strict requirements of equal total or equal per capita expenditures on men's and women's athletics in institutional contexts. The operative principle should be equal concern and respect for all participants, and this may sometimes justify differences in actual treatment, including differences in expenditures between men's and women's athletic programs. In particular, the proportionality requirement has been criticized as too rigid and as a poor tool for achieving equity, since it can be satisfied by cutting opportunities for men without increasing them for women.

Our discussion also has implications for our view of gender equity beyond athletics. In particular, it suggests that equal respect and concern sometimes are compatible with the recognition of difference. Recognizing difference, conversely, does not necessarily require relations of subordination and dominance. In sports, sex equality does not require forgetting sex.

6

Sports on Campus

On the surface and to the casual observer, intercollegiate athletics may appear to be a healthy segment of the American sporting scene. The NCAA men's basketball Division I championship is one of the most popular sporting events in the United States and attracts attention throughout the world. Big-time college football has long held the national limelight, and programs such as those at Notre Dame, Florida, and Penn State have national as well as regional followings. In the 2002–2003 season, the popular University of Connecticut women's basketball team set a record for consecutive wins by a women's team and, over the years, has contributed significantly to the growing attention received by women's college basketball, perhaps due to intense competitions with its rivals from the University of Tennessee. College athletics have provided sports fans with many thrilling moments, including the then relatively unknown Michael Jordan's shot that gave North Carolina the 1982 NCAA basketball championship over Georgetown and the memorable victories in football Bowl games, such as the last minute win by Ohio State over Miami in the 2003 Fiesta Bowl in a game that decided the national championship.

But are exciting contests and superb athletes the whole story about college sports? Is there an ethically questionable side to intercollegiate athletics? What about the scandals that continually seem to surface in college sports? Do intercollegiate athletics actually harm the academic and educational functions of the university?

Public criticism of intercollegiate athletics in the United States goes back at least to 1905 when President Theodore Roosevelt summoned the presidents and

football coaches of Harvard, Yale, and Princeton to the White House in an attempt
to reduce the extreme level of violence then prevalent in the game. In our own day,
criticism has focused on the scandal-plagued programs of the large Division I institutions that offer athletic scholarships and that tend to dominate intercollegiate
sports. Such scandals have involved academic fraud, the alleged coddling of athletes
who have behaved outrageously, and cheating in the recruiting of highly talented
high school athletic stars. In contrast, intercollegiate athletics at the level of the Ivy
League, the highly selective liberal arts colleges, such as those that are members of
the New England Small Colleges Athletic Conference (NESCAC), and academically
respected but athletically competitive universities such as Duke and Stanford are
still thought of as relatively pure examples of what college sports at their best
should be. But even that view has come under challenge.

Thus, only a few months after North Carolina's victory over Georgetown in
1982, the game that brought Michael Jordan to national attention, another national
basketball power, the University of San Francisco (USF), which in the past had been
represented by such great players as Bill Russell and K. C. Jones, announced that it
had dropped intercollegiate basketball to preserve its "integrity and reputation." According to the Rev. John Lo Shiavo, then president of USF, people at the university
(presumably in the athletic program) felt that they had to break NCAA rules in an
attempt to remain competitive in big-time intercollegiate athletics.[1]

A particularly shocking and perhaps extreme example of abuse was provided
by former Clemson basketball coach Tates Locke in the book *Caught in the Net,* also
published in 1982. As Locke describes the situation at Clemson during his tenure
there, there was tremendous pressure on him to win. Clemson is a member of the
highly competitive Atlantic Coast Conference, which includes such college basketball powers as North Carolina, North Carolina State, and Duke. Some of these institutions not only have fine academic reputations but have locations that made it
easier for them to recruit black athletes from the inner cities than it was for Locke
in the somewhat more rural Clemson area.

It appeared to Locke that Clemson could not win as long as it abided by the
recruiting rules laid down by the NCAA. As he acknowledges in *Caught in the Net,*
Locke at the very least failed to prevent (and possibly turned a blind eye to) under-
the-table payments to players by boosters. He also may have condoned deception
in luring recruits to Clemson. To attract black athletes to Clemson, which was virtually all white, blacks from Columbia, South Carolina, were paid to pretend to be
student members of a fictitious black fraternity on weekends when black athletic
recruits visited the campus. A false picture of extensive on-campus social life for

blacks was created on what was then in truth a predominantly white campus. Locke confessed to his wrongdoing and wrote primarily to expose the pressures that may promote the violation of rules. But although Locke may have turned his career around, violations of fundamental principles continue to plague intercollegiate sports, particularly at the level of the elite Division I men's basketball and football powers.[2]

For example, in one of the most serious of recent abuses involving academics, an NCAA investigation of the University of Minnesota men's basketball program found that from 1994 to 1998, a secretary in the athletics academic counseling office, who was also employed as a tutor for the team, was involved in preparing about four hundred pieces of course work, including providing substantive material for papers, for student athletes in the program. The head coach of the basketball team, Clem Haskins, was found to be "knowledgeable about and complicit in the academic fraud" involved. According to the NCAA investigation, "The violations were significant, widespread, and intentional. More than that, their nature—academic fraud—undermined the bedrock foundation of a university and . . . damaged the academic integrity of the institution."[3]

Other problems have plagued college athletics as well. These range from low graduation rates for male athletes in major sports at many Division I institutions to the kind of not only embarrassing but also dangerous misbehavior and sometimes criminal activity of academically marginal athletes in some big-time intercollegiate programs. Although there are many fine athletes and coaches in major college sports, too often a concern for winning, and the status and income that go with it, have taken priority over the academic mission of the university. Thus, the 2002 NCAA Men's Championship game featured a win by the University of Maryland over the University of Oklahoma. But according to NCAA statistics, neither basketball program was able to graduate over 20 percent of its scholarship athletes, and Oklahoma did not graduate even one player out of the seven classes reported on by the NCAA, arriving as freshmen from 1989–1995.[4]

In his announcement in 1982 of the termination of the USF's basketball program (since reinstated at a lower level of competition), the Rev. John Lo Shiavo surely raised a fundamental ethical question about college sports when he asked, "How can we contribute to the building of a decent law-abiding society in this country if educational institutions are willing to suffer their principles to be prostituted and involve young people in that prostitution for any purpose and much less for the purpose of winning some games and developing an ill-gotten recognition and income?"[5]

It would be a mistake to think, however, that the problems with intercollegiate athletics simply involve outrageous behavior by athletes, recruiting violations, and academic fraud. Many critics believe the problem lies deeper. The moral questions that can be raised about intercollegiate athletics go well beyond an examination of violations of NCAA rules. We can ask questions about the rules themselves. For example, should colleges and universities be allowed to give athletic scholarships at all? Does the NCAA permit teams to play too many games to the academic detriment of the athletes?

At an even more fundamental level, we can question whether intercollegiate sports even belong on campus in the first place. After all, shouldn't colleges be educational institutions rather than minor leagues for professional sports? Is the academic mission of the university compatible with a commitment to intercollegiate athletics? Is commitment to excellence in athletics in conflict with commitment to academic excellence?

These questions suggest what might be called the "Incompatibility Thesis." This thesis states that intercollegiate sports are incompatible with the academic functions of colleges and universities. The strong version of this thesis asserts that the incompatibility is between academic values and *any* serious form of intercollegiate athletics. A weaker version holds that the incompatibility lies only between academic values and elite Division I athletic programs, those that offer athletic scholarships and whose teams, particularly in high-profile sports, regularly compete for national rankings.

This chapter is an examination of the Incompatibility Thesis, and more broadly, of the value, if any, of intercollegiate athletics. Its central question is what place an athletic program should have on a college or university campus. We shall be concerned not only with the proper role of athletics on campus but with the very nature and mission of the university.

The Role of Sports in the University
All Jocks Off Campus

Why should a university support an intercollegiate athletic program? After all, some distinguished institutions, including the University of Chicago, Emory, and the California Institute of Technology, have well-deserved reputations for academic excellence yet at various times in their history have not supported a full intercollegiate athletic program or, in some cases, have not had any such program at all.

In evaluating the role of intercollegiate athletics in the academy, it will be useful to distinguish three separate questions:

1. Is it wrong for colleges and universities to have an intercollegiate athletic program? Are any athletic programs morally impermissible?
2. Is it desirable for colleges and universities to have an intercollegiate athletic program?
3. If colleges and universities should have an intercollegiate athletic program, what kind of program is most justifiable?

It may be, for example, that it is not wrong for colleges and universities to support intercollegiate athletics programs, but such programs are undesirable because the money spent on them could be better spent elsewhere. Perhaps all sorts of intercollegiate athletic programs are not equally desirable. For example, intercollegiate athletic programs may be desirable if run along the lines of Ivy League or Division III programs but not if run more expansively.

Is there any reason for thinking that intercollegiate athletics programs are wrong? Should intercollegiate sports be prohibited? The question here is a broad one for many sorts of programs, ranging from those of Division III schools (such institutions do not offer athletic scholarships, they compete regionally rather than nationally, and they emphasize athletics less than schools in Divisions I and II) right up to the athletic giants such as Michigan, Oklahoma, Texas, and Notre Dame. One argument for the view that it is wrong for universities to support serious intercollegiate athletic programs rests on the Incompatibility Thesis. The wrongness arises from the corruption of academic values by athletic values.

Perhaps it is best to begin by considering an idealized but important model of what the university should be in our attempt to ascertain just what academic values ought to be regarded as fundamental. By assessing this model and seeing its relationship to various forms that intercollegiate athletics can take, we may be able to offer a judicious assessment of the proper role, if any, of intercollegiate athletics.

The University As a Refuge of Scholarship

Why have the college or university at all? What would be lacking in an educational system that devoted the elementary and high school years to imparting basic skills in reading, writing, and mathematics? After high school, students would either seek employment or go on to specialized professional training. Does a college education serves a function that such a system would fail to satisfy?

Traditionally, the role of education in the liberal arts has been thought to fill an important gap that is ignored by merely professional training and that is not fully approachable by those still mastering basic skills. Education in the liberal arts exposes students to "the best that has been thought and said" in their own and other cultures. By reflecting critically and analytically on the significant works, including artistic achievements, that the best minds have produced throughout human history, students should become better able to acquire a broad perspective on the human situation, learn to analyze difficult problems critically, and appreciate excellence in the arts, humanities, and sciences. And although there is often controversy about what works should be studied and what counts as "best," debates over that issue can themselves have enormous educational value.

Similar rhetoric can be found in the catalogs of most colleges and universities, for behind the language lies an institution that, though evolving, traces its heritage from ancient Greece, through the medieval universities of Europe, to the modern colleges and universities of our own time. The most important function of these institutions, it can be argued, is to transmit the best of human intellectual achievement, to subject different viewpoints to critical analysis, and to add to human knowledge through research.

Although today's huge "multi-universities" have many functions, including provision of professional training in medicine, business, education, nursing, and law, it can be argued that the most important function of the university still is to transmit, examine, and extend the realm of human knowledge. This function often places the university, or at least some of its members, in an adversarial relationship with the rest of society, because the university's function commits it to the often critical examination of popular ideas of a given time and culture. If that function were not performed, many bad ideas would not be subjected to criticism, and even good ideas would be less appreciated or understood because their advocates would never have to modify or defend them in the face of objection.[6]

Critical inquiry, then, is a major function of colleges and universities; it is fundamental to a democratic society because it gives citizens the information and skills they need to function as citizens. And by exposing ideas to critical scrutiny, it allows for the kind of correction of errors and checks on power that are lacking in tyrannies and dictatorships.

Accordingly, let us consider critical inquiry as a normative claim about what the principal function of the university should be. Can a case be made for the inclusion of an intercollegiate sports program in the university conceived not as a business or as a training ground for tomorrow's professionals but as a center of scholarship, critical thought, and training for citizenship in the democratic state? Is intercollegiate athletics at least compatible with the major educational mission of the university? Can athletics actually contribute to or enhance that mission?

Athletics As Education: A Reply to the Incompatibility Thesis

Why are athletic programs thought to be incompatible with academic values, particularly the kind of education involved in critical inquiry in the arts, sciences, social sciences, and humanities? Some of the points already touched on support the Incompatibility Thesis, especially when applied to elite Division I athletics.

First, the enormous pressures to win, often generated by the need to keep jobs, produce revenues, and promote the visibility of the institution, all too often generate cheating. The academic fraud we have seen at Minnesota and other institutions testifies to the strength of these pressures and to the values associated with victory at all costs.

Second, even if we ignore the abuses in some major intercollegiate athletic programs, there seems to be a basic contradiction between the aims of education and the aims of athletics; thus, the time students spend on the athletic fields is time spent away from their studies. Likewise, athletes either uninterested in academic work or unprepared to do it undermine the academic mission of many institutions.

Finally, many of the values associated with athletics, such as obedience to the orders of coaches, seem at odds with the kind of inquiring and questioning minds professors attempt to develop in the classroom; indeed, some critics see athletics as a mindless activity in which only physical skills are developed. Thus, to many college and university faculty, athletics are at best a necessary evil, perhaps useful in allowing students to let off steam, but in basic conflict with educational values.

One way to reply to such criticism is to acknowledge the existence of serious abuses but maintain that academic and athletic values are much more compatible than critics acknowledge. In fact, the place of athletics in the university traditionally has been defended on educational grounds. If it could be shown that athletics, particularly intercollegiate athletic competition, has significant educational value, a strong case can be made that colleges and universities should support such activities. Whether such a case could support the major athletic programs of the elite Division I institutions that offer athletic scholarships is a separate issue.

If intercollegiate athletics can be defended as an educationally valuable element of the academic community, the Incompatibility Thesis would be called into question. Such a defense is normative, not descriptive, in that it justifies a position athletics *ought* to hold rather than describing the actual operation of all "big-time" intercollegiate athletic programs.[7] But an account does not lack value because it is partially prescriptive; rather, it can be the basis for criticism because it tells us what ought to be rather than what actually is.

Let us consider such an argument and how it might apply first to "big-time" college athletics and, second, to schools in the Ivy and Patriot Leagues in Division I and the members of Division III, the largest division of the NCAA.

The Problems of "Big-Time" Intercollegiate Sports

The ideal of intercollegiate athletics as a model for excellence in the face of challenge is at best only partially adhered to, even by athletic programs that most resemble the ideal. When we turn to practices in major intercollegiate athletic programs, the resemblance may be minimal at best. In view of the abuses that have been detected within many such programs, we need to ask whether big-time college athletics can be justified at all. Many major college and university athletic programs are run honestly, and student-athletes in such institutions do get an education and develop athletically as well, but the reported abuses are sufficiently serious and the incentives for abuse sufficiently great to justify our concern.

The Corruption of Intercollegiate Sports

In many of the athletically prominent colleges and universities of our land, sports have become big business. Television revenues and the visibility and support accompanying success in the major "visibility sports," such as men's football and basketball, seem to many to undermine the educational ideal of sports. To gain visibility, and the revenues and support that go with it, a program must be successful. But "success" in this context means "winning," and so the temptation is to do what is necessary to win. For example, coaches who teach their athletes effectively and who recruit only academically qualified players may not be as valuable to an institution interested in athletic success as a coach who wins, who can handle the media, and whose scruples about recruiting are less strict. Corners get cut. Other schools feel they, too, must cut even more corners, just to be competitive, and soon real abuses become far too common.

Violations of NCAA rules and the misbehavior of athletes who are only marginally qualified as students get much of the publicity. However, perhaps the most significant form of abuse goes deeper: If the purpose of participation becomes winning for the sake of external goods, such as visibility and financial support, won't players come to be viewed as mere means to that end rather than as students to be educated? Indeed, to keep players eligible, athletic programs could view education as an obstacle that must be overcome; many players could be inadequately educated and perhaps never graduate. Former star Minnesota Viking lineman Alan Page has described a meeting of eight defensive linemen to go over the team's playbook:

> We had each spent four years in colleges with decent reputations
> . . . and I remember that two of us could read the playbook, two
> others had some trouble with it but managed, and four of my team-
> mates couldn't read it at all. . . . The problem seems to be that these
> athletes—and there are many more like them, blacks and whites—
> were never expected to learn to read and write. They floated
> through up to this point because they were talented athletes.[8]

Various reforms made by the NCAA in the last twenty years may have contributed to some improvement since Page was a player. The overall graduation rate for student-athletes at NCAA institutions is higher than for students at large. However, serious problems remain, particularly in the high visibility sports of men's football and basketball. Although highly regarded institutions such as Penn State and Duke report high graduation rates even in those sports, other programs seem to be a disaster area. For example, for students entering college in 1995–1996, the overall graduation rate was 58 percent. The graduation rate for all athletes was 60 percent and for all male athletes 54 percent. However, male basketball players graduated only at a 43 percent rate and African American basketball players fared even more poorly, graduating at a 35 percent rate (although that rate was comparable to the overall graduation rate for black male students). Some individual institutions did far worse; the University of Oklahoma and the University of Nevada at Las Vegas graduated no male basketball players, and Florida State and the University of Cincinnati graduated no male African American basketball players. In fact, forty-two institutions failed to graduate *any* black male basketball players between 1991–1992 and 1994–1995.[9]

Thus, perhaps the morally most damaging charge brought against major intercollegiate athletics is that it exploits the participating athlete. Such athletes are ostensibly offered scholarships to play their sport in return for an education, but too often, the athlete is expected to give everything on the field, sometimes to the huge financial benefit of the university, but little or no time or effort is taken to insure success in the classroom.

For example, football at major universities, and often at smaller schools as well, is virtually a year-round sport. Practice starts in late summer. The season can extend into December, and even further if postseason competition in the major bowls is involved. The season itself may be followed by an off-season "informal" weight training program; this goes through winter and may, in turn, be followed by spring practice. Not only does the time devoted to practice leave athletes little time for the nonathletic aspects of university life but it also affects academic achievement and, as we discussed earlier, encourages academic fraud.

The Problems of the Black Athlete

The problems discussed above, especially those involving the alleged exploitation of athletes, may apply particularly to the black athlete. Although blacks constitute about 12 percent of the population of the United States, they constitute well over a third of college football and basketball players, about 40 percent of professional football players, and about two-thirds of professional basketball players. Disproportionate representation is even greater in the major intercollegiate programs and at the very top levels of major professional sports, where all-star teams often are dominated by black players.

What explains the disproportionate representation of black athletes in certain sports? Theories of innate or genetic physiological racial differences have been used to explain this phenomenon; however, explanations that are largely or entirely environmental seem simpler and more plausible. A plausible explanation for the unusual representation of black athletes in many sports is discrimination and lack of opportunity in inner city areas. If blacks perceive many doors as closed to them because of discrimination, sports may seem the best escape route from poverty and the ghetto. The effects of discrimination and the focus of the mass media on athletes may also lead to there being a dearth of nonathletic role models in the black community, a gap filled by successful black athletes. Or such alternate role models may exist but may be less appreciated than is warranted because of the attention focused on such black athletic superstars as Michael Jordan, Shaquille O'Neal, and Kobe Bryant. As a result, success in athletics may come to be more highly valued in the black than in the white community. Thus, blacks become disproportionately involved in athletics, especially such sports as basketball, track, football, and baseball, which normally do not require large investments in equipment and for which inexpensive facilities are widely available in urban areas. As one African American scholar has argued, "To assert that Afro-Americans are superior athletes due to the genetic makeup of the original slaves would be as naive as the assertion that the determining factor in the demonstrated excellence of white pole vaulters from California over pole vaulters from other states is the physical stamina of the whites who settled in California."[10] Just as the climate and facilities available in California can account for the success of the pole vaulters, so can a different set of environmental factors account for the success of young African Americans in many sports.

The following quotations from interviews with black baseball players tend to support the environmental hypothesis:

> It has been an avenue for me out of the ghetto. Hadn't I played baseball, I probably would have finished school but I doubt seriously I would be doing exactly what I wanted to do. Blacks just don't get an opportunity to do what they always want to do.

> Very definitely, I escaped through sports. For poor blacks there aren't many alternative roads. Sports got me into college and with college I could have alternatives. . . . I've worked hard at baseball to get away from the way of life I led growing up.

> Yes. . . . It's helped a lot of blacks. There ain't too many other things you can do. There are other things, but you don't have the finances to do it.[11]

If it is true that sports are more often viewed as the path of choice to upward mobility in the black community than the white, we might worry whether black athletes are more vulnerable to the dangers of big-time college athletics, particularly the failure to get a rigorous education, than whites. For example, as many black youngsters might tend to see sports as the major and perhaps only avenue to success open to them, they may be more likely to neglect their studies than others. The hope of obtaining an athletic scholarship and of playing professional sports may interfere with developing the educational tools that make for success in other areas. Some writers have argued that, since it may disproportionately steer African American youngsters away from focus on education to focus on sports practice instead, the dream of success in athletics may be harmful to the African American community. Once in college, black athletes in football and basketball may overestimate their chances of making the professional leagues or not even be concerned about graduation because they hope or expect to be drafted early by a professional team.

Although athletic scholarships are available for many athletes, including under-privileged blacks and whites, the odds of obtaining them are not high. The odds of achieving a career in pro sports not only are even lower, they are astonishingly small. According to one estimate, the chances that an African American youngster will succeed at making a professional team in a major professional sport is roughly 1 out of 18,000.[12]

Unfortunately, it appears that African American youngsters have a greater tendency than whites to overestimate their chances of playing college and professional sports and so may assign a higher priority to athletic than academic success.[13] Not without reason, some writers argue that the athletics in the United States, often considered in popular thought as a road to equal opportunity for African Americans, has been harmful to them.[14] Although such a thesis may be overstated, for many of those who neglect educational opportunities, athletic talent may be far more likely to lead down a dead-end street than to the pot of gold at the end of the rainbow seemingly provided by professional sports.

The Case Against Major Intercollegiate Athletics

To review, the criticisms of "big-time" intercollegiate athletics arise from the change of emphasis from athletics as an educationally valuable activity supplementing the normal academic curriculum to athletics as a source of revenue, support, and high visibility. These benefits—revenue, support, and visibility—depend upon winning, which, in turn, depends largely on recruiting the best athletes. The pressure to win can become so intense that coaches and athletes as well as university administrations (often under pressure from influential alumni boosters) make decisions that reflect athletic rather than educational priorities. At their worst, the pressures lead to recruiting violations, to misbehavior, and even to crime and other abuses, all of which have too often dominated the sports pages of our daily newspapers. Moreover, athletes may be given the opportunity to get an education but lose the opportunity because of their own lack of educational commitment.

The kind of disrespect for the educational mission of the university, along with violations of NCAA rules and misbehavior by athletes themselves, undermines overall respect for the university. If the ideal of the university is that of an institution concerned for the discovery and preservation of truth and the recognition of human excellence, isn't that ideal compromised by sacrificing the education of athletes for athletic victories, and even more so by outright cheating? Even though it is true that the modern university has become what has been called a social service station, fulfilling a variety of social needs, its most important function is still to formulate, test, teach, and evaluate achievement in the arts, sciences, humanities, and professions. How can the university claim to represent such fundamental values when it subverts them in its own practice?

Reasonable people may doubt, then, whether intercollegiate sports should be played at the level of national competition and intensity found in the major football and basketball conferences of our nation. Many would argue that the only reputable intercollegiate athletic programs are those resembling the Division III or Ivy League levels where no athletic scholarships are given, athletes are expected to be students, and competition is normally regional rather than national. Perhaps this level of intercollegiate competition is the only kind compatible with respect for the athlete as a person, with respect for the educational value of athletic competition, and with respect for the integrity of the university.

Reforming Major Intercollegiate Athletics

Before we accept the conclusion that major intercollegiate athletics at the national level are inherently unethical, important counterarguments need to be considered. In particular, proponents of major intercollegiate athletics maintain that providing entertainment for the campus community and for regional and national audiences is not inherently wrong, especially when it results in financial and other kinds of support for the university. After all, it can be said with considerable justice that many critics of intercollegiate athletics would not complain if the university's drama or dance companies received national recognition by providing a huge television audience and many evenings of enjoyment. If it is permissible for the university to be a social service station in other areas, why shouldn't it provide entertainment to society, in return for rewards, in athletics as well?

A Consequentialist Defense—Nonacademic Benefits

Can major athletic programs be justified by their good consequences? This appeal to consequences is utilitarian; it appeals to the greatest good of those affected by an action or practice as a whole. Utilitarian arguments, although arguably not the only moral considerations, are not irrelevant to moral evaluation. After all, we surely ought to consider whether major athletic programs promote more good than harm when morally evaluating them.

What are the consequences that defenders of major intercollegiate athletics programs might cite? First, there is the fun that major college sports provide not only for segments of the college or university community but for local, regional, and sometimes national audiences. Sports teams also may generate allegiance to a college or university. Surely part of the support that large universities, such as the University of North Carolina at Chapel Hill, Penn State, Michigan, Notre Dame, and Duke, is due to the visibility and competitive success of their athletic teams. Visibility in turn may lead to increased applications, greater selectivity, support from state legislatures and sometimes from alumni, and overall indirect benefit to the institution's academic mission.

Moreover, highly visible men's teams in sports such as basketball and football, and some women's basketball teams such as those at Tennessee and Connecticut, may generate considerable revenue that can be used to support the rest of the athletic program or be applied to academic needs as well. Although, as we have seen in Chapter 5, there is doubt that most major college programs generate revenues, surely the most successful programs often do. Sometimes what counts as a profit and loss in this area is controversial: Should we stick to counting just gate receipts? What about sales of apparel bearing the institution's logo? (One can hardly go to a campus in the United States without seeing apparel with the logo of such schools as North Carolina or Notre Dame.) On the other hand, are expenditures counted properly, such as costs of stadiums and athletic facilities? Should all the costs be attributed to varsity teams if these facilities are shared with other students and faculty?

For the sake of argument, let us assume that some athletic teams at major schools do generate substantial revenue. If we add this benefit to the others mentioned above, is there a utilitarian argument sufficient to justify major intercollegiate sports in the face of the case against them?

The problem is that if defenders of major intercollegiate athletic programs are to appeal to utility, they must consider all the relevant consequences. Do the negatives outweigh the positives?

The issue becomes more complex if we don't restrict ourselves to purely utilitarian arguments, especially those that emphasize the alleged direct nonacademic benefits of intercollegiate athletics. As we have seen, utility alone does not normally override other ethical considerations involving fairness and individual rights. On the contrary, rights function as constraints on the direct pursuit of utility. Without the protection provided by individual rights, individuals could be unduly sacrificed for minimal gains in the good of society as a whole. Because one of the charges against major intercollegiate athletic programs is that they too often sacrifice educational values for athletic ones, or cheat and commit fraud for athletic advantages, utilitarian arguments alone will not carry the day.

This suggests that major intercollegiate athletic programs are morally required to operate within strict ethical restraints to be ethically defensible. But what restraints should be in place? Can educational values and respect for persons be preserved in intercollegiate athletics without losing the quality of excellence and the levels of intensity and enthusiasm characterizing the NCAA basketball championships or Big Ten football?

Should College Athletes Be Professionals?

One proposal, defended by former Senator Bill Bradley, himself a former college and professional basketball star, and proposed most recently in 2003 by a member of the Nebraska state legislature (to apply to football players in the Big 12 Conference) is that college athletes playing major sports in "big-time" intercollegiate programs should be professionals.[15] According to one version of such a proposal, the athletes would be paid to play and need not be students. Such individuals could attend classes and obtain a degree if they fulfilled the normal requirements for admission to the academic program, but they would not be required to do so. Rather, they would be employees of the college or university for which they played.

This proposal would have several advantages. First, it would be honest. Since the athletes would be openly paid a fair salary, illegal payments to them would be unnecessary. Second, the fiction that all players are "student athletes" need not be maintained. Athletes not academically qualified to attend classes and those not interested in doing so would not be expected to perform academically. Third, athletes would not be exploited. They would share in the profits produced by their play, and their pay would be set by the market. Fourth, such athletes could enroll in classes and earn a degree if they wished to do so, but only by meeting the same academic standards of admissibility and performance as other students; thus, athletic excellence and the academic integrity of the university would be preserved.

Although such a proposal has virtues, it may be a matter of throwing out the baby with the bath water. If it were adopted, what we would have is not intercollegiate athletics but just another professional minor league. Critics might object that "just another professional minor league" is what we have now, but perceptions, and sometimes the reality, differ. In spite of the abuses, many, perhaps most, athletes in major intercollegiate programs are working towards degrees and are students at the schools for which they play. Many, perhaps most, institutions in Division I do not cheat, and their athletes also earn degrees in reputable areas of study. Female athletes, including female basketball players, have significantly higher graduation rates than other students, including female nonathletes. So even at the level of elite Division I athletics, the bleak picture presented by critics is far from the whole story.

Moreover, the enthusiasm of the crowds and the spectacle of college sports make them different from professional sports, and part of this difference arises from the belief that college teams in some sense represent their institutions. Students, alumni, and other members of the university community generate enthusiasm because of their loyalty to their institutions and because they believe the players have a similar relationship to the schools. It is an open question whether the distinctive character of college sports would survive professionalization.

Of course, critics could object that the fans' perceptions are often distorted and that college athletes in high-visibility sports in major programs really are (poorly paid) professionals; however, the issue is whether we should further encourage this development, openly and honestly, or try to make college athletes comply with the academic mission of colleges and universities. The latter policy has the advantage of preserving the distinctive character of college athletics and the educational values of a good intercollegiate athletics program.

Another serious problem faces professionalization. Once the university enters professional sports with the primary goal of making a profit, isn't there even greater danger than at present to the educational priorities of the institution? Will favorite players be traded or let go if their salary demands are too high? Will games be scheduled off campus whenever possible to insure high attendance by those most able to pay high prices for tickets? Will students be treated as second-class spectators and have even more limited access to tickets than currently provided at some profit-hungry institutions because they can afford to pay relatively little for them? Will making a profit on high-visibility sports be regarded as so important that the educational lessons to be learned from good competition are lost? Won't winning be the bottom line, regardless of how it is achieved? Although some of these circumstances exist already in major intercollegiate sports, professionalization may only accelerate them even further.

Moreover, will professionalization really avoid the exploitation of athletes? Will universities be able to pay athletes large salaries without diverting funds from education? On the other hand, if salaries are low, won't athletes still be underpaid but have even less chance of getting an education than at present? And if, as critics claim, relatively few big-time programs actually do generate profits, where will the funds come from for salaries? Before we decide whether professionalization is the best alternative, other options ought to be considered as well.

The Academic Reform Movement

In the late 1980s, throughout the 1990s, and into the early years of the current century, widespread disgust with the state of major intercollegiate athletics led to a reform movement within the governing body of college athletics, the NCAA. Headed by a commission led by selected presidents of NCAA institutions, a series of reforms were proposed, debated, and sometimes adopted. The goal of these reforms was to reaffirm the priority of educational values in intercollegiate sport. Although proposals arising from this reform movement undoubtedly will continue to be proposed and debated, reasserting the primacy of educational values over profits and won-lost records deserves examination as an alternative to professionalization.

The reform movement has focused on such goals as tightening academic standards for eligibility, restricting the amount of time that can be devoted to practice, and trying to control the length of seasons.

However, the difficulty of achieving incremental reform is significant. For example, a series of propositions were adopted by the NCAA in the 1980s and early 1990s requiring that freshmen achieve a minimal SAT score (or, in a later version, a combined index of SAT scores and grades in core courses) to be eligible for intercollegiate athletic competition. But, since African Americans tend to score lower on the SAT than others, such requirements proved highly controversial.

Are the SATs culturally biased against minorities? What are the effects of socioeconomic status on standardized test scores? A disproportionate number of African Americans are economically disadvantaged; therefore, as socioeconomic status tends to correlate with test scores, are the tests stacked against them? Some observers believe proposals to require a minimal SAT score for eligibility were unfair to African American athletes. Former Georgetown basketball coach John Thompson was so outraged by the NCAA propositions that he walked out of a game with Boston College in protest.

In opposition to such charges, some educators, including prominent and hardly conservative African American scholars, have argued that the standards set by Proposition 48 are too low. If, as suggested above, socioeconomic factors predispose black youngsters to overemphasize athletics at the expense of acquiring basic academic skills, the setting of a standard by legislation such as Proposition 48 may create an incentive for reversing priorities. As sociologist of sport Harry Edwards has argued,

> Rule 48 communicates to young athletes . . . that we expect them to develop academically as well as athletically. . . . Further, were I not to support Rule 48, I would risk communicating to black youth in particular that I, as a nationally known black educator, do not believe they have the capacity to achieve a 700 score on the SAT . . . when they have a significant chance of scoring

460 by a purely random marking of the test. Finally, I support the
NCAA's action because I believe that . . . the black community
must insist that black children be taught and that they learn whatever subject matter is necessary to excel on diagnostic and all
other skills tests.[16]

Whatever the merits of the issue, the attempt to raise academic standards by
working with limits on standardized test scores proved impossible to sustain. Attention has now shifted to requiring students to achieve minimum grades in core
courses in high school and to maintain academic standing while in college. More
promising proposals include depriving intercollegiate teams of athletic scholarships
if their athletes do not graduate at approved rates. The problem with such proposals
is that graduation or even grades themselves may not be significant markers of academic progress if the athletes are not enrolled in demanding programs (thus, the
former emphasis on the SAT, which provided a standard separate from the grading
practices of individual institutions).

Rather than focus on individual incremental attempts at reforming big-time
intercollegiate athletics, it may be more useful for us to examine broader issues and
themes. Such a discussion may generate principles that can be used as a framework
for assessing proposals for incremental reform.

Awarding Athletic Scholarships: An Immoral Practice?

One possibility, not officially considered by the NCAA but well worth examination,
is that all institutions conform to rules like those presently in place in Division III or
in such Division I conferences as the Ivy League. In this view, there should be no
special financial aid for athletes. Prospective athletes would then pick a college or
university that would best fulfill their educational needs, not for the athletic scholarship they would receive. Financial aid would be awarded only according to need,
not athletic ability. Moreover, although admissions officers might give special
weight to a candidate's athletic talents, roughly similar weight would be given to the
nonathletic talents of other applicants, such as ability in music or drama. Colleges
and universities would look for true student athletes, not just those looking for
cost-free exposure to professional scouts.

This is a very attractive proposal. It would avoid the objection that major intercollegiate sports exploits athletes because only athletes who are concerned with
the education an institution can provide would enroll. Moreover, athletic programs
would be run as part of the institution's educational program rather than as revenue

producers. For example, coaches might be given faculty status and be judged primarily as teachers rather than according to their record of wins and losses. Generating income and support would not be the program's primary purpose. Because athletes would be admitted on the same basis as other students, much of the motivation for the recruiting abuse and academic fraud that have plagued major college athletics would have been removed.

Nevertheless, although this proposal might express the most desirable framework for conducting intercollegiate athletics, it has serious defects. For one thing, it is impractical in the sense that it is unlikely ever to be adopted. Given the visibility and, sometimes, the revenue generated by the most successful big-time athletic programs, as well as entrenched support by alumni and fans for their favorite teams, a sudden radical de-emphasis of intercollegiate sports probably could not be achieved.

The policy of de-emphasis still might be morally justifiable even if is difficult or impossible to carry out. But even though there is much to be said for the moral justifiability of this approach, there are moral objections to it. According to these objections, some de-emphasis on athletics is justified, but radical de-emphasis, including the elimination of athletic scholarships, is not.

In particular, it is far from clear that the award of athletic scholarships or the use of athletic programs to generate revenue and support is inherently immoral. Athletic scholarships can be used to attract top talent to particular programs and make competition exciting. They also allow talented athletes to acquire an education that might otherwise be beyond their grasp. In addition to tangible benefits, such as money, athletics can enhance the visibility of the university, create cohesion within the university community, and create enjoyment for the region and sometimes the entire nation. Major college athletic events are entertaining, demonstrate a quest for excellence through challenge, and can generate a sense of pride in one's institution and loyalty to it that might carry over into support for it in many other ways. What is immoral in this view is not major intercollegiate competition but specific abuses resulting in the exploitation of athletes and the violation of academic ethics. Reforms should aim at cleaning up big-time intercollegiate athletics, not eliminating it.

How are these positions to be evaluated? Each seems to rest largely on empirical or factual assumptions that are difficult to confirm. The proponents of de-emphasis doubt whether incremental reforms can curb the abuses arising when money and status are at stake. Proponents of incremental reform are more optimistic. They believe that specific changes short of major de-emphasis, some of which will be discussed below, can work. At present, it is unclear which of these factual assumptions is true.

In addition to consequentialist arguments about the effect of reform, there is another sort of argument for the view that awarding athletic scholarships is immoral. Why, a critic might ask, should an athlete receive financial aid to attend a college or university when an educationally better qualified student is turned away? Why should limited openings in a college class be filled by those whose primary talent is athletics, instead of by those who could do best in the classroom? Why should a disadvantaged but not athletically talented student be denied financial aid, and therefore denied an opportunity to receive an education, in favor of an athlete who may not even need the money and who may be uninterested in obtaining an education?

In particular, many athletic scholarships are awarded by large, generally unselective universities that enroll large student populations. Admission need not be a zero-sum game where each scholarship awarded to an athlete means that a needy academically qualified nonathlete is denied financial aid (although athletic programs that run up huge losses may well impose severe burdens on the rest of the academic community). Although it is widely agreed that athletes who are not educationally qualified should not be admitted, athletes can be given some special consideration in admission because of the overall goods they provide for the whole community. Similarly, if other kinds of students can provide similar benefits for the university as a whole, they should receive special scholarships as well. After all, it is unclear whether standardized test scores, high school grades, and class rank should be the only determinants of admissibility to even the most selective institutions. A diverse class, including the athletically talented, may provide educational benefits as well as enhance life in ways that benefit a broad segment of the university community.

Moreover, although some major intercollegiate athletic programs have poor graduation rates, particularly in men's high-profile sports, others have quite high graduation rates for athletes. Some groups of athletes, females and those in lower-profile sports, often do as well academically as other students. Finally, athletes in an entering class often are not given preference over academic superstars but are accepted instead of students who may not have vastly superior academic credentials and who sometimes might not have performed better in class than the scholarship athlete.[17]

These rejoinders may be defensible. In particular, if the benefits provided by high-visibility sports in major college athletic programs can also benefit other members of the university community, such programs, including the awarding of athletic scholarships, may be morally permissible if the incremental reforms proposed by the NCAA are effective. In short, the practice of awarding athletic scholarships is open to serious question, but the questions may be answerable through an effective reform program.

Three Proposals for Reform

It is important to consider proposals for reform for, even if they are not ideal, they may constitute a second-best solution to the problems of intercollegiate athletics if the ideal solution proves unattainable. Let us consider the idea of reform further.

First, it seems entirely justifiable to set academic standards that prospective athletes recruited for elite Division I programs must meet to be eligible for athletics. These standards should in part consist of satisfactory grades in academically sound core high school courses in core subjects, such as English and mathematics. However, the courses offered by different schools can vary in quality, and sometimes there are legitimate concerns that athletes may not be held to the strictest standards so that they can remain eligible to play.

Thus, I suggest there is a role for the SAT to play, in spite of fears that it may unfairly disadvantage minorities. However, rather than require athletes to attain an across-the-board minimal SAT score, we could consider relativizing the score to their institutions. That is, athletes should achieve a score on the SAT comparable to that of, say, the lowest third of accepted applicants to that particular institution who are not athletes. Moreover, failure to achieve this relativized score could be overcome by evidence of superior academic achievement as shown by grades or class rank. Finally, failure to achieve the minimal SAT score would not prevent a prospective athlete from being recruited or being offered a scholarship, only from being eligible to play until academic achievement was demonstrated while in college.

Second, the strategy of restricting travel, length of season, and time devoted to off-season practice for Division I programs is a good one and should be extended further. In particular, it is hard to see how athletes can achieve the full benefits of a university education if they are constantly on long road trips playing games. Although specific proposals might differ from sport to sport, national nonconference competition should be restricted to vacation periods or postseason play in national championships.

Critics have complained about the amount of time today's college athletes are expected to practice out of season. Although the NCAA has restricted the amount of off-season practice that institutions can officially require, the critics charge that allegedly voluntary "captain's practices" held in the off season, supposedly at the initiative of the players themselves, are in fact mandatory because coaches will penalize players who don't attend. This is a tricky issue, however, since many highly motivated athletes (some of them academically successful) do want to practice on their own in the off season. Isn't it an unjustified restriction on their liberty to prevent them from doing what any other student may do; namely, practice a sport on their own time? (Former Olympic swimmer Janet Evans, who carried a 4.0 or A grade-point average at Stanford, was said to have left school because she felt she could not prepare adequately for world class competition under the NCAA rule adopted in 1991 limiting required practices to twenty hours each week.) At a minimum, restrictions on the liberty to practice in the off season need to balance the protection of the athlete against the freedom to engage in a valued activity, and so must be drawn in a manner sensitive to both sets of values.

A third proposal is to hold institutions responsible for the academic progress of their athletes. Different versions of this proposal are under consideration, but the general idea is that athletic programs within an institution be penalized by loss of future athletic scholarships if the graduation rate and academic progress of participating athletes were deficient. This approach would have two desirable consequences: It would provide incentives for institutions to recruit only athletes who could succeed academically and to insure their athletes did learn once they matriculated.

All this presupposes that athletes are taking legitimate courses and are involved in academically satisfactory programs of study. To insure this, faculties need to exercise significant oversight on the courses chosen by athletes. For example, course selection for athletes should be handled the same way as it is for other students; that is, through faculty or academic advisers, not coaches or employees of the athletic department. Course selection by athletes should resemble that of other students unless there was an appropriate educational reason for the difference. For example, athletes might take more education courses than other students if they were interested in becoming teachers and coaches after graduation, or specialize more than others in economics if they had a greater interest in entering the business world. But faculty monitoring and control would do much to insure that the academic ethic was not being undermined by athletics. Surely the contribution athletics can make to the overall community in elite Division I programs should not be at the price of athletes' academic progress.

Finally, as noted earlier, athletes must take advantage of the educational opportunities offered them. The academic deficiencies of some athletes sometimes may not be the fault of the institution at all but of the athletes' priorities. Although incremental reforms of the kinds suggested above might do much to make academics and big-time intercollegiate athletics compatible, reforms can only provide a better opportunity for individuals to receive an education; the individuals themselves must take responsibility for achieving it.

Can Athletics Enhance Academics?

At most, our argument so far shows that athletics at the level of major intercollegiate sports, given appropriate and effective regulation, can provide benefits such as a sense of community, fun, visibility, and perhaps revenue without undermining the central academic mission of colleges and universities. Skeptics may question whether regulations can be effective given the incentives to win and claim that the argument shows athletics to be a necessary evil, but that response may well be too bleak. Most athletes in elite Division I programs graduate, often, as we have seen, at higher rates than other students. Female athletes do particularly well, but many athletes in high-visibility men's programs also graduate at high rates at institutions whose athletic programs have achieved national prominence.[18] Although graduation rates are not always an indication of the rigor of the programs in which athletes are enrolled, greater faculty control would surely enhance the quality of education received by athletes at high-profile institutions.

But even if this limited defense of elite Division I athletics has force, an even stronger kind of argument should also be considered. This argument claims not merely that, under suitable conditions, big-time athletics and academics can be minimally compatible and so should be accepted for their utilitarian benefits, but that intercollegiate athletics in the right circumstances can enhance or contribute to the academic mission of colleges and universities.

Athletics As Education

In particular, if we consider the model of athletic competition as a mutual quest for excellence through challenge as developed in Chapters 2 and 3, it has several features that make it a desirable supplement to a broad liberal arts education. On this model, athletic competition can be thought of as a test through which competitors commit their minds and bodies to the pursuit of excellence. To meet such a test, they must learn to analyze and overcome weakness, to work hard to improve, to understand their own strengths and weaknesses, and to react intelligently and skillfully to situations that arise in the contest. In the sports contest, they must use judgment, make decisions that are open to reflective criticism (often known as second-guessing), apply standards of assessment, critically analyze play, and exhibit perseverance and coolness under pressure. During a season, athletes can learn and grow by understanding their physical and psychological weaknesses and trying to improve.

Many of these same traits are also required for successful study in the humanities and sciences. An important part of education is learning to know and understand oneself, and that kind of self-knowledge is one of the most valuable kinds of knowledge that can emerge from participation in sports. In calling for the best that is within each participant, a good athletic program can provide educational experiences that are unusually intense and unusually valuable, and that reinforce and help develop many of the same traits that promote learning elsewhere. But even leaving aside such consequences, the good sports contest is a crucible in which important learning takes place and involves the discipline, understanding, and analysis that are related to learning in other parts of the curriculum.

Critics might object that even if these points are correct, they do not show that intercollegiate athletics is a necessary part of an educational curriculum. After all, if the same values are directly promoted, taught, and exemplified in the classroom, the additional indirect reinforcement provided by athletics is at best marginal and at worst distracts students from more academic pursuits where the most important aspects of education are dealt with. At most, critics might argue, intramural programs may well be warranted, but not the kind of intense activity found in varsity intercollegiate athletics.[19]

This sort of critical rejoinder is not decisive. As philosopher Paul Weiss has pointed out, students, particularly undergraduates, are novices in the academic disciplines they study. At best, the more advanced undergraduates may become apprentices by assisting professors in research, but they rarely have the chance to be at the cutting edge of achievement in a discipline until later in their careers. Athletics, along with the performing arts, are perhaps the only areas in most colleges and universities where students can achieve and demonstrate excellence—and not just as apprentice learners but in performances that rank among the best at a high level of comparative judgment.[20]

Perhaps more important, appreciation of achievement in athletics is widespread, far more so than understanding of achievement in mathematics, physics, philosophy, or other specialized disciplines. Because of this, athletics can and should serve as a kind of common denominator that allows people from vastly different backgrounds, cultures, social classes, and academic interests to experience together the lessons of striving to meet challenges. These experiences can be not only educationally valuable to the participants but also can inspire, teach, and inform other members of the wider university community who also enjoy the competition. Moreover, because athletics is accessible to and attracts the interest of wide segments of the population, it can be a unifying force in an intellectual community often split along ideological, ethnic, religious, socioeconomic, and disciplinary lines. Although this function is perhaps distinct from its primary educational functions, intercollegiate athletics can help create bonds that allow communication to persist when it might otherwise break down because of differences within the university.

Thus, because of the intensity and high level of the competition, intercollegiate athletics can serve as a common medium through which large and diverse segments of the academic community can demonstrate and appreciate excellent performance and the struggle to meet challenge. Michael Oriad, a professor of English at Oregon State University, captured the effects of his institution's basketball program and its coach, Ralph Miller, when he wrote

> My colleagues and I recognize the most important functions of the university to be teaching, research, and service. . . . But on Friday or Saturday night from December through March, we cannot conceive of a finer place to be than in Gill Coliseum watching what the locals have termed the Orange Express. . . . These games are the major social events of our winter months, and our enthusiasm for the team is compounded of many elements. Some of us have had players in class and usually have favorable reports of the experience. . . . Most of us never appreciated the art of passing until we saw how O.S.U. executes it. . . . It is a particular kind of excellence that our basketball team exhibits and that most appeals to us. Ralph Miller speaks the truth when he calls himself not a coach but a teacher, and we teachers in other disciplines appreciate what his pupils have learned to do.[21]

Our discussion suggests, then, that although intercollegiate athletics are not strictly part of an education in the way the classroom experience is, they can and should add a desirable educational component to the university. Of course, our account has been highly intellectual and is not meant to deny that intercollegiate athletics can provide other benefits to the academic community as well. These benefits include opportunities for relaxation, to make new friends and meet different kinds of people, and to promote a sense of community on campus. Although these other benefits are significant, it is important to consider the educational benefits of athletics as well if we are to determine their proper role in the university. For example, one might argue that if athletics have educational value, coaches should be evaluated primarily as teachers rather than according to their record of wins and losses or their ability to generate funds for the university.

In all fairness, this model of athletics does not easily fit the major intercollegiate athletic programs found at the athletic pinnacle of Division I. The institutions that come closest to meeting it most probably are schools like those in the Ivy League, perhaps major universities that do award athletic scholarships and have strong academic reputations—such as Duke and Stanford—and many of the institutions in Division III (the largest division within the NCAA), where athletic scholarships are not awarded, where athletes take the same courses as other students, and where athletics is regarded as an adjunct to the educational program.

But although it may be comforting to think of intercollegiate athletics at such schools as pure and pristine, at least compared to the kind of problems that have plagued big-time intercollegiate athletics, some recent criticism has called even that assumption into question. This criticism goes directly to the heart of the claim that athletics can enhance academics and has a significant educational role to play at many institutions of higher education.

Do Intercollegiate Athletics Fail the Game of Life?

In their recent book, *The Game of Life,* James L. Shulman and William G. Bowen, officers of the prestigious Mellon Foundation (Bowen is also a former president of Princeton University), use material from an extensive database comparing the academic performance of athletes and nonathletes as well as their careers after college and conclude that intercollegiate athletics is even more harmful at the Ivy League universities and highly selective liberal arts colleges.[22]

Critics point out that because the smaller, more academically selective schools tend to offer more intercollegiate sports than others, athletes constitute a high percentage of their student body, as much as 30 percent to 40 percent. In the late 1950s, athletes at the schools studied by Shulman and Bowen performed well academically, often better than their peers. This, they maintain, is no longer so. Rather, they suggest that if athletes are given too great an admissions advantage and if they perform much worse academically than their classmates, they can drag down the academic atmosphere of the whole institution. Moreover, they suggest that a "culture of athletics," a kind of "jock culture" exacerbates this problem and, apart from its consequences, may be inherently in conflict with academic values.

Although the highly selective schools in the book's database may not be typical of the majority of institutions of higher education, these schools have an importance larger than their numbers would indicate. Not only are they widely regarded as academic standard-bearers, but they also appear to have resisted the temptations inherent in major intercollegiate sports. Many observers will conclude that if intercollegiate sports are harmful even in such a context, nowhere in higher education can they be a positive educational and ethical influence.

Much of the argument of *The Game of Life* rests on statistical comparisons between the academic performance while in school or achievements after graduation of athletes versus nonathletes. Because the argument is based on an exhaustive analysis of a major database, it cannot fully be analyzed here; however, we can look at some of the questions about methodology that go well beyond one particular study.[23]

Although it may seem methodologically sound to compare the academic performance of athletes to those of nonathletes at colleges and universities, we need to be careful about what conclusions we draw from such a comparison. Suppose the athletes do worse than nonathletes. Does this mean the academic stature of the student body could be raised if we stopped giving preference in admissions to talented athletes who apply?

Not necessarily. Much depends, not only on how much preference is given, but on who would have been accepted if athletic talent was not taken into positive consideration in the admissions process. If schools are comparing academically less-qualified athletes not to potential academic superstars but to applicants who are academically weaker, then the applicants who would have replaced the athletes might not have done all that well either.[24] In other words, how strong academically were the candidates who would have been accepted had some degree of preference not been extended to athletes in the admissions process?

To assess the effect of athletics on the academic stature of the student body, we would also need to consider another issue (one not given significant attention in *The Game of Life*), namely, the extent to which a competitive athletic program might attract athletes who are outstanding students and who want to participate in intercollegiate athletics at a respectable level of competition. This was brought home to me in the spring of 2001 when an excellent student in my seminar, who was also a top player on our women's basketball team, remarked after I had summarized *The Game of Life* for the class that "I would never have come here if I hadn't been a recruited athlete." Thus, in evaluating the effect of athletics on academics, one must consider not only weaker students who would not have been admitted if they had not been athletes but also top students who would have attended another institution if they had not been attracted by the opportunities for athletics, either as a participant or spectator, at the school where they matriculated.

Finally, it is important to remember that the academic performance of many, perhaps most, athletes does not differ significantly from the performance of other students, as suggested by data in *The Game of Life* itself. In fact, data from the book suggest that female athletes do as well academically as other students and that the academic performance of male athletes in sports other than men's football and basketball does not differ much from that of other students. The widest divergence from the performance of the overall student body probably is in male high-profile sports, where the population of student athletes is also more socioeconomically diverse than the student body as a whole.

This raises the issue of whether the recruitment of athletes might contribute to the diversity of an institution's student body. We have already seen, for example, that African Americans are disproportionately represented on the major sports teams of athletically elite Division I schools. In their analysis in *The Game of Life,* Bowen and Shulman find a much more modest contribution at the schools in their sample, presumably because less weight is given to athletics in recruiting at those schools than in big-time college athletics and because the majority of student athletes at such schools play lower-profile sports, such as golf, lacrosse, tennis, and crew, that historically have not always attracted or been open to minority participation.

However, by considering diversity among all athletes, the study may have underemphasized how high-profile men's sports can contribute to diversity. In particular, male athletes in high-profile sports such as football do disproportionately tend to come from different socioeconomic backgrounds than other students.[25] As we have seen, the high-profile men's sports are the very ones where the academic performance of the student athletes is least satisfactory. If athletes in high-profile sports do tend to do less well than others academically, this may be due to a complex combination of factors, including their somewhat different educational backgrounds combined with the amount of time required by serious commitment to intercollegiate athletics.

Our discussion suggests that measuring the effect of athletic recruitment at academically selective schools is complex. Because some of these complexities may not have been given adequate attention by the authors, the quantitative analysis underlying *The Game of Life,* while raising issues of concern, arguably is less than compelling. But rather than focus simply on quantitative analysis, important as it is, let us turn to more philosophical criticisms of the claim that athletics and academics can be mutually reinforcing.

The "Culture of Athletics" and Academics

At a large state university, athletes may constitute a small percentage of students simply because the institution is so large. As we have seen, that may not be true at smaller Division III schools, such as liberal arts colleges, or even at Ivy League undergraduate colleges. If athletes have different values and attitudes than other students, and these are inimical to the educational mission of the institution, a critical mass of athletes can negatively affect the educational atmosphere of an institution apart from their academic performance as individuals. In other words, "jock culture" and academics may be in conflict.

Thus, Bowen and Shulman identify a cluster of traits they identify with a culture of athletics. Although this culture is not precisely defined, it shows a tendency for athletes to socialize mainly with other athletes, to pursue majors in proportions different from the rest of the student population, and, male athletes especially, to focus more on financial success after college than other students. This culture of athletics has been fostered by youngsters' early specialization into particular sports, recruiting policies by admissions officers that reward such specialization (the search for a well-rounded class rather than well-rounded individuals), and the consequent estrangement of athletes from the academic mission of their institutions.

Although the idea that a culture of athletics adversely affects athletes' academic performance may be plausible as a partial explanation, it is doubtful whether it is the whole story, or even the most significant part. This kind of explanation suggests that athletes even at highly selective and academically demanding institutions lack a true commitment to academic success. But surely the picture may be more complex.

Institutional factors built into selective colleges and universities may also play a significant role, as might cultural factors having little to do with athletics. For example, athletes whose parents did not go to college or who attended different sorts of institutions may be unaccustomed to interaction with faculty, particularly during their freshman year. These are the very students who might be most in need of academic support from professors but may not know how to go about getting it.[26] Even worse, if too many faculty exhibit outright disdain for intercollegiate athletics or, more likely, are indifferent to athletes, players may sense this and be more reluctant than other students to seek help from those faculty. Again, because review sessions or outside lectures may be scheduled during practice or game times, athletes may be more likely than others to miss them. Moreover, the amount of time and energy that goes into athletic training may be more demanding than many other kinds of extracurricular commitments. It is unclear, then, just how much "jock culture," assuming it exists, affects academic performance and whether it has a greater or lesser effect than other explanatory factors.

Should the culture of athletics be viewed primarily negatively, as in *The Game of Life,* or is a more positive assessment plausible? Is there an ideal distribution of students across concentrations, let alone of values or career goals, that institutions should seek to foster? If not, why should we regard the culture of athletics as negatively as the critics suggest?

The Game of Life suggests that athletes, both male and female, increasingly tend to have more conservative values than their peers; surely the different values attributed to some athletes can be a contribution to diversity on campus, at least if "diversity" is not understood in a narrow and partisan way. If so, athletic recruiting can contribute not only a degree of socioeconomic diversity, as suggested above, but also contribute to a potentially intellectually fruitful mix of values within the academic community as well.

Athletics and Educational Values

Let us return more directly to what might be called the academic defense against the Incompatibility Thesis. According to this defense, athletics, properly structured, is not only compatible with academic values but may enhance and reinforce them. This point was defended earlier when it was argued that an athletic contest, conceived of as a mutual quest for excellence through challenge, is educational or has educational components closely related to academic virtues. Let us return to this point from another direction.

Surely, a major part of intellectual inquiry is a willingness to question what often is taken for granted, including one's own cherished beliefs. I find that my own students, at least when they are new to philosophy, are quite good at articulating their own views but less than satisfactory at anticipating serious objections to their own positions and meeting the challenges that would be presented by a thoughtful critic. Similar behavior on the athletic field can lead to the serious underestimation of an opponent or overestimation of one's own ability, misjudgments that are often made all too visible to participants and spectators alike through exposure in competitive contests.

That is, the kind of intellectual honesty and respect for truths so crucial for intellectual inquiry are closely related to similar virtues necessary for athletic success and personal improvement in sport. Participation in competitive athletics can require intellectual honesty and a concern for truth, including accuracy about one's own values and talents, in ways parallel to academic inquiry.

Thus, participation in competitive athletics conducted within a defensible educational and ethical set of requirements can be educational in its own right. And although there need not always be a causal relationship between the development of these virtues in one context (say in athletics) and in the other (say academics), there also is no reason why these qualities should not be mutually reinforcing, given the proper emphasis by coaches and professors. More generally, by emphasizing how the pursuit of excellence in athletics requires the development of virtues that also apply in academic pursuits, and by involving coaches more directly in motivating student-athletes educationally, athletics and academics might be seen more as mutually reinforcing than in total conflict. Perhaps if coaches made a more direct attempt to indicate how qualities that promote success on the athletic field also do the same in the classroom and professors encouraged student-athletes, particularly in the high-visibility men's sports, to apply the personal qualities that lead to athletic success to academics, athletics and academics might come to be seen as mutually re- . inforcing rather than antithetical to each other.

Our discussion so far may have assumed that we are all in agreement about just what the academic mission of undergraduate education in the liberal arts and sciences, which are central to the ideal of critical inquiry, should be. Our discussion has associated that mission with the promotion of critical inquiry, which involves understanding major achievements in different fields, mastery of critical tools needed to assess them, and the ability to apply those tools in evaluating and assessing major positions in a variety of fields and disciplines.

This does not mean, however, that colleges and universities should have as their primary role the replication of more and more professors. It is important and even essential that students develop enthusiasm for some intellectual pursuit or activity, but it does not follow that the goal of undergraduate education is simply to produce scholars.

Surely one additional major function is to train people to function as intelligent citizens in a democracy. If so, many of the skills learned in sport and developed through competition (and expressed to spectators through scheduled contests) can contribute to such a goal. These would include appreciation of teamwork, including cooperation with those very different from oneself in pursuit of a common enterprise, and learning to appreciate achievement (including that of opponents) as well as learning to view opponents as persons who contribute to one's own development.

Our democracy might be much healthier if many of the attitudes the ethical athlete would have towards a worthy opponent, as outlined in Chapters 2 and 3, were also applied toward those who engage in reasonable debate within the democratic process.

Finally, let me suggest, however tentatively, a contribution competitive athletics make to liberal arts colleges that in my view is too often ignored. The contribution I have in mind is *ethical*. Competitive sport is by its very nature a value-laden activity. If carried out properly, such sports involve fair play, respect for opponents, and understanding and appreciation of (even reverence for) the traditions, practices, and values central to one's sport. Sport at its best is an unalienated activity participants engage in for its own sake, as well as for whatever external rewards participation may promote. As many scholars of sport have argued, concern for external rewards crowd out the love of the game and its internal values often corrupt sport and lead to many of the excesses of commercialized big-time sport in the United States.

However, the kinds of institutions that are best equipped to promote harmony between athletics and academics, such as many of the institutions studied in *The Game of Life,* are just the ones where the participants play primarily for love of the game and where commercialization is minimal. Although it remains controversial whether participation in athletics at these institutions actually makes the participants more ethical than otherwise (whether in sport or in unrelated activities), competitive sport arguably can express or illustrate these values to a wider community. Thus, competitive sport at such institutions exemplifies the pursuit of an activity for its own sake and illustrates the attempt to meet challenges simply for the sake of testing oneself and learning from the test. As such, it stands in contrast to a crude sort of utilitarianism approach that asks what everything is good for in terms of immediate payoffs, or to a view that rejects achievement and standards of excellence as arbitrary or mere matters of opinion. Of course, other activities, especially in the arts, also do the same. The suggestion here is not that athletics is unique in the way suggested but only that its role in illustrating, expressing, and possibly reinforcing important values is significant and should not be ignored. The French philosopher Albert Camus was making an important point of general educational importance when he remarked that the only context in which he really learned ethics was sport.[27]

Concluding Comment

In this chapter, we have argued that although academic values and intercollegiate athletics may often be in conflict, especially at the athletically elite colleges and universities that pursue national recognition at the top of Division I, this conflict is far from inevitable. Athletics can too often be the tail that wags the academic dog, as was indicated by one university president who, when seeking funds before a state legislature, was said to have stated, "We need to build a university our football team can be proud of." But athletics, properly integrated into the academic community, can also fill important and valuable functions. In the proper context, intercollegiate athletics can even enhance and reinforce the academic mission of the institution.

This academic defense is probably best realized within the framework of institutions that do not offer athletic scholarships and that tend to integrate athletics into the overall academic community, perhaps by evaluating coaches primarily as teachers and insuring that students who are athletes take rigorous academic programs similar to those of nonathletes.

This does not mean that the athletic programs, even at colleges and universities that best exemplify the model, are fine just as they are. Perhaps too much weight is given to athletics in admissions even there, or seasons are too long, or preseason training has become too demanding. However, our discussion has also suggested that broad criticism of athletics at such institutions, such as found in *The Game of Life,* may draw a bleaker picture than is warranted of the academic consequences of intercollegiate athletics in the academy. The role of athletics in academia can and should continue to be examined, but criticism of athletics, although sometimes well taken, should not obscure the contribution a properly structured athletic program can make to the college and university community.

7

The Commercialization
of Sport

At its very best, competitive sport can express a quest for human excellence, exhibit beauty, and create excitement and drama that fascinate millions of people throughout the world. But is its popularity its Achilles heel? High-profile sporting events, top athletes, dramatic athletic contests, at least in popular sports, are in demand. People want to see such events, sometimes identify with sports stars, and show tremendous loyalty to the teams or individuals with whom they identify. But because elite sports are in demand, they becomes something people will pay to see. In other words, sports have become more than a mutual quest for excellence: Market forces have transformed them into a commodity.

Top professional athletes and coaches in popular sports often make many millions of dollars in a season, often many, many times more than teachers, college presidents, oncologists, to say nothing of the president of the United States. Professional sports franchises can be worth hundreds of millions of dollars. Even at the level of college sports in the United States, high-profile Division I football and basketball are referred to, if sometimes inaccurately, as "revenue producing" sports. High-profile athletes provide entertainment, and, like other entertainers, can have a huge impact on younger fans. Sports dominate the mass media, and television rights to major events, such as the NCAA Men's Basketball Championships, sell for billions. Sport, then, is not only engaged in by athletes at various levels of play; elite sports, including major professional sports, also have become commercial institutions with governing bodies and business other than sporting interests.

Has this commercialization of sport been for good or ill? What sort of ethical problems does it raise? Has sport, as many critics have charged, been corrupted by its role in the world of commerce and markets? Has it become just another commodity, something to be bought and sold, and has this commercialization not only robbed it not only of its purity but has it damaged the values central to what makes sport a significant area of achievement and endeavor?

In this chapter, we will examine selected issues arising from the commercialization of sport. In particular, we will explore claims that the commercialization of sport has led to its corruption, and then look at specific issues raised by attempts to "market" sports to a mass audience.

The Corruption of Sport By Commerce

A persistent theme in the writings of many critics of modern sport is that sport today has been corrupted by the marketplace.[1] What does this claim mean? The term "corruption" refers to decay, a falling off from an original and perhaps noble purpose. We can understand corruption to mean that the values central to sport, such as those of fair competition, sportsmanship, and perhaps the mutual quest for excellence, are being or already have been undermined by the growing commercialization of sport.

One area of concern, although it is perhaps connected as much to the emphasis on elite sport as much as commercialization (at least as far as their effects can be separated), is the relationships between the mass marketing of sport and participation by masses of people. Critics have argued that the emphasis on elite athletes and the marketing of elite sports contests, along with coverage by mass media, have had a harmful effect on participation in sport by the ordinary person. For example, in his provocative and readable book, *Sports in America,* James Michener warned that "we place an undue emphasis on the gifted athletes fifteen to twenty-two, a preposterous emphasis on a few professionals aged twenty-three to thirty-five, and never enough on the mass of our population aged twenty-three to seventy -five"[2] Since Michener's book was published in 1976, we have seen a drastic reduction in the physical education classes given in public schools in the United States and an epidemic of obesity among American youth that exposes millions of children to premature hypertension and Type II diabetes, diseases previously thought to afflict only the middle-aged and elderly.

Perhaps the greatest concern is that the commercialization of sport actually corrupts the sport itself. For example, rule changes can be introduced that make the game more entertaining for the mass of fans who do not understand the nuances of the game. These changes can make the game more marketable but also can take away from the subtlety of the game or the skill needed to play it. For example, the introduction of the designated hitter into Major League Baseball (in the American League) may have made the game more exciting to fans who wanted more action and more frequent home runs; but, arguably, it minimized subtle strategic decisions such as whether to pinch hit for a pitcher or whether to have the pitcher sacrifice through a bunt, and it may also have contributed to the cheapening of the home run. Perhaps an even better example is the kind of loose officiating that observers claim has become commonplace in the National Basketball Association. Critics charge that NBA officiating allows stars to score more points but also allows them to get away with what ordinarily would be rule violations—such as traveling with the ball—thus minimizing skills but maximizing sales.

Commercialization can affect sporting contests in other ways. For example, "TV time outs," designed to stop play to allow the showing of commercials on televised broadcasts, disrupt the flow of many games, particularly in professional and college basketball, and can even affect outcomes by allowing less well-conditioned teams to recover during the many additional breaks in the action.

But the role of money in sport can cut even deeper, especially in professional sports, because the wealthiest teams often find it easier to win. As some critics of sport have concluded, "Commodification is pathological when it leads to the violation of the . . . meanings of the central culture of the game."[3] Isn't the entire ethic of competition undermined when the richest teams can buy the best players and in effect field a vastly superior team before the game has even begun? Although the success of the New York Yankees over decades has led to the phenomenon of Yankee hating, especially virulent in Boston and dramatized in the well-known musical, *Damn Yankees,* it seems more understandable in recent years when the Yankees, as one of the wealthiest franchises in Major League Baseball, can simply outbid other teams for the best players.

Similarly, the desire for profits can lead to longer and longer seasons; this in turn can create incentives for athletes not to play every game to the limit and thus save their bodies for the long haul and season-ending playoffs when championships are decided. Thus, the value of a regular season game is cheapened as athletes "pace themselves" (that is, not play their hardest for the whole game), and the regular season is seen simply as a preliminary for postseason play. At the same time, fans are often asked to pay more and more to attend the devalued regular season games, and many are priced out of the market altogether.

The influence of money can also change the relationship between fans and players. As professional sports become more and more commercially oriented, players can be viewed as commodities who are bought, sold, and traded from team to team. As a result, they may be seen less as persons and more as products who are viewed as defective if they do not produce high performance on the field. As the income available to sports stars surpasses that of the average fans many times over, fans may become alienated from players, who may be viewed (sometimes, but far from always, with justification) as spoiled, inaccessible, and remote. Since professional teams aim at making a profit, tickets may be priced beyond the means of traditional fan bases, thereby creating even more alienation.

As sports become more entertaining but perhaps less nuanced, they draw new fans to the game who lack knowledge and respect for its traditions and ethos.[4] These less-educated fans may contribute to a steamroller effect in which their sport is changed more and more frequently to become ever more entertaining, but at the price of important principles that make the game challenging and important traditions that have been part of its history. Thus, it has been charged that baseball authorities may be reluctant to enact strict rules for testing players for performance-enhancing drugs because such drug use may lead to stronger players and more home runs.[5] Home runs are exciting, and so more home runs may be thought to lead to greater attraction for fans; but, in the long run, drug use may cheapen the value of the home run, lessen the challenge of the game, and make comparison to the performances of stars of the past impossible.

These remarks suggest what might be called the "corruption thesis." This thesis states that the commercialization of sport, the transformation of elite sport into a product that can be bought and sold, corrupts sport. This is because the kinds of values that broad internalists (see Chapter 3) would regard as central to sport can conflict with the market value of sport. As William J. Morgan has argued, commercialization installs market values, such as the pursuit of money and fame, "as the proper ends of sporting practices thereby depriving their practitioners of any reason, let alone a compelling one, to value or engage the particular competitive challenges they present, the select athletic skills they call upon, and the human qualities and virtues they excite."[6] Athletic excellence, according to Morgan and other proponents of the corruption thesis, becomes only an instrument to achieving external goods of sport such as fame, power, and wealth. The importance of internal goods, those skills and excellences created by the practice that are intelligible only by references to its rules and the challenges they present, is diminished or regarded as only instrumental to more important extrinsic rewards. What is entertaining is what sells, but it might not necessarily be good sport.

Is the corruption thesis defensible? Has commercialization spoiled sport, as the remarks above suggest, or has it broadened its appeal and made elite sport accessible to millions of spectators through greater coverage in the media? Let us consider the commercialization-of-sport critique in more detail.

Examining the Corruption Thesis
Participation and Elite Sport

Let us begin with the line of criticism suggested by Michener that we are a nation of spectators rather than participants. Critics of American sports point out that millions of us spend our weekends glued to the television screen, watching football, baseball, and golf rather than playing a sport ourselves. Moreover, most of us watch sports in relative isolation, as networks such as ESPN bring more and more major games into our homes, rather than in the communal setting of a local high school game. The time devoted to observing sports rather than participating in them is seen by critics as unfortunate, not only because of ill effects on the health of those who only sit and watch, but also because spectators miss out on the other basic benefits of participation. According to this view, the true result of the "star" system is to drive people from participation on the playing field to the grandstand, or more often the living room couch, instead.

Is this aspect of the critique of American sports justified? Note that it rests on at least two hidden assumptions, neither of which is clearly correct. First, it is assumed that watching sports tends to preclude participation: Spectators tend not to play precisely because they are spectators. But this assumption is hardly obvious.

It is far from clear that being a fan has a negative effect on participation. On the contrary, many fans, particularly youngsters, may be motivated to try to emulate the moves of the successful athletes they see on television. What schoolyard basketball player has not tried to copy the moves of Michael Jordan? Spectators may promote participation rather than lower it because they often observe the techniques of top players and apply them to their own games. As commentator Christopher Lasch has noted, "It is by watching those who have mastered a sport . . . that we derive standards against which to measure ourselves."[7]

What about the fan who is a spectator only? Here we must be careful not to jump to the conclusion that such individuals are not participants simply because they are fans. Perhaps they wouldn't be participants even if they weren't fans. Maybe they enjoy watching skilled performers but would not be motivated to play themselves even if there were no top athletes to watch. Or perhaps there are inadequate facilities for participation in their area, as is true for many golfers in metropolitan areas. Accordingly, the simple assumption that emphasis on big-time sports and on the skills of an athletic elite reduces mass participation is open to serious question. Thus, the growth in women's participation in athletics since the passage of Title IX indicates that increasing presentation of elite events in the mass media do not necessarily reduce participation. Similarly, increasing participation in outdoor recreational activities supports the same conclusion. For example, one major survey indicates that the number of people participating in walking as a form of recreation grew from about 93 million in 1982 to over 133 million in 1994–1995. Similarly, there was a 14 percent increase in those running or jogging and a 16 percent increase in those swimming during the same period. Although the population also grew during this period, and perhaps even more people would have participated if they had not been glued to the couch watching games on television, data suggest that the effect of elite sport on participation may be much more complex than critics have postulated.[8]

A second assumption about the relationship between participation in sports and watching them is open to even more serious question. According to a moderate version of this second assumption, being a participant in sports is of greater value than being a spectator. Playing is better than watching. In its most extreme form, this assumption characterizes watching sporting events as a passive, almost slothful activity that requires minimal intellectual and emotional capacities. The stereotype of the beer-drinking, overweight football fan who spends the whole weekend in front of the television set watching games expresses the disdain in which mere fans are sometimes held.

In rebuttal, none of us can participate in everything. Most of us are spectators of some practice or other; theater, music, and dance come immediately to mind. After all, we don't sneer at spectators, commonly known as audiences, at the ballet or a play, even though few members of the audience are also dancers, actors, or musicians.

Moreover, spectators of sports, like audiences in other areas, are often called upon to exercise critical judgment and apply standards of excellence. As Lasch has pointed out, "Far from destroying the value of sports, the attendance of spectators makes them complete. Indeed, one of the virtues of contemporary sports lies in their resistance to the erosion of standards and their capacity to appeal to a knowledgeable audience."[9] Consider, for example, a fine double play executed at a crucial point in a pressure-packed baseball game. An observer unacquainted with baseball might appreciate the grace and fluidity of the players' movements; however, such a spectator could not see the movements as examples of excellence at baseball. To such an uninformed spectator, a botched double play would be indistinguishable from a well-executed one, since the failure of the fielder to, say, pivot properly while throwing from second base to first base would be unappreciated.

Thus, it is unclear that watching games is of less value than playing in them, just as it is unclear that appreciating a ballet is less valuable than dancing in it. Indeed, audiences and performers often feed off each other, and superb performers in the arts as well as sports find their performances enhanced by the reactions of spectators.[10]

Even if there is less value in watching than participating, it is far from clear that the intelligent observation of sports, or other human activities in which excellence is demonstrated, is without value at all. Spectators at sporting events can be rude, ignorant, or passive, but so can audiences of other kinds. On the other hand, appreciating a competitive athletic contest requires intelligence, observation, and the critical application of standards of excellence.

A critic might respond that although such points have force, they are an intellectualized account of what it is to be a sports fan. Spectators don't just appreciate good performances; they also root for their teams to win. Indeed, the atmosphere at an important college basketball game often far more resembles the atmosphere at a revival meeting than that of a seminar on excellence in sports. As the critics of commercialization have argued, mass audiences have become less appreciative of excellence and more interested in partying and being entertained. More and more fans see themselves as consumers out to get their money's worth and have fun, which perhaps explains the increase in their boorish behavior.

Loyalty to our favorite team and players, and expressing emotion in support of them, surely do and should play a major role in sports. As in other areas of life, we develop special relationships with those we care about. Nevertheless, loyalty and emotion should not get out of hand. The behavior of fans who go on rampages, destroying property and threatening life, should not be tolerated. Even where overt violence is absent, the partisan, hostile character of crowds at many sporting events threatens to intimidate visiting players and referees alike. Thus, it is true that commercialization, along with excessive partisanship, may often attract mass audiences unfamiliar with the nuances of the game and just out for a good time. When combined with the easy availability of alcohol at many contests, the combination may just be a recipe for trouble.

Although the critical perspective towards sports, which was attributed to fans, is only part of the story, and undoubtedly idealized at that, it serves as a moral and intellectual constraint on the emotionalism generated by excessively provincial fan loyalty, ignorance of the traditions and nuances of the sport, or just plain bad behavior. A moral requirement of good sportsmanship for fans is that they retain their critical perspective. Even though we need not be ashamed of caring about our team's fate and wanting them to win, when we care so much that we become unable to appreciate good play by the opposition, not only are the opposing players shown disrespect as persons but the justification of athletic competition is undermined. If competition in sports should be conceived of as a mutual quest for excellence, spectators should retain enough detachment to appreciate who best meets the challenge. Otherwise, sports are reduced to a mere means for satisfying our own egos rather than constituting an area where spectators and athletes alike can learn and grow by understanding and meeting ever increasing challenges to their athletic and critical skills.

We must not forget the positive side to commercialization. Commercialization and the mass media have made athletic contests available to large audiences all over the world and arguably have made sport more open by making it more accessible to all. The trick is to enjoy this benefit while minimizing the deleterious effects of mass consumption. More will be said about how this might be accomplished later in the chapter.

Our discussion does suggest that, first, it is unclear whether emphasis on elite sport in the mass media lowers participation. Second, watching athletic contests may have value of its own. Sporting audiences, no less than other audiences, are called upon to appreciate excellence and to apply critical standards of judgment. Emotional bonds to favorite teams and players, when constrained by the norms of respect for persons and appreciation of excellence, can enrich our existence and motivate us to do our best.

The Internal Goods of Sports

We have considered the claim that too much emphasis has been placed on the star athlete and too little on participation by the many. It may remain controversial just how much emphasis is too much, but some important distinctions have emerged from our discussion among the kinds of goods that sport can promote.

Michener and others who worry about lack of participation in sport seem focused on what might be regarded as the *basic benefits* of involvement with sport.[11] These benefits involve better health through exercise, the fun of recreation, and the joy of competition. Presumably, they are available to all participants, not just elite players. The basic benefits are to be contrasted with what have been called the "scarce benefits," or goods of sport; namely, fame and wealth. By their very nature, these are available only to elite stars at the highest levels of athletic competition.

Those who worry that we have overemphasized the performance of elite athletes fear that the majority of people will lose out on the basic benefits by becoming passive observers of the pursuit of fame and fortune by the elite. Those worried about commercialization fear that emphasis on the scarce benefits will corrupt sport.

Our discussion suggests that emphasis on the basic and the scarce benefits of sport alone sets up far too narrow a framework for discussion. Discussing the distribution of the scarce and basic benefits only immediately suggests tension between the athletic elite and the greater bulk of the population, who often lack adequate opportunity to pursue the basic benefits. But emphasis on opposition between an elite and the rest of us may be misleading. In philosophy, the questions we ask may determine the answers we consider. In restricting ourselves only to questions about scarce and basic benefits, we may have cut ourselves off from considering the relationships that exist between outstanding performances by the few, and the enjoyment and appreciation of the many.

In particular, scarce and basic benefits are external to sports; that is, each logically can be conceived and obtained apart from sports themselves. They are what we call "external goods." Goods, such as health, fun, fame, and wealth, can be understood and obtained by those who have no understanding of or relationship to sports.

In addition to such external goods, there are also goods that are *internal* to sports. Goods are internal to a practice or activity when they logically cannot be understood or enjoyed independently of that practice or activity. For example, the concept of a "home run" is unintelligible apart from the practice and rules of baseball; the elegance of a winning combination in chess cannot be understood or enjoyed without an understanding of the rules and strategy that characterize the game of chess.

The distinction between internal and external goods of sports is central to our concerns in this chapter because the conformity to standards of excellence implicit in various sports creates shared internal goods available to the whole community. Spectators appreciate and share in the enjoyment of the internal goods created by top performers at all levels of athletic competition. Thus, often ignored by those who fear overemphasis on an athletic elite is that skilled participants in sports are as capable of creating internal goods, shared by large numbers of people, as are skilled participants in, say, dance or theater. As argued in the previous section, audiences who can appreciate these goods are no more passive than those who appreciate the arts and humanities.

Thus, when it comes to an evaluation of the corruption thesis and the degree to which sport has become commercialized, we need to look at positive as well as negative aspects of commercialization. Perhaps, as argued above, the alleged conflict between benefits for an elite and benefits for large numbers of others has been overstated and the role of top athletes in creating internal goods that can be appreciated and enjoyed by unprecedented numbers of observers has not been given the attention it deserves by critics of the current sporting scene.

Does Commercialization Undermine Internal Values?

One of the principal arguments in favor of the corruption thesis is that the transformation of elite sport into a commodity is in conflict with the very internal goods that make sport so valuable. This is largely because sport needs to be entertaining if it is to sell. But for it to be entertaining to mass audiences, it needs to enjoy mass appeal. Therefore, sport becomes cruder, perhaps more violent, and certainly less nuanced. Players come to value external goals over internal ones, thus sport is further corrupted. For example, since salaries are based more on scoring averages than fitting into a team, the offense on a basketball team must insure that a star player gets his quota of shots. More generally, professional players come to see their sport as a business and personal profit becomes more important than the good of the game. Many young stars are too immature to handle their wealth and celebrity status and stories of self-destructive and criminal behavior by star athletes have become far too common.

Although even the casual observer of contemporary sport will acknowledge that this critique has much force, it is not the whole story. For one thing, as just noted above, the presentation of major sporting events by the mass media have allowed millions of spectators to observe top athletes at the highest levels of competition, something that might well have never been possible without commercialization. Of equal importance, not all changes in the rules of sport have been for the worse, even when one of the reasons for the change was to make the sport more entertaining. For example, the introduction of the shot clock and the three-point field goal in basketball did make the game more entertaining, but also arguably made it better and more challenging. The three-point shot helped open the court for fast, fluid play, gave teams more options on both defense and offense, thereby making the game more nuanced, and produced more chances for comebacks and exciting finishes. Similarly, the shot clock did make the game more entertaining by limiting the extent to which teams with a lead could stall rather than attempt shots, but it also made it faster by bringing out the tremendous athleticism of top players.

Critics of commercialization also argue plausibly that the big money available to top athletes has had a corrupting effect on many young players (although it has also lifted many athletes out of poverty). It also is true that many players have become transients, going from team to team as market forces dictate, through trades and free agency agreements. This may well have had a deleterious effect on fan-player relationships as professional players are far less likely to be viewed as members of a common community. Rather, they are too often seen as mere products or resources whose function is to provide wins; they quickly lose the support of fans and may even open themselves to abuse when they fail.

An example of this change involves a comparison of fan reaction to Gil Hodges's failure in the 1952 World Series and Bill Buckner's famous error in the 1986 Series. Hodges, later to become a World Series winner as manager of the New York Mets was, in 1952, a star slugger and top fielding first baseman for the National League champions, the Brooklyn Dodgers. The Dodgers had led the way in breaking the color line on Major League Baseball in the late 1940s, and Jackie Robinson, the first African American to play Major League Baseball, was a star of the 1952 team, along with Roy Campanella, Pee Wee Reese, and Duke Snider. The team was beloved in Brooklyn and indeed gave Brooklyn much of its identity. The series was against the arch enemy, the crosstown New York Yankees, a team with its own stars, including Mickey Mantle, Yogi Berra, and Phil Rizzuto. Feelings ran high in Brooklyn, which had never won a World Series, and which loved its team. (I even remember my parents letting me stay home from school for several days to watch the games on television!)

The Dodgers lost in a thrilling series that ran seven games. Throughout the series, Hodges time after time failed to get a hit. However, as his hitless streak continued, fan support for him became more and more vocal. The fans suffered with him rather than regarding him as a failed product to be treated with derision and disgust. The Dodgers might well have won if Hodges had gotten just a few key hits, but he went hitless throughout the series. Nevertheless, fan support for Hodges by the Dodger faithful throughout the off season was overwhelming. Hodges responded by having an outstanding season for Brooklyn in 1953 and the Dodgers ran away from the rest of the league to win the pennant once again.

Contrast this with the treatment given to Red Sox player Bill Buckner after his crucial error in game six of the 1986 World Series contributed to Boston's loss of the series to the New York Mets. The Red Sox led in the ninth inning of the sixth game. One more out would give them a victory in the World Series. A ground ball was hit toward first base that would have ended the game if fielded cleanly. Although the grounder was not routine, it should not have presented extraordinary difficulty to a major leaguer; however, Buckner, the Red Sox first baseman, failed to field the ball, the Met batter was safe on first base, and the Mets went on to win the game, and, the next day, the series.

Although Buckner lived in Boston, he was reviled by fans during the off season. The harassment became so great that Buckner felt he had to move from the area and leave the Boston team. In effect, Buckner was driven out of Boston by reaction of the fans to his error. In contrast, Hodges was supported by his fans, in spite of his failure in the 1952 World Series, and remained a star for many years. What accounts for the difference in treatment?

Although an explanation for the difference in treatment would be complex, some critics of contemporary sport might argue that the growing commercialization of the game since Hodges's time as a player was a contributing factor. True, Red Sox fans were frustrated by a long series of perceived failures by their team, but the Dodgers had never won a World Series before 1952. Dodger fans were also frustrated, but they still treated Hodges with compassion.

It is plausible to think that because fans in 1986 were not as close to players as those of the 1952 Dodgers, they tended to regard them more and more as high-priced products who were expected to produce, and less and less as fellow members of a sports community. Surely, the critics would argue, the Buckner example is just one instance of a disturbing trend towards more and more abusive behavior by fans, which in turn is at least partially the result of the increasing commercialization of sport and the consequent split alienating fans not only from players but from the traditions and principles of the game.

Although the force of any explanatory hypothesis is empirical rather than purely philosophical, the claim that commercialization of sport and its marketing as a product has frequently been harmful has the ring of plausibility; but it, too, can be overstated. Commercialization may have had a corrupting effect on many athletes, but it does not seem to have affected others' love of the game. Many great professional and top amateur athletes retain a tremendous work ethic, and are exemplars of respect for their games. Michael Jordan, Tiger Woods, Sue Bird, Lance Armstrong, Annika Sorenstam, and Grant Hill are among the many who come immediately to mind. And although the behavior of spectators and players alike has deteriorated in many respects in recent years, it is doubtful whether all the blame can be placed on the commercialization of sport. What of the general decline in ethical standards throughout society? These, in turn, may be due to strains on the family, inadequacies in the educational system, declining economic insecurity, alcohol and drug abuse, and a variety of complex factors that go well outside the world of sport. Indeed, it is not in the interest of professional teams, sports organizations, or top athletes to encourage abusive behavior among fans or in society at large.

How, then, are we to assess the corruption thesis? First, is it simply a matter of adding up the benefits and harms caused by commercialization in a kind of utilitarian cost-benefit analysis? Do the benefits produced outweigh the bad effects or does the bad outweigh the good? Or does commercialization violate some fundamental moral principle so that it is wrong, at least if carried too far, regardless of the results of the utilitarian calculus?

Our own discussion suggests that the transformation of elite sport into a commodity does present real dangers to an ethic of sport. We also have argued that there are compensating benefits and the criticism of commercialization may sometimes be exaggerated. Rather than engage in a purely consequential analysis of the effects of commercialization, it may be more profitable to ask what moral principles should apply to professional and elite sports in our society. In any event, commercialization is so entrenched that it has probably become a permanent feature of the sporting scene, one with positive as well as negative aspects. Let us consider, then, whether there is an ethical framework that would regulate the effects of economic markets in sport so that the benefits of commercialization could be enjoyed while also maintaining respect for the internal values of sport. Perhaps we can arrive at such a framework by considering ethical issues that arise in the business of sport.

The Ethical Responsibilities of Sports Management
Business and Social Responsibility

What ethical principles should constrain the commercialization of sport? On whom do the responsibilities for applying these principles fall?

The second question is crucial. Part of the process of commercialization has been the transformation of many professional sports franchises into corporations, some with international connections in the recruiting of players and marketing of their products. Equipment companies, such as Nike, are transnational corporations as well and exert enormous influence on the world of sport. We also need to consider the role of sports regulatory organizations, such as the National Football League, the Professional Golfers Association, and Major League Baseball, which, through officials such as the Commissioner of Baseball, are supposed to serve as a check on corporate interests that might be harmful to the game.

Some might think the answer is relatively easy, at least as far as corporations are concerned. Professional sports franchises on this view are no different than other business organizations. Their role is to make a profit; to expect them to do otherwise is to ask them to disregard their obligations to stockholders or to in effect requisition the money of private owners for public purposes without their consent. As Milton Friedman, winner of the Nobel Prize, economist, and defender of the free market, once put it, "There is one and only one social responsibility of business—to use its resources and engage in activities designed to increase its profits as long as it stays within the rules of the game, which is to say, engages in open and free competition, without deception and fraud."[12]

Friedman's view is open to criticism, however; in a way, it is in part similar to the claim that the only moral responsibility of the athlete is to try to win within the rules. As we have seen, athletes may well have other moral responsibilities, such as respecting the principles presupposed by their sport, showing appropriate respect for their sport, and carrying out both negative and positive obligations to bring about good competitive contests. Can similar points be brought against the thesis that the only social responsibility of business is to make profits?

To begin, consider what arguments might support Friedman's view. One may be utilitarian; the economy simply works best if business aims at profits, for this promotes the most efficient allocation of resources. Second, where corporations are concerned, it can be argued that the managers have a moral responsibility to use the stockholders' funds in the way intended by the investors themselves, which surely is to get the best financial return possible. Wouldn't the allocation of funds for other purposes, including the pursuit of moral goals, in effect be taking from the investors without their consent? Wouldn't this be stealing? Accordingly, don't professional sports teams, equipment companies, and other sports-related businesses have exactly the duty Friedman specifies—to make as much of a profit as the market allows?

The utilitarian argument, although important, is not decisive; even if a totally free market could be achieved and did promote economic efficiency, economic efficiency is not always the only value at stake in morally evaluating social policy. The most efficient system, for example, may not be the most just. Friedman's own analysis conceded this point by acknowledging that profits may be pursued subject to the constraint of other values; namely, nondeception and avoidance of fraud. But why should those be the only values corporations take into account? What about workers' safety, the safety of products, and concern for the environment?

What about the second defense of the view that the only moral obligation of corporations is to make a profit? This defense claims that for managers to appropriate investments to secure ethical goals is to divert money from the purpose stockholders intended when investing, which is to make a profit, and is in effect stealing from them?

This assumes the very point at issue; namely, whether it is correct to regard making a profit the only obligation of a business. If businesses have other obligations, such as promoting workers' safety and not committing injustices, and stockholders have good reason to be aware of those obligations, then the balancing of profits against appropriate ethical constraints is an obligation of business, not an improper distraction from its true goals.

Although the issue here is complex, several writers have suggested that the relationship between business, particularly corporations, and society is contractual, or at least based on a kind of reciprocity. The terms on which a corporation can exist, what legally counts as a corporation, and its various privileges and powers are defined by society through the legal system. In short, society grants business a certain sphere of legitimate activity but has a right to expect it to honor certain duties in return. The political scientist, Robert A. Dahl, expressed this sort of view:

> Today it is absurd to regard the corporation simply as an enterprise established for the sole purpose of allowing profit making. We the citizens give them special rights, powers, and privileges . . . and benefits on the understanding that their activities will fulfill purposes. . . . Every corporation should be thought of as a social enterprise whose existence and decisions can be justified only insofar as they serve public or social purposes.[13]

As Norman E. Bowie comments, "The corporation must not only benefit those who create it, it must benefit those who permit it (namely society as a whole)."[14]

The point here is that large corporations don't operate in a social vacuum. Rather, the legal and political order often lays downs the constraints under which corporations can operate. Even more, it provides benefits that enable them to prosper through tax codes and provision of other forms of public support. Thus, sports stadiums in which professional teams play may be funded in part by the public. Since corporations are not purely private entities and since they benefit from public support in a variety of ways, reciprocity requires that they also pay appropriate attention to broad values of central concern to the public in the democratic state. As one prominent approach to business ethics puts it, corporations have responsibilities to "stakeholders," those whom corporate actions might seriously harm as well as stockholders.[15]

But doesn't this view itself start from the questionable assumption that society has a right to dictate the terms on which those who have legitimately acquired wealth may invest it? After all, isn't it the stockholder's or owner's money? On what grounds can society regulate what they do with it?

These questions reflect a position in political philosophy often referred to as "libertarianism." Libertarians believe that the fundamental human right is the right not to be interfered with by others, particularly not to be used for the purposes of others. In their view, at least in an extreme form, the appropriation of property without consent is unjust interference with personal freedom. Thus, libertarians would regard any income tax used for redistributive purposes, such as provision of education, health care, or basic welfare benefits for the poor, as a gross violation of our most fundamental right.[16]

However, if it is conceded that society does have a right to regulate the economy to an appropriate extent, as happens in Western democracies, including the United States, the contractual analysis of business responsibilities seems defensible. Regulation can be seen as defensible to the extent that it enhances social welfare and recognizes nonlibertarian basic rights, such as the right to public education, compatible with a reasonable and significant degree of economic freedom.

Although a full exploration of libertarianism and its critics would take us too far afield, further reflection may well support the modern welfare state's rejection of libertarianism and its endorsement of a broader set of economic as well as liberty rights.[17] The same reasons that may lead us to defend the right to the kind of personal liberty libertarians rightly defend, and to embody versions of it in our basic constitution, may also support broader welfare rights to basic necessities. For example, libertarian rights to personal liberty seem important because we justifiably view persons as centers of autonomy entitled to make their own choices about how they should live. But welfare rights are also important to preserve autonomy and choice. How autonomous can one be without food, shelter, education, or health care? How much control over one's life would one have then? Libertarianism can be reasonably rejected, then, as arbitrarily regarding only liberty rights to freedom from interference as fundamental while rejecting all welfare rights, even though some form of welfare rights seem as necessary to securing our control over our destinies as liberty itself.

We can approach this point from the ideal social contract we considered when assessing the use of performance-enhancing drugs in Chapter 4. Reasonable and impartial people (following John Rawls's idea of choosing the principles of society as if in ignorance of one's position in it as well as of personal characteristics that might contribute to personal success or failure) arguably would reject a society organized entirely around the freedom of market transactions, since they would (being impartial) need to consider the disabled, the poor, the frail elderly, children in need of education and health care, and (especially relevant for our purposes) the commitments of many to social practices regarded as having value over and above their value as commodities, such as the practice of sport itself.[18]

Accordingly, although libertarians are right to emphasize liberty and the preservation of freedom that protects us from exploitation by society, it is reasonable to think that limitations on the economic market designed to preserve fundamental values and rights are also justifiable. This implies, to return to the social responsibilities of corporations, that business is not entitled to do anything it pleases to increase profits, but it can be constrained to operate according to reasonable principles designed to protect fundamental rights and values. Stockholders, therefore, have no right to expect that corporations in which they invest may do anything to increase profit, no matter how ethically repugnant. Rather, business, including corporate entities in businesses connected to sport, such as professional teams, can and should be expected to pursue profits within reasonable ethical constraints.

Moral Responsibilities of Business to Sport

But although we might agree that business has some ethical obligations, such as not deliberately marketing unsafe or defective products, what are the obligations of businesses closely connected with sport? In particular, what moral constraints, if any, apply to major league professional sports teams?

According to one view, sports teams may have the same obligations as other businesses with respect to safety and the environment but have no special obligation to preserve and protect important principles of sport. If making sport more entertaining sells, then, since they are in business, sports teams ought to do it. What sells is what pleases fans; making sport more entertaining and therefore more profitable increases overall utility by making fans happy and also by increasing financial returns for owners and players alike.

But should professional sport be regarded as only a form of entertainment? Focusing only on what sells, and never on the competitiveness or integrity of the game, may not even be in the best financial interests of owners and players. Suppose, for example, that newer football fans want to see more and more violence in the game. To sell more tickets, professional football eliminates rules that protect vulnerable players such as quarterbacks and punt returners, moving in toward and even beyond the so-called Extreme Football League experiment of the late 1990s. The result is likely to be a rash of injuries to star players, less exciting contests as a result, and probably fewer sales. Pro football might come to be regarded as more like professional wrestling, a form of unsophisticated entertainment than a thrilling sport, and fans might turn their attention from it to sports perceived to be truer to the idea of competitive challenge. (In fact, Extreme Football did not sell.) Similarly, if professional basketball players become more and more focused on great individual moves that look good on televised highlight films, and less and less on fundamentals and team play, fans may lose interest in the professional game and turn to college basketball instead.

Thus, it may be to the *mutual advantage* of sports teams in a common league or sport to agree to arrangements that limit their freedom to tamper too much with the integrity of the game. Leagues may create an official bureaucracy, such as the Office of the Commissioner of Baseball or the PGA Tour, that has the explicit function of protecting the good of the sport. Although it is important for such officials to be truly independent of owners and players, each of whom may become too focused on short-term financial gain, such independence may be difficult to achieve. However, the creation of official regulatory institutions, which have as at least part of their mission the preservation of the integrity and competitiveness of the game, is a structural mechanism for preserving some of the values of sport as a mutual quest for excellence even in the professional arena.

This sort of argument from mutual advantage suggests that it is in each team's overall interest to set limits on the pursuit of profits. If all teams engaged in the unlimited pursuit of profit, sport may be so diminished by commercialization that it attracts less and less interest, and so everyone loses.

Mutual advantage aside, would it be morally wrong on other grounds for the sports industry to turn a sport into a form of entertainment, even though that would severely diminish the key principles of skill and competition central to the game? In fact, it is doubtful whether the moral obligations of business can be reduced to considerations of mutual advantage alone. What if one team is so dominant that it is not to its advantage to cooperate in setting limits? Or what if one group—say traditional sports fans interested in preserving the integrity of the game—are so weak that it is not in the interest of more powerful business interests to negotiate with them? Considerations of mutual advantage, in many areas, seem to conflict with rather than exhaust the demands of fairness and other fundamental moral principles.[19]

Let us apply this to examples. Suppose that major league baseball introduces a much livelier ball than the one used at present that led to home runs becoming routine. It becomes common for teams to score twenty runs in a game. For some reason, fans find this entertaining and buy more tickets. What has been lost, however, is the balanced contest between pitcher and hitter that always has been central to the game. Or, even worse, suppose professional basketball games come to have scripted endings, just as professional wrestling matches are now said to have. Games become less like contests and more and more like dramatic plays that follow exciting and entertaining scripts. Thrilling comebacks, last-minute shots, and comical mistakes help fill arenas but they are all choreographed in advance, the outcome decided by the writers of the day's screenplay rather than the play of the game.

What, if anything, is wrong about such scenarios? After all, the owners profit as do the players (perhaps better referred to in the last example as "actors"), and masses of fans enjoy the entertainment provided. The "purists" who object that true sport no longer exists are powerless and ignored. Such changes might be to the mutual advantage of many, but are they justifiable ethically?

It is probably true that if sports were transformed in such a manner, they would not remain interesting to many people. Good sport is entertaining precisely because it demonstrates human skills and virtues in meeting difficult challenges to mind and body alike. To the extent that professional wrestling or partially scripted exhibition games, such as those of the talented Harlem Globetrotters, are popular, it is because they are parasitic on genuine competitive sport where the outcome of game depends on the performances and skills of players and coaches. In other words, it is activity governed by the underlying principles of sport as a mutual quest for excellence that make sport of interest in the first place. (That is why it is to the mutual advantage of members of the sports industry to preserve those values rather than allow them to diminish or disappear.)

More important, something of great value would be lost if sport were transformed solely to a commercially viable form of entertainment at the cost of losing its basic character; namely, the value of sport as a mutual quest for excellence through challenge. Although professional sports do not exactly fit this model, and in many ways (sometimes justifiably) try to appeal to mass audiences, their appeal has value precisely because it reflects the underlying principles of sport, not entertainment.

Another way of making this point is by asking who would be harmed if commercialization were allowed to transform sport too radically in the direction of pure commercial entertainment. Surely it would be members of the broader sports community: players, officials, and fans devoted to the principles of the sport and who respect the game. If sport, as argued in earlier chapters of this book, embodies and expresses values of enduring significance, such as the importance of dedication in overcoming challenge or the value of standards of excellence, than the broader community would lose as well.

It might be objected that even if commercialization, when carried to an extreme, *harms* others, it does not follow that it *wrongs* them. (Thus, the police may harm a robber in preventing a crime, but it does not follow they have wronged the robber or treated him unjustly.) Since it is not clear that depriving people of something of value is a form of wronging them, it is controversial whether the commercialization of sport that significantly undermines the fundamental principles of sport does involve wronging others. If popular forms of music so dominated markets that the opera no longer remained economically viable, opera lovers may have been harmed, but were they wronged? On the other hand, if a valuable social practice of enduring human significance is diminished by the growth of commercial interests or even lost, is it implausible to conclude that a wrong has been committed as well as harm? Even if no one is wronged, which is doubtful, a wrong still might have been committed.

If it is justifiable to regard corruption in the values of sport as a wrong as well as a harm, or, more simply, if it is wrong to corrupt values of such fundamental importance, there is an argument for concluding that the sports industry is more than just a marketer of sport; it can also be regarded as having a fiduciary relationship to sport. This means the industry has some responsibility for preserving the integrity of sport and respect for its central values. This may not only be in the best interests of the industry, as indicated by the argument from mutual advantage, but may extend beyond self-interest to the protection of what is of deep value as well.

An Example: Technology and the Good of the Game

The growth of technology and its application to sport has raised a host of ethical issues that bear on our discussion. One of them concerns the possibility of conflict between the marketing of technologically advanced equipment and what is good for the game. Advanced technology, if it is available only to some competitors, can tilt the playing field in a way that is arguably suspect. If an individual or team wins a contest because of access to technology unavailable to opponents, has the best team or player really triumphed? Norwegian philosopher Gunnar Breivik has suggested that performance-enhancing technology should be made available to all competitors if it is available to any.[20] Otherwise, the wealthiest teams (or countries if we are thinking of the Olympics) would have competitive advantages unrelated to athletic ability. Sport would become as much a competition between teams of scientists and engineers as between athletes.

If one issue concerning new technology concerns access to it, another concerns threats to the challenge of the game itself. Might new technological breakthroughs in equipment, even if available to all competitors, simply make the sport too easy by significantly reducing the challenges it faces? Let us consider this second issue in more depth by considering an alleged example of making the game too easy through technology.

For some time, the United States Golf Association (USGA), the chief rule-making body for golf in the United States, Mexico, and Canada, has had growing concerns about whether technological advances in golf club design might reduce the challenges of the game, particularly by making existing golf courses too easy because of the greater distance the newer clubs allow golfers to hit the ball. Recently, the organization adopted a standard limiting the "spring-like effect," or the extent to which the clubface of drivers might rebound, in an effort to keep technology under control. However, the Royal and Ancient, the rule-making body in England that has authority over the rest of the golfing world, did not agree, and as a result for several years (1999–2002), clubs that conformed to the rules for tournament play elsewhere failed to conform in the United States and other countries where USGA rules apply. (Both associations agreed to a common standard in the fall of 2002.)

Although smaller companies had been marketing nonconforming drivers in the United States for some time, and others have been purchased abroad for use here, the stakes have gone up once industry giant Callaway challenged the USGA by offering a nonconforming driver for sale on the American market. In a spirited defense by its innovative founder, the late Ely Callaway, the company argued that the effect of nonconforming drivers on elite golf was marginal but that they could make the extremely difficult game of golf more fun for recreational golfers by allowing them to hit the ball farther than they could with conforming clubs. After all, it can be argued, if the nonconforming clubs help a segment of the golfing-challenged public to hit the ball farther and score better (the two may not even go together, since longer shots may simply go deeper into the woods!), who is hurt? (Perhaps, as a kind of compromise, rules for tournament play among professionals and top amateurs could still prohibit the use of clubs that supposedly make the game easier for elite golfers while making an often too difficult game more manageable for others.) In this view, since no one is hurt and many are helped, Callaway's action increases the net welfare of the golfing community and so is to be applauded rather than condemned.

But is this argument decisive? This kind of reasoning maintains that the ethical thing to do is what provides the most benefit and the least loss for all affected and therefore seems utilitarian. But before we accept the results of this kind of moral cost-benefit analysis, at least two questions need to be asked. First, have the costs and benefits been correctly assessed? Second, are consequences all that is relevant? Do other sorts of moral considerations, such as fairness or respect for our opponent, also need to be considered?

It may be useful now to consider briefly the kind of argument advanced by the great sixteenth-century British philosopher, Thomas Hobbes, who tried to show us why we would have had to invent the state even if it had not evolved on its own. Hobbes argued that in the absence of a central authority, we would find ourselves in what he called the state of nature. With no enforceable common standards left to soften rivalry and restrain our baser impulses, competition would be unbridled and life would end up "nasty, brutish, and short."

Although the consequences in sport are not nearly so dire, critics argue that the kind of argument presented by Callaway threatens to plunge golf as we know it into an analogue of the Hobbesian state of nature (and may also have implications for national concerns about the erosions of standards).

If some golfers decide it is permissible to use a club that violates the rule, why can't other golfers use a nonconforming ball that goes farther than conforming balls under the same conditions? Why can't still other golfers decide that it is all right to carry fifteen clubs instead of the fourteen allowed by the rules? Eventually, each group of golfers will be playing their own version of golf and none will be playing the standard version. (In fact, isn't it a mystery why anyone would spend many hundreds of dollars on an illegal club when the same results can be obtained for only a few dollars by playing an illegal ball or, for no money at all, by teeing off a few yards ahead of the marker indicating the beginning of each hole?)

But is this Balkanization of golf so bad? Why shouldn't different groups of golfers play by their own rules? Of course, we need a set of uniform rules for serious competition among elite professional and amateur players, but the vast majority of players are recreational golfers who rarely, if ever, play in highly competitive events. What harm is done if nonconforming clubs are used in recreational but not in competitive play?

This rejoinder has at least two flaws, the second of which may be of social significance that goes well beyond golf. First, it assumes that there is a sharp line between competitive and recreational play, when in fact there are many competitive levels, ranging from a course championship through regional, state, and national amateur competitions, to the professional tours, that are not always clearly distinct.

Let us consider a more fundamental difficulty that applies beyond golf to many other competitive sports. As our discussion in earlier chapters has suggested, what makes sport so fascinating is that its rules are designed to create a challenge that, if the sport is well designed, can test our heart, mind, and physical ability to the limit. Golf has long been known as particularly challenging: a game no one ever fully conquers. If equipment is allowed to make the game too easy, the challenge, if not lost, is significantly reduced and achievement becomes too easy to obtain.

Consider the golfer who buys a nonconforming club, uses a nonconforming ball, and places the ball in easy positions to hit rather than "playing it as it lies" as the rules require. Suppose this golfer breaks 90, that is, completes the round taking less than 90 strokes, for the first time.[21] Well, did the player really break 90 at golf? Arguably, the player was playing another game having some resemblance to golf—lets call it modified golf—and although the player broke 90 in modified golf, it is far from clear that 90 was broken in golf.

That is, the cost of making the game too easy is that achievement is cheapened. Even worse, focus is placed on a result, the score, which in this case is breaking 90—rather than the process of achieving it. In an effort to make ourselves feel good—"Guess what! I broke 90 for the first time today!"—we have eliminated the conditions that give a score of below 90 its significance. (Grade inflation might have the same unintended consequence in higher education.) This is more than—or at least different from—a utilitarian point about which practices tend to satisfy or frustrate people's preferences; rather, it is a point about the value of striving for achievement and challenge in a difficult enterprise and even more about our nature as persons. By reducing standards to make success ever easier, we lose the opportunity to try to meet challenges that force us to stretch the limits of our abilities, a point that applies to a variety of areas, especially education, as well as golf.

But, skeptics might retort, your argument against nonconforming clubs is grossly overstated. Other advances in equipment, ranging from the introduction of the sand wedge to the use of graphite shafts and introduction of large-headed titanium drivers, and, most especially, the evolution of the golf ball, have already made the game easier for the average player. Similar advances have been made in other sports, where changes in the composition of tennis racquets, cross-country skis, poles for vaulting, and other equipment have resulted in creating new standards of achievement in many sports.

Moreover, in golf, players have traditionally modified the rules for friendly play. To think that the average golfer totally conforms to the rules of golf is about as naive as expecting to find a Platonic form of the golf swing sitting on the foot of your bed when you wake up tomorrow morning.

These points have force but also are not the whole story. Surely some technological changes are welcome and improve the sport. The pertinent issues, however, are where lines are to be drawn—how much improvement alters the nature of the game—and who is to draw the line, the governing bodies of various sports or equipment companies? And although it is true that golfers sometimes modify the rules in friendly or recreational play, the rule changes are made by consent, usually due to unusual conditions, and apply the same to all.[22] In any event, rules cannot be amended by consent in formal competition.

The real price of widespread recreational use of the nonconforming clubs, then, is devaluing the challenge of golf and weakening the bonds of solidarity that unite golfers by dividing them according to which version of a series of games resembling golf they choose to play. Life in the golfing state of nature may not be "nasty, brutish, and short," as it would be in the Hobbesian one, but the true significance of one's score will be a mystery, since it will not be clear what version of modified golf one will be playing. Some golf companies may gain financially from the promotion and sale of nonconforming drivers. But their policies arguably harm the game by reducing its challenge. They make it easier for golfers to gain self-esteem, but at the cost of losing respect. Critics warn that we would be weakening the very conditions that entitle us to take pride in our athletic achievements. In the golfing state of nature, good scores may come more easily, but what are they worth?

An Ethical Compromise

In the debate, points of some merit have been made by both sides. The equipment companies surely are correct to point out that technological advances are part of sport, have often made sport more exciting, and can benefit recreational as well as elite players by bringing the game within the grasp of ordinary participants. But surely governing bodies of sports are also correct to say that equipment companies should not be the judge of when technological advances cease to be good for the game, or even harm it by reducing its challenges, and that a line sometimes may need to be drawn, even if not always in a perfect place.

The challenge of where to draw the line is significant. Preserving the integrity of the challenges of a sport is only one consideration that needs to be taken into account. Safety may be another. Thus, the use of aluminum rather than the traditional wood bats in baseball has raised concerns because the velocity with which the ball rebounds from such bats is so high that the safety of pitchers is threatened. A ball hit sharply right back at the pitcher's mound may come so quickly that the pitcher has no defense against being hit and perhaps suffer a serious injury. Cost is another factor. In golf, courses may simply be lengthened to mitigate the impact of "hot" clubs and balls. But longer courses are more expensive to build and maintain, and extra costs may be passed on to participants. This can make the game less accessible to many players, thereby reducing their numbers and actually hurting the equipment companies in the long run by reducing the size of their market. (Remember the argument from mutual advantage discussed above.)

Although there often will be no perfect place to draw the line about when technologically advanced equipment is and is not permissible, all these factors suggest that it is best to have a line drawn rather than have none at all. Otherwise, we might find ourselves in the sporting analogue of Hobbes's state of nature where the unconstrained pursuit of commercial interests is all too likely to undermine the good of the sport.

Hobbes's own solution to the problem of the state of nature was to argue that all power should be conceded to a sovereign who would make the rules for all. But, as proponents of democracy have long argued, such a solution has grave dangers of its own: Sovereigns may rule arbitrarily and need not focus on the best interest of their subjects.

In sports, a more desirable solution would be for governing bodies to have control of where the line on technology is set, but to operate in an open manner that takes into account the interests of the constituents of the sporting community, including fans, equipment companies, sports teams, recreational and elite athletes, and the principles of the game itself. When there are disagreements, different points of view need to be expressed and heard by the governing authorities. Finally, the sports governing bodies, such as the USGA in golf and the commissioners and official structure of various professional sports, need to make decisions constrained by concern for the basic values underlying their sport and the more general constraints set by the value and nature of competition in sport.

These authorities will not always make the best possible decision; however, as in drawing a line with respect to performance-enhancing drugs, decisions must be reasonable and nonarbitrary, must be based on dialogue among different constituencies of the sport, and must give due weight to underlying principles of sport that apply to the situation.

This does not mean that business concerns should always give way to reasonable interpretations of principle. Great increases in the entertainment value of a sport and its interest to a wide audience may sometimes justify modifications in the rules, even those that make the game less nuanced but more accessible to the casual fan. (Perhaps the introduction of the designated hitter rule in baseball might be such a modification.) How the balance is to be struck when interests or values conflict may depend heavily on contextual factors specific to each sport. Nevertheless, our discussion supports the view that sports organizations properly exercise a fiduciary responsibility to preserve the integrity of competitive sport.[23]

Reassessing the Corruption Thesis

We began this chapter by considering the corruption thesis. We have taken this thesis to be making an empirical claim about causality; namely, that as sport becomes more and more commercialized, market forces tend to subvert the central principles of an ethic of good competition and replace it by what sells, by what has entertainment but not necessarily sporting value. What does our discussion suggest about the truth of the corruption thesis?

First, the growing commercialization of sport does sometimes represent a threat to its integrity. The argument of earlier chapters suggests that sport does have an internal morality of its own that is centered around principles presupposed by a mutual quest for excellence through challenge. Moreover, the internal principles or values of sport can be threatened by commercialization. For example, skills central to a sport can be reduced in significance by rule changes designed to make the sport more entertaining to relatively unsophisticated mass audiences. Or a professional sport can be structured so that the wealthiest teams can dominate competition season after season. The pursuit of wealth can lead teams, as well as individual athletes, to sever their roots with local or regional communities in an attempt to reach larger audiences but at the price of creating alienation and disaffection in the serious sports community.

Nevertheless, our discussion also suggests that commercialization is not always harmful on balance, and that proper governance of elite, commercially viable sports has the potential to reduce significantly the conflict between commercialization and the integrity of competitive sport.

First, commercialization allows the internal goods created by elite athletes to be available to enormous numbers of people. Elite sport, including professional sports, has the potential to play a positive social role in this regard by exhibiting and expressing standards of excellence, achievement, and commitment.

But commercialized sport can play a predominately positive social role only if it operates within ethical boundaries that set parameters for the pursuit of profit. Thus, a second point suggested by our discussion is that the sports industry has a fiduciary moral responsibility towards the practices with which it is involved. This requires that governance of elite sports, especially professional sports, should reflect more than commercial interests concerned with generating wealth from the game. Governance should also give voice to and reflect the concerns of those whose allegiance is to the basic principles of competitive sport. If the argument of this chapter has force, this is not only because sports industries stand to lose if sport is cheapened beyond repair (the argument from mutual advantage), but because impartial reasoning suggests that the values central to good sporting competition are of sufficient weight to set moral limits on the pursuit of private interest.

8

Sports Values Today

In previous chapters, we have examined whether and under what conditions competition in sport is ethical as well as ethical issues that arise within competition, such as those involving fair play, violence, and the use of performance-enhancing drugs. In addition, we have looked at questions involving the relationship of sports to issues of equality, participation, education, and commerce. It is fitting that we conclude our examination by briefly considering some of the broader social implications of the ethical values that should apply in sport.

In particular, we should ask whether sports can and should play a significant role in broader spheres of moral development, especially in education and in our personal lives. Because claims for the moral import of sports have often been exaggerated and because of many abuses within the practice of competitive sports, many people regard sports as a symptom of our moral decline rather than a positive moral influence. But perhaps such a negative view has been overstated. Do sports have an important role to play in our moral lives after all?

Values, Morality, and Sports
The Reductionist Thesis

How are values in sports related to values in the larger society? According to one influential thesis, which we can call reductionism, values in sports are reflections and perhaps reinforcers of values in the broader society. This view is "reductionist" in that it attempts to explain all values in sports as expressions of dominant social values, thereby reducing the values in sports to those of the wider society. This kind of reductionism asserts that if a society is intensely competitive and stresses the advancement of individuals over that of the group, sports will reflect and perhaps reinforce adherence to those values. If, in another society, competition is frowned upon, and loyalty to the group is held to be more important than individual advancement, there will be less emphasis on the importance of winning and more on teamwork than in the first society. Some reductionists might add that the emphasis on such values in sports may reflect back on the prevailing social values and reinforce commitment to them in the broader culture.

Reductionism can be understood as an explanatory theory if its claim is that the nature of values in sports is fully explained by the existence of values in society. It can also be understood as a normative theory if it holds that the worth or justification of values in sports is no different from the worth or justification of more fundamental social values.

We have already encountered an example of reductionism in sports in our discussion in Chapter 4 of Paul Hoch's critique of football. Hoch, a critic of American society, sees it as too militaristic, capitalistic, and egoistic. In his view, football reflects and reinforces these values, which he regards as prevalent in our society. Some forms of Marxism also tend to be reductionist not only in their view of values in sports but also about values generally; some Marxists tend to view all social institutions as reflecting the values of the economic structure of society. An emphasis on individual moral rights, according to this kind of Marxist analysis, is not part of a universal, objective morality, but is characteristic of capitalistic, competitive societies in which individuals compete with one another for success in the market. Individuals "stand on their rights" against others precisely because the free market puts them in cutthroat competition with each other in the first place. Thus, claims about equal individual rights might well be unintelligible in a feudal society, where the hierarchical structure emphasizes the morality of one's station and its duties, or in tightly-knit communities where the individual, rather than being viewed as an autonomous unit, is in part defined by his or her place in the communal structure.

The reductionist position faces some serious objections if it is extended to cover all ideas and values. If ideas, moral codes, and social practices are mere reflections of underlying and more fundamental economic relations, isn't that true of the reductionist thesis itself? If so, and if reductionism is used to debunk the universalist claims to objectivity and truth, the reductionist thesis cannot claim to be an objective truth applying in all times and places but can itself be dismissed as a parochial belief fostered by a particular economic system.[1]

Of course, reductionism, or even Marxism, need not be based on so crude a form of economic determinism.[2] Moreover, such a criticism does not apply to limited reductionist analyses that apply only to values in sports because such analyses do not claim that all values are mere reflections of a more fundamental underlying basis. Rather, their claim is only that values in sports are expressions of dominant social values, not all values everywhere.

Perhaps the major objection to reductionist analyses of the values in sports is that sports often seem to express values that go counter to prevailing moral beliefs. An interesting example is given by Drew Hyland, a former Princeton basketball star and now a philosopher. Hyland has suggested that the emphasis on the merits and skills of the basketball players on local playground basketball courts can help to overcome racial prejudice and suspicions. When the only way to retain one's place on a crowded neighborhood court is to put together a winning team, whether other persons are good players will tend to count far more than their race, religion, or even sex. "In this situation, the preservation of . . . racism has a clear price, the likelihood that you will lose and have to sit."[3]

Our own discussion throughout this book also indicates that some values internal to sports are not necessarily mere reflections of a prevailing social order. For example, if dominant ideologies within a society were to disvalue excellence and challenge, the values expressed in good sports contests, conceived of as mutual quests for excellence through challenge, would conflict with rather than reflect dominant social values. If so, sports might be an important source of moral values and even have a significant role to play in moral education, a topic we will explore later in this chapter.

The Inner Morality of Sport

Suppose a person claims to be a serious athlete committed to competitive success but, in spite of having time to practice, virtually never does so. In addition, this person shows no desire to learn about his weaknesses in his sport or to analyze strategies that might be used successfully against opponents. Surely, in the absence of a special explanation, this individual's behavior would undermine his claim to be a dedicated athlete.

This example suggests that certain values, such as discipline and dedication, are central to competitive sports in the sense that an individual or team concerned with competitive success would have strong reason to act upon them. As noted above, in a society in which little emphasis was placed on achievement or hard work, those committed to competitive success in sports would be endorsing and acting upon values that conflicted with the prevailing values of their culture. If such athletes become sufficiently influential, their values may change and even replace the prevailing value system.

Other values also seem closely connected with a desire to compete in sports and athletics. Consider concern for playing by the rules. Although some athletes may be tempted to cheat and may even do so on occasion, no athlete can normally endorse disrespect for the rules as a universal value to be held by all athletes. For if cheating becomes a universal practice, there is no athletic competition in the first place. The very idea of such a competition is that of an activity governed by the appropriate constitutive rules, which at least partially define the game.

Concern for excellence and recognition of excellent performance are other values intimately connected to competitive sports. Even if a competitor's main concern is winning rather than achieving excellence, such an athlete must intend to play better than the opposition. This presupposes a conception of better and worse play, and therefore a conception of standards for evaluating performance.

Some values may be so intimately connected with sports that they are internal to it. Goods are internal to a practice or activity just when they logically cannot be understood or enjoyed independently of that practice or activity. For example, the value of being a skilled playmaker cannot even be understood without some understanding of the constitutive rules of basketball and appreciation of its strategies and nuances. In a society where such external goods as fame and wealth are highly valued by the majority, athletes who value securing the internal goods of sports may exemplify a way of life that conflicts with the norms of the majority, and might undermine or question them.

To cite one last example: Although there are different and competing conceptions about which ethical principles should apply to competitive sports, an ethics of competition can stand apart from and even conflict with moral principles widely accepted in other domains. Thus, the ethic of competitive sports such as a mutual quest for excellence conflicts with the view that competitive values are bad, wrong, or always to be abjured and the view that defeating others should be the only fundamental goal of the competitive athlete.

These illustrations strongly suggest not only that the reductionist thesis is seriously flawed but also that the practice of competitive sports and athletics is value laden in important ways. Some values, such as concern for excellence, discipline, and dedication, are traits that all competitive athletes have strong reason to commend and act upon themselves. Others, such as respect for the rules, are values that all competitive athletes have good reason to maintain; they should be part of the universal set of norms upon which all athletes should act. Still other values, such as the excellences of particular sports, are internal goals that all serious players of the sport normally seek to exemplify and that reflect standards for evaluating the play of oneself and others. Finally, conceptions concerning the ethic of competition, such as the mutual quest for excellence, constitute moral standards purporting to be morally justified.

These different normative features constitute what might be called the inner morality of sports. They may be more or less in harmony with the ethic of some cultures, or subgroups within cultures, but they can conflict with the moral codes of others and may promote change in existing moralities. Although there may be different interpretations of the inner morality of sports, and perhaps even different and conflicting inner moralities of sports, such a moral code (or codes) seems capable of profoundly influencing social and individual moral development.

This does not mean that an internal morality of sport is totally unique to the context of sport. For example, achievement in many areas, including medicine, scholarship, and teaching, requires dedication and commitment. An artist may value excellence just as much if not more than an athlete.

The importance of the inner morality of sport, then, is not that it is a totally unique approach to ethics. Rather, our analysis of the inner morality of sport indicates that athletics at its best involves core values that are attractive, defensible, and related to important fundamental principles such as respect for competitors as fellow persons, appreciation of excellence, and the value of subjecting ourselves to stimulating mental and physical challenge. Even professional sports, normally engaged in for financial gain as well as for (or sometimes instead of) the love of the game, are parasitic on the internal values, for it is precisely the fascination of seeing top professional athletes exposed to challenge that contributes to the widespread interest in professional athletics. Moreover, these values are internal in that they arise from the core character of competitive sport and are not mere reflections of wider social values, which can in principle and sometimes in practice diverge significantly from those found in competitive sport. Sports may well be value laden, and many of these values may also be endorsed by such approaches to ethics as utilitarianism and Kantianism, but at least some of those values are independently grounded in the domain of sports and can conflict radically with values found elsewhere in the social order.[4]

If athletes can act upon an inner morality (or moralities) of sports that can be expressed through their actions on the field, we can ask what its broad social role might be. Such a question is too broad to deal with exhaustively here, but one issue is worth our special attention. Sport, as some of our earlier discussions have indicated, has long been thought to influence character development. Accordingly, the role sport can play in moral education is well worth further consideration.

Sports and Moral Education

Because moral values play a large role in sport, it is not surprising that sports are often thought of as an area where values can and should be taught and transmitted to the next generation. We have seen in Chapter 2 that a traditional defense of athletic competition rests on its allegedly good effects on character. In Chapter 6, it was argued that intercollegiate and interscholastic sports can have educational value when conducted properly.

Many people see a decline in values in our society. Random violence seems to be all too common. Drugs, gangs, and urban decay create risks for youngsters that seem to be higher than those faced by children of the previous generation. With the rise in the divorce rate and the decline of the nuclear family, many children seem to be receiving less attention at home than in previous generations. The schools increasingly are asked to take on extra responsibilities, such as sex education, which used to be left, however wisely or unwisely, to the home, church, or synagogue. It is natural to ask, then, whether the schools should provide moral education and direction. Should sports have a role in moral education? If so, what should that role be?

Should schools be involved in teaching values? If so, whose values should be taught? Should there be formal courses in moral instruction? What, if anything, gives public schools, and through them the state, the right to decide upon an "official" morality to be taught to our children?

These questions suggest two important difficulties with the idea that schools should be responsible for moral education. The first might be called the problem of partisanship and the second the problem of indoctrination.[5] According to the first, the public schools have no business teaching values because there is no one set of values that all agree upon. The schools, and through them the state, have no business deciding on a particular set of values and making them the official ideology of the land. Imagine how you would feel, for example, if you were a political and social conservative (or liberal) and the schools taught liberal (or conservative) values as the correct morality. Even if we could agree on the values that should be taught, we would be indoctrinating many of our students. Since many students are not yet sufficiently mature to evaluate complex moral systems rationally, we would be imposing a value system upon them without their autonomous consent.

Because of these difficulties, existing programs of moral education may have emphasized either teaching students to clarify their own values or teaching procedures of moral reasoning, such as trying to see things through the perspective of others, rather than endorsing substantive moral principles. Such views attempt to avoid the charges of partisanship and indoctrination by restricting themselves to the form rather than the content of moral thought and by encouraging development of autonomy. Even these approaches have been severely criticized on various grounds, including the charge that they express the hidden agenda of an abstract but highly partisan morality. Thus, advocates of such approaches have been accused, in the case of values clarification, of teaching a disguised moral relativism ("It doesn't matter what values you hold as long as you can clearly articulate them and authentically accept them"); or, in the case of concern for the form of moral reasoning, of presupposing a "male-oriented" universalist ethic of impartiality (as opposed, for example, to a communitarian ethic or "female-oriented" ethic of caring).[6]

Whether or not these criticisms are justified, our discussion of the inner morality of sports suggests that informal moral education is going on in the schools all the time. For example, coaches of athletic teams normally stress dedication, discipline, teamwork, concern for excellence, and respect for the rules. Indeed, it is hard to see how they could avoid teaching such values, since some values are presupposed by the attempt to succeed in competitive sports. Coaches may also teach related values associated with their conception of the ethics of competition, including sportsmanship, fair play, and the principles required by conceiving of sports as a mutual quest for excellence by the participants.

Classroom teachers are also involved in informal moral education. Related to the inner morality of sport, one can argue that there is an inner morality of scholarship, which minimally requires civility in the classroom, respect for evidence, willingness to consider the views of others, and respect for them as fellow participants in critical inquiry. Dedication, discipline, and respect for the rules of evidence apply not just to sports but to intellectual inquiry as well. Thus, elementary school teachers who insist on civility and nonviolent behavior in the classroom encourage their pupils to discuss their differences rather than simply allow them to beat up opponents.

Not only do teachers and coaches often stress such values, it seems entirely appropriate that they do so. An emphasis in the classroom on concern for evidence and willingness to listen to other points of view clearly is not neutral in the sense of being value free; rather, it seems to be presupposed by the educational process itself. Similarly, an emphasis on the playing field on teamwork, discipline, striving for excellence, and respect for the rules seems to be presupposed by competition in sports and athletics. Accordingly, such values may be neutral in a sense other than that of the value of freedom; that is, it is reasonable to suppose that such values would be agreed upon by all concerned with the practices at issue (education and competition in sports). The inner morality of sports (and of scholarship) are neutral rather than partisan in that they concern values that all committed to the activities in question have good reason to support.

If this last point is justifiable, the inner morality of sports seems to avoid the charge of partisanship directed against the idea of moral education in the public schools. But is it really free of ideological bias? Aren't we trying to have it both ways here? On the one hand, the claim is that there is an inner morality of sports that is independent of and can even conflict with prevailing social values; on the other, it is claimed that such values are nonpartisan and, in some sense, neutral. Are these claims mutually compatible?

Thus, critics of competitive sports agree there is an ideology of athletics but reject it as overly competitive, egoistic, and conservative. We have seen in Chapter 4 that some critics of current practices in competitive athletics identify adherence to the rules with blind subservience to the existing order, regardless of its moral standing. The critics are correct if they are pointing out that sports can be used to transmit messages about values extrinsic to athletic competition. For example, a conservative coach can call for blind loyalty to the team regardless of the behavior of the players and equate that with the sentiment of "my country right or wrong."

Although such values as discipline and respect for the rules might be central to an inner morality of sports, it can be argued that blind loyalty is not. The difference is that the former values, but not the latter, are presupposed by the practice of competitive sports. Discipline, unlike blind loyalty to a team, is a value anyone interested in competing well in sports has reason to pursue regardless of ideology. Similarly, respect for the rules cannot be equated with blind loyalty to the status quo; rather, respect for the rules is a way of recognizing the equal moral standing of others by abiding by the public conditions for competition that every competitor is entitled to believe will apply. Respect for the equal moral standing of others is not value free because it is incompatible with viewing the interests of others as of less moral significance than one's own, but it does seem to be presupposed by the idea of fair and meaningful competition.

Similarly, the classroom teacher who insists that students discuss differences rationally rather than force their opinions on others through violence is rejecting some values, such as intimidation as a means of settling disagreements; however, rationality and willingness to respect others as participants in the discussion is central to education in a way that intimidation is not. Thus, we can argue plausibly that in applying the inner morality of sports and of scholarship, the schools are not imposing a partisan "official" ideology upon pupils but are teaching values that are presupposed by activities properly included in the educational curriculum.

What about the charge of indoctrination? Many coaches and teachers do not explicitly discuss the core moralities they are acting upon but simply impose them on students, many of whom are themselves too young or immature to make competent and autonomous decisions about morality. Teachers who insist that the bigger children in their elementary school classes do not beat up smaller ones are not offering a philosophical defense of civility but simply commanding their pupils to be civil. Similarly, by simply disciplining young athletes who loaf in practice, coaches are not engaging in Socratic dialogue about the value of commitment and dedication but rather insisting that their players show discipline and commitment. If this isn't indoctrination, what is? In particular, what gives athletic coaches the right to impose such values on players?

We need to ask if what is going on is indoctrination in a pejorative sense of that term. In particular, as some writers have suggested, perhaps not all values can be autonomously adopted; rather, some may be presupposed by the practice of autonomous reflection itself.[7] For example, before one can autonomously evaluate the justifiability of conflicting points of view, one must acquire the disposition to evaluate evidence and consider arguments rather than merely go along with one's friends or popular opinion. The acquisition of such a disposition cannot itself be the result of critical inquiry and autonomous reflection because one must already have the disposition needed to engage in critical inquiry and autonomous reflection. Training that helps immature and not yet competent individuals develop such traits is not the harmful indoctrination that subordinates critical thinking, but instead is part of a social process that develops critical and autonomous persons.

Similarly, the inner morality of sports, insofar as it forms part of a defensible practice of moral education, does not place athletes in intellectual blinders. Values such as commitment, discipline, respect for the standing of others, and appreciation of excellence are also presuppositions of moral and rational development.

If this position can successfully withstand critical examination, what are its implications for educational policy? In particular, they suggest that moral education of a limited sort is properly the function of our schools and that organized athletics can and should be part of it. Moral education of the kind at issue is limited to promoting those dispositions of mind and of character that can reasonably be regarded as prerequisites of the capacity to engage in autonomous critical inquiry with others. Just which values are to be cultivated will often be controversial, but a strong argument can be made for those core values constituting the heart of what we have called the inner morality of scholarship and sports.

If this approach is defensible, it provides an important reason why athletic programs should be considered a significant part of the curriculum of public education and not just a "frill" to be done away with as soon as school taxes get too high. By reinforcing values taught in the classroom, athletic competition in which people from diverse backgrounds and perspectives engage in a common quest for excellence can help promote and illustrate values that all committed to fostering development of autonomy and reason in both public and private life have reason to support.

Sports and Moral Responsibility

If sports can play an important moral role in society, does it follow that individuals involved in sports have special moral responsibilities to the rest of us? What about the duties of leaders in the world of sport, or of highly visible elite athletes? Let us consider the role of the coach in interscholastic and college athletics.

Coaching and Its Duties

Coaching can take different forms at different levels of sport or different areas of competition. In individual sports such as golf and tennis, the coach can be virtually an independent contractor hired by the athlete to provide technical advice on mechanics or, as a sports psychologist does, to work on improving mental aspects of the game. Thus, famous golf instructor Butch Harmon has been hired by Tiger Woods to bring his game to an even higher level. Harmon's relation to Woods is different from that of, say, the coach of a high school team to her players since, for one thing, the contract between Harmon and Woods can presumably be dissolved by either party. The high school coach, on the other hand, may have to be a team leader in a way that Harmon is not, be responsible for team behavior, set practice schedules, and perform many duties in addition to teaching mechanics or form. Although an individual coach such as Harmon also may perform some of these duties at the highest levels of elite individual sports, and the difference therefore is one of degree, there surely is a substantial distinction between coaches of team sports at the high school and college level, and the golf or tennis professional.

Coaches of teams may be asked to perform many duties and be evaluated on various factors. Often, in American sport at least, coaches are judged primarily by their wins and losses. At the level of elite intercollegiate sports, coaches in high-profile sports with losing records may not bring in sufficient revenue or create sufficient visibility for the institutions that employ them. At the professional level, winning relates to profits even more. Coaches are often expected to promote their program to the general public, be great recruiters, and at the same time keep their players in good academic standing and out of trouble.

Many of these functions are legitimate and important, but they can also conflict. Perhaps the coach can improve the team's competitive record by recruiting marginal students, or by not enforcing disciplinary codes when star athletes misbehave. At the extreme, as happened at the University of Minnesota (discussed in Chapter 6), the coach might tolerate academic fraud to keep players eligible and the team winning. In other words, if the main function of the coach is to win, important values may have to be ignored and basic ethical principles violated when necessary to achieve that goal.

Perhaps the coach's goal should be to win, but only when the pursuit of victory is limited by appropriate ethical constraints. My suggestion is that the constraints suggested by the basic argument of this book are sufficiently stringent that although coaches should surely strive for competitive success, they should be regarded primarily as educators and evaluated as such as well as on their record of wins and losses.

In particular, if competition in athletics is best regarded as a mutual quest for excellence through challenge, and the experience of meeting challenges is one in which we learn about ourselves and others, coaches should, as part of their role, facilitate this experience. This involves not only teaching the mechanical skills needed to play well but also clarifying the principles behind strategies and setting guidelines about commitments and responsibilities; in this way, athletes will be able to play hard and well in contests while also being successful in class. Most young people play sports to have fun, although serious athletes have fun, not by playing loosely or carelessly, but through focused training that enables them to reach their potential in competition. Coaches, therefore, should be evaluated primarily on how well they facilitate this development as well as on how well they promote understanding and love of their sport. Indeed, our argument in Chapter 6 suggests that in educational institutions, coaches can play an important academic role in integrating academic and athletic values and in insuring the success of student-athletes in both areas.

Thus, a coach can be successful as a teacher even if he or she does not have a winning record, although it is sadly true that, at many levels of intercollegiate and even interscholastic sports, losing coaches may have trouble keeping their jobs.

Sometimes, though, a continual run of losses or losing seasons may suggest the coach is a bad teacher, but that is not always so.

Even if we do regard the coach primarily as an educator, many ethical issues arise in coaching. Should a coach always play the best players or always aim at winning, even if it means that some players always ride the bench? How is participation to be balanced against excellence? Should a college or high school coach play a talented freshman over a senior who is less talented but who has been loyal to the program for years? Ethical issues that arise within coaching are extensive and deserve thorough treatment of their own.[8]

For our purposes, however, perhaps the supreme imperative for a coach is to treat the players with concern and respect and not regard them as mere means either for self-promotion or for pursuit of revenue or visibility for an institution. Winning is not unimportant for many reasons and, as argued earlier, often indicates whether one has met the challenge of a competitive contest. As the level of competition gets higher, greater emphasis appropriately is placed on competitive success. But athletes are not just means for achieving victory; they are persons in their own right. Constraints on the coach that arise from the status of the players hamper the pursuit of victory at all levels of sport, although they may apply differently to those at elite levels than to youths and children. Thus, emphasizing participation for all players may be highly desirable in youth sports when players are developing skills and competition should teach all participants about the nuances of play and how to meet challenges. At the level of elite sports, which athletes freely engage in precisely because of the challenge and the desire for competitive success, a coach normally has good reason to put his or her best players on the field in key situations.

As an aid to developing a broader theory of the rights and responsibilities of coaches and athletes, we might ask what coaches and athletes would expect from one another if they considered the roles impartially. Although it is unclear what a full hypothetical social contract between players and coaches would look like, surely there are some fundamentals that neither party could reasonably reject. Thus, it is reasonable for coaches, like other teachers, to expect their athletes to be dedicated, to be willing to learn, and to abide by appropriate team policies. Athletes, on the other hand, reasonably should expect the coach to be focused on their development and to treat them as persons, not simply as resources to be used in the pursuit of victory. How these guidelines play out in specific contexts will often be debatable, but perhaps such an account can provide an ethical framework that can be brought to bear on specific controversies.

Should Athletes Be Role Models?

In considering the moral responsibilities of athletes, Pete Rose comes immediately to the minds of many observers of sport. Rose, formerly a star Major League Baseball player for the Cincinnati Reds, became known as "Charlie Hustle" because, through hard work and effort, he was able to turn what many regarded as less than extraordinary athletic ability into a distinguished major league career. Rose ended his career having recorded more base hits than anyone else who had ever played the game. His place in the Baseball Hall of Fame seemed assured. To many, Rose was not only a star player but also a symbol of what dedication and commitment to excellence could accomplish.

Following an investigation of charges alleging that Rose, then manager of the Reds, had gambled extensively on baseball games, he was banned from baseball for life in 1989 (although the lifetime ban might now be reconsidered if Rose acknowledges the extent of his involvement in gambling). Not only was Rose claimed to be a compulsive gambler, he was convicted of felonies involving tax evasion, presumably committed to support his gambling habit, and served a jail sentence in 1990. In addition, Rose was precluded from election to the Hall of Fame.

Did Pete Rose, as a star athlete and presumably a hero and role model to many youngsters, have a special obligation to behave ethically because of his participation in sports? Do athletes in general have special responsibilities to be good role models for the rest of us, particularly for the children who look up to them as heroes? Or are athletes simply ordinary people with special skills who have the same legal and moral responsibilities as anyone else but have no special obligation to be models for the rest of society?

What does it mean to claim that athletes have special moral obligations to the rest of us to behave ethically? Although it is not always clear what proponents of such a view might be claiming, they might mean that there are reasons over and above those that apply to us all for athletes to behave ethically. A second thing they might mean is that if an athlete behaves unethically, it is somehow more seriously wrong, perhaps because it is more harmful than if someone else commits the same unethical act. These might not be the only interpretations of what is meant, but we can work with them in exploring the scope of the moral responsibilities of athletes.

Why should we believe that athletes have special moral responsibilities? Athletes, it might be argued, are just people who have particular skills but in other respects are the same as the rest of us. All of us have obligations not to wrong others. Why should the possession of a special talent, such as athletic skill, carry with it an additional moral obligation to be a moral exemplar for others? Athletes may indeed have special moral obligations within competition to, say, follow the rules and play hard so as to provide a challenge for opponents, but it is quite another thing to say they have a special responsibility to be ethical generally. Surely, from the premise that certain individuals have unusual athletic talents, it doesn't logically follow that they have special moral obligations outside of competition as well.

It can be argued, however, that athletes occupy a special place in our society. They are often regarded as heroes by children and young people. To many disadvantaged youth, particularly minorities, many star athletes may illustrate that escape from deprivation is through success in competitive sports. Because athletes are revered by a large portion of the population, they are regarded as models to be emulated. Therefore, they have a special reason to behave morally—the unusually great influence they can have on others. They can do more harm through their influence on others than the ordinary person when they behave immorally. Thus, athletes who are users of addictive drugs, for example, may, however unintentionally, convey the message that it is "cool" to take drugs and so induce their fans to become "copycat" users.

This sort of argument is open to many objections. Instead of expecting athletes to live up to the perhaps unreasonable expectations of many of their fans, the fans ought to become more realistic. Indeed, as we have seen, the hero worship of athletes can be harmful, especially when it leads youngsters to try to develop their athletic rather than academic skills in the grossly unrealistic hope of becoming professional athletes. In any event, why should fans, particularly youngsters, regard athletes rather than physicians, nurses, teachers, scientists, or their parents as their heroes? From the perspective of the athletes, why should they have any more responsibilities to be moral exemplars than other entertainers, such as movie or rock stars, who often not only fail to be desirable role models for young people but also are not usually assigned any special moral blame for their derelictions?

These points surely are worth our consideration. But are they decisive? It can be argued that sports not only do but should play a central place in our society because of their concern with excellence and because appreciating sports does not require the special training or background often needed to appreciate excellence in such fields as medicine, science, mathematics, and even the fine arts. If so, sports is a practice which, by its very nature, is accessible to large and diverse portions of the population yet expresses and illustrates a concern for excellence. Given the attention paid to sports by the media and the love many people, particularly the young, have for sports, it is doubtful whether fans will suddenly become "realistic." It is far more likely that they will continue to have special regard for national sports figures as well as local athletes.

What has this to do with the moral obligations of athletes off the field? Arguably, because of the special connection between competitive sports and the quest for excellence and because of the broad accessibility of sports, it is not unreasonable for many segments of the population, particularly children and young people, to hold athletes in high regard and seek to emulate them. Top athletes profit from this emulation and are often represented to the public as having exhibited special virtues on the field. For example, Pete Rose was known for his dedication and hustle, Michael Jordan is loved for his enthusiasm for the joy of competition, and Tiger Woods is known for his ability to perform his best under the greatest pressure. Indeed, our own discussion of an inner morality of sports, and of the function of sports in expressing values, suggests there is an unusually intimate relationship between participation in athletics and ethics.

If so, and if it is therefore not unreasonable for the general public, particularly youngsters, to regard top athletes as heroic figures, and given that many top athletes accept and welcome the benefits of their position resulting from the way they are regarded, then perhaps it is not unreasonable to conclude that they have special reasons for at least avoiding the kind of immoral behavior, such as drug and alcohol abuse, cheating, and law breaking, that impressionable young people are likely to emulate. If athletes are regarded as role models in part because of the values expressed through their play, they can do unusual harm if their misbehavior leads their fans either to emulate their misdeeds or to become skeptical of the original values for which the athletes were thought to stand.

Perhaps a more important reason for thinking athletes have special moral obligations rests not upon controversial empirical claims about their effect as role models but on the special place values have in sports. If there is an inner morality of sport in which such values as dedication, concern for excellence, and fair play are central, then athletes express such values through their play and benefit from adherence to these norms by other competitors. Without such commitment, we couldn't have the good sports contest and the basic, scarce, and internal benefits it provides. To express such values and benefit from them in a central area of one's life and then undermine them elsewhere seems wrong. Similarly, it is wrong for a professor to claim to value intellectual integrity in scholarship and yet fail to do so outside the classroom, for example by ignoring evidence in political debate.

Thus, it is not just that sports fans often do look up to and emulate star athletes that underlies the claim that athletes have special reasons to be role models. It is also that the athletes owe much of their fame and fortune to the esteem in which they are held. This esteem arises in significant part not just from their athletic performance but also from the way it expresses an inner morality of sport, encompassing such virtues as dedication, commitment, excellence, coolness under pressure, and respect for the game and its challenges. If athletes willingly benefit from their exhibition of such virtues, which are part of their performance as athletes, it is not unreasonable to expect them to respect such virtues off the field as well.[9] This does not mean that athletes must be saints, but at least suggests that they do have special reasons to avoid morally immature behavior, to say nothing of criminal actions or the abusive treatment of others; such behavior not only can have harmful effects on young fans but is arguably hypocritical.

Although these suggestions need fuller support than has been presented here and are intended as invitations to reflection rather than as decisive argument, they may have sufficient force to show that the claim that athletes have special moral responsibilities is worth taking seriously. Again, the point is not that athletes should be saints, but that they have special reason not to violate minimal standards of good behavior or discredit values central to the inner morality of sports. Although we could take the opposite tack and argue that athletes should not be our heroes and should be respected only for their physical skills, the role of athletes in illustrating and expressing important values through their play suggests that their role in sports tends to thrust them into the moral spotlight in a way carrying some obligation with it.

Perhaps, then, we need to reflect not simply on the fun and beauty that can be provided by good sports but on the values embedded in the practice of athletic competition. What specific implications this might have for our actual practices, especially within educational institutions, needs further consideration, but at least two possibilities are worth mentioning. First, our discussion suggests that coaches in educational institutions ought to be evaluated more as teachers than according to their won-and-lost records. If appropriate standards of competitive sports have implications for life outside the playing field as well as on it, we need to reward instructors who can teach us to play according to a plausible version of an inner morality of sports rather than foster an amoral indifference to ethics in the pursuit of victory. For example, coaches in colleges and universities might be accorded faculty status and be judged for retention and promotion. Second, we should expect athletes in our schools not simply to satisfy minimal standards of behavior and academic progress but to be good citizens and committed students as well. Although such specific suggestions may or may not have merit, an emphasis on the inner morality of sports and the lessons it can teach may have a role to play in moral education and, more broadly, in our moral life.

Sports and Fundamental Values: A Concluding Comment

The principal theme of this book is that sports raise a host of significant ethical issues. At their best, sports are a stimulating challenge to mind and body; at their worst, they can be a joyless endeavor where losing is equated with being a failure as a person and winning becomes just a means to egoistic self-posturing over others.

However, our discussion suggests that sports properly conducted provide values of enduring human significance. Through sports, we can learn to overcome adversity and appreciate excellence. We can learn to value activities for their own sake, apart from any intrinsic reward they provide, and learn to appreciate the contribution of others, even when we are on opposing sides. Through sports we can develop and express moral virtues and demonstrate the importance of dedication, integrity, fairness, and courage.

In particular, sports presuppose the importance of standards; standards of excellent play and standards for appropriate conduct. Whether or not we accept some version of the ethic of the mutual quest for excellence, some moral standard is needed to distinguish sports as they should be conducted from degradations of the sporting ethic. These standards can be arrived at and examined only through the kind of critical reflection that is characteristic of philosophic inquiry.

Moreover, if there are justified standards that really do distinguish excellent from poor play as well as ethical from unethical behavior in sports, they provide reason for questioning the claim of many theorists that all standards are merely subjective and arbitrary preferences, simply reflecting our race, gender, socioeconomic status, religion, or cultural upbringing. Although what we learn surely arises from the particular social and historical perspective in which we find ourselves, whether our beliefs are justified is another question. Our discussion about sports suggests that the search for justified standards is not necessarily fruitless. Our particular positions at a given time may always be fallible and subject to criticism, but the claim that there are justified standards of excellence in play and in the ethics of playing morally indicates that the search for justifiable standards need not always be in vain.

We could do worse, then, than conclude with the remarks of Socrates in Plato's *Republic,* whose remarks about music and gymnastics may apply to creative activity and to sports generally when he asserts that "there are two arts which I would say some god gave to mankind, music and gymnastics for . . . the love of knowledge in them—not for the soul and body incidentally, but for their harmonious adjustment."[10]

Notes

Chapter 1

1. According to one of the most extensive studies done in this area, the *Miller Lite Report on American Attitudes Towards Sports,* completed in the 1980s, 96.3 percent of the American population frequently plays, watches, or reads articles about sports or identifies with particular teams and players. Moreover, nearly 70 percent follow sports every day and 42 percent participate daily. *Miller Lite Report on American Attitudes Towards Sports* (Milwaukee, Wisc.: Miller Brewing Company, 1983).

2. In a penalty kick, an offensive player attempts to shoot directly against the other team's goalie in a one-on-one situation. No other players other than the kicker and the goalie participate.

3. This incident is described in George Vecsey's column, "Backtalk: When Is It Gamesmanship and When Is It Cheating?" *New York Times,* 8 August 1999, sec. 8, p. 13.

4. Edmund Pincoffs of the University of Texas told me this story some time ago.

5. Allen Bloom, *The Closing of the American Mind* (New York: Simon and Schuster, 1987), 25.

6. My discussion of relativism draws heavily on distinctions made by James Rachels in *The Elements of Moral Philosophy* (New York: McGraw-Hill, 1993), 17–25, particularly the distinctions between various forms of relativism. Errors in their use or in my criticism of crude forms of relativism are entirely my own.

7. There may be a temptation to reply that because science is different from ethics, the example in the text is irrelevant. Disagreement in science doesn't show the impossibility of a rational resolution of a dispute, but disagreement in ethics does. But what entitles the skeptic to assume that science is rational but ethics isn't? The skeptic needs to show just how science and ethics differ in ways that are relevant to supporting skepticism and not simply assume the difference to be self-evident when that very assumption is being challenged. In any event, the logical point still stands. Disagreement on an

217

issue by itself does not establish that we can never tell whether one side has better reasons for its views or is more justified than the other.

8. There are other difficulties with ethical relativism as well. For example, what counts as a culture? Is the sporting community a culture? Is there such an entity as Western culture, or are there only loosely related cultural subgroups within the West? What should we do if we belong to different cultures, each of which makes conflicting moral recommendations? What if our religious culture tells us that abortion is wrong but the secular culture of our peer group says it is permissible? Ethical relativism, which tells us to follow the dictates of our culture, would seem to be useless when the dictates of the cultures to which we belong clash. Finally, cultures rarely speak with one voice. Thus, the genital mutilation of females, practiced in some African cultures, is not only criticized by many Western observers but also by those within the culture itself who oppose the practice. Ethical relativism, by assuming that cultures speak with one voice, obscures the ethical diversity and moral disagreement that exists within them. Doesn't the important issue concern not just what a culture asserts but whether the assertion is or can be supported by critical rational inquiry?

9. I discuss the issues raised by this comment, particularly the reluctance by some students to make moral judgments, in "The Paralysis of Absolutophobia," *The Chronicle of Higher Education* (27 June 1997): B5–B7.

10. *Nichomachean Ethics* bk. 1, chap. 2, sec. 25, trans. W. D. Ross, in *The Basic Works of Aristotle,* ed. Richard McKeon (New York: Random House, 1941), 936.

11. See, for example, R. M. Hare, *Freedom and Reason* (New York: Oxford University Press, 1965) and his more recent *Moral Thinking* (Oxford: Clarendon Press, 1981).

12. John Rawls, *A Theory of Justice* (Cambridge, Mass.: Harvard University Press, 1971).

Chapter 2

1. What Lombardi is claimed to have said is "Winning isn't everything, but wanting to win is." Scott Morris, ed., *The Book of Strange Facts and Useless Information* (New York: Dolphin, 1979).

2. The statement by Rice is from *John Bartlett's Familiar Quotations* (Boston: Little, Brown, and Co., 1951), 901, and the remark from Evashevski is from *Sports Illustrated* (23 September 1957): 119. For discussion, see James Keating, "Winning in Sports and Athletics," *Thought* 38, no. 149 (1963): 201–210.

3. Judy Cooperstein as quoted by Gerald Eskanai, "Judy Cooperstein Still Has the Tempo," *New York Times,* 2 July 1981, B12.

4. Quoted by John Loy and Gerald S. Kenyon, *Sport, Culture, and Society* (New York: Macmillan, 1969), 9–10.

5. Utilitarianism is really the name of a family of related positions. For example, utilitarians disagree among themselves over whether we ought to evaluate the consequences

of specific actions (act utilitarianism) or of general compliance with rules or social practices (rule utilitarianism). There are different versions of both act and rule utilitarianism.
Some philosophers believe that each approach will evaluate the same act differently, as
when a specific violation of a promise will have good consequences even when it breaks
the rule that promises ought to be kept. Others suggest that a defensible set of rules will
have so many exceptions that the very distinction between act and rule utilitarianism blurs
or even collapses. For a helpful introductory discussion of utilitarianism, see James
Rachels, *The Elements of Moral Philosophy* (New York: McGraw-Hill, 1993), 90–116.

6. Bruce C. Ogilvie and Thomas Tutko, "Sports: If You Want to Build Character,
Try Something Else," *Psychology Today* (October 1971): 61–62.

7. James L. Shulman and William C. Bowen, *The Game of Life* (Princeton: Princeton
University Press, 2001).

8. Walter E. Schafer, "Some Sources and Consequences of Interscholastic Athletics," in *The Sociology of Sport*, ed. Gerald Kenyon (Chicago: Athletic Institute, 1969), 35.

9. Harry Edwards, *Sociology of Sport* (Homeward, Ill.: The Dorsey Press, 1973),
324.

10. The idea of an expressive function of punishment is suggested by Joel Feinberg
in "The Expressive Function of Punishment," in his *Doing and Deserving* (Princeton:
Princeton University Press, 1970), 95–118. The idea of an expressive function of sport
is examined by David Fairchild in his article, "Prolegomena to an Expressive Function
of Sport," *Journal of the Philosophy of Sport* 14 (1987): 21–33.

11. John Schaar, "Equality of Opportunity and Beyond," in *Equality,* Nomos IX, ed.
J. Roland Pennock and John W. Chapman (New York: Atherton Press, 1967), 237.

12. Michael Fielding, "Against Competition," *Proceedings of the Philosophy of Education Society of Great Britain* X (1976): 140–141.

13. Richard Harding Davis, "Thorne's Famous Run," in *The Omnibus of Sport,* ed.
Grantland Rice and Harford Powel (New York: Harper and Brothers, 1932), quoted by
Edward J. Delattre, "Some Reflections on Success and Failure in Competitive Athletics,"
Journal of the Philosophy of Sport 2 (1975): 134–135.

14. Delattre, "Some Reflections," 134.

15. Ibid., 135. Similar themes are developed by Paul Weiss in his *Sport: A Philosophic
Inquiry* (Carbondale, Ill.: Southern Illinois University Press, 1969), one of the pioneer-
ing works in twentieth-century philosophic study of sport.

16. A. Bartlett Giamatti, *Take Time for Paradise: Americans and Their Games* (New York:
Simon & Schuster, 1989), 35–36.

17. Robert Nozick, *Anarchy, State, and Utopia* (New York: Basic Books, 1974), 240.

18. Can't we just see whether our current performance improves relative to our
past performance? Thus, if I shot a 90 in golf last month and an 89 today, haven't I
shown improvement? Perhaps so, but whether that improvement is significant or worth
noting depends on comparisons with an appropriate reference group. If players of simi-

lar athletic ability and training "normally improve from 90 to 82 in one month, I may have no justification for regarding my "improvement" as worth noting, or of significance at all.

19. However, it need not always be so. Winning may breed egotistical behavior or generate excessive self-confidence that may ultimately lose friends or lead to dangerous risk taking. It can cause a young athlete to neglect academic work and overemphasize athletic success. Whether or not winning is in one's overall self-interest is an empirical question and depends upon the circumstances at hand.

20. Ronald Dworkin, *Taking Rights Seriously* (Cambridge: Harvard University Press, 1977), 227.

21. Ibid., 272.

22. Ibid., 272.

23. Ibid., 272. For an excellent book-length treatment of desert, see George Sher, *Desert* (Princeton: Princeton University Press, 1987).

24. Based on my memory of a televised postgame interview with University of North Carolina running back Kelvin Bryant in 1981.

25. *The New York Times*, 3 February 1999, D4.

26. William J. Bennett, "In Defense of Sports," *Commentary* 61, no. 2 (1977):70.

27. Ibid., 70.

Chapter 3

1. Mike Ammann, goalkeeper of the Metro Stars of Major League Soccer, quoted by George Vecsey, "Backtalk: When Is It Gamesmanship and When Is It Cheating?" *New York Times*, 8 August 1999, sec. 8, p. 13.

2. As used here, "sportsmanship" will designate a virtue that can be exemplified equally by males and females of all races, ethnic groups, and socioeconomic backgrounds.

3. James W. Keating, "Sportsmanship As a Moral Category," in *Philosophic Inquiry in Sport,* ed. William J. Morgan and Klaus V. Meier (Champaign, Ill.: Human Kinetics Press, 1995), 144–151.

4. Ibid., 146.

5. Ibid., 147.

6. Ibid., 147.

7. Ibid., 149.

8. This distinction will be criticized later in the chapter. For additional criticism of Keating's position, see Randolph M. Feezell, "Sportsmanship," in *Philosophic Inquiry in Sport,* ed. William J. Morgan and Klaus V. Meier (Champaign, Ill.: Human Kinetics Press, 1995), 152–160.

9. William J. Morgan, *Leftist Theories of Sport: A Critique and Reconstruction* (Urbana, Ill.: University of Illinois Press, 1994).

10. A series of works by Bernard Suits has been particularly influential in developing the idea of constitutive rules as central to the idea of games (and most sports). See Bernard Suits, "What Is a Game?" *Philosophy of Science* 34 (1967): 148–156, and "The Elements of Sport," in *Philosophic Inquiry in Sport,* ed. William J. Morgan and Klaus V. Meier (Champaign, Ill.: Human Kinetics Press, 1995), 8–15. See also Suits's instructive and often amusing book, *The Grasshopper: Games, Life, and Utopia* (Toronto: University of Toronto Press, 1978). For criticism, see Klaus Meier, "Triad Trickery: Playing with Sport and Games," in *Philosophic Inquiry in Sport,* ed. William J. Morgan and Klaus V. Meier (Champaign, Ill.: Human Kinetics Press, 1995), 23–35.

11. This kind of example, with a squash player who forgets her racquet rather than a golfer whose clubs are lost was employed by Robert Butcher and Angela Schneider in "Fair Play as Respect for the Game," *Journal of the Philosophy of Sport* 25 (1998): 6, but for an even earlier use of it, see A. S. Lumpkin, S. Stoll, and J. Beller, *Sports Ethics: Applications for Fair Play* (St. Louis, Mo.: Mosby, 1994).

12. See, for example, Warren Fraleigh, "Why the Good Foul Is Not Good Enough," in *Philosophic Inquiry in Sport,* ed. William J. Morgan and Klaus V. Meier (Champaign, Ill.: Human Kinetics Press, 1995), 185–187.

13. For example, see the influential paper by Fred D'Agostino, "The Ethos of Games," in *Philosophic Inquiry in Sport,* ed. William J. Morgan and Klaus V. Meier (Champaign, Ill.: Human Kinetics Press, 1995), 36–49.

14. For Dworkin's criticism of Hart, see "The Model of Rules," in Dworkin's *Taking Rights Seriously* (Cambridge, Mass.: Harvard University Press, 1977).

15. Much of what follows in this section is taken from and more fully developed in my "Internalism and Internal Values in Sport," *Journal of the Philosophy of Sport* 27 (2000): 1–16.

16. Robert Butcher and Angela Schneider, "Fair Play as Respect for the Game," *Journal of the Philosophy of Sport* 25 (1998): 9.

17. Ibid., 11.

18. Ibid., 18.

19. J. S. Russell, "Are Rules All an Umpire Has to Work With?" *Journal of the Philosophy of Sport* 26 (1999): 27–49.

20. Ibid., 28.

21. Ibid., 14.

22. Ibid., 15.

23. Morgan's *Leftist Theories of Sport* is in part an argument for this conclusion.

24. *New York Times,* 3 February 1999, D4.

25. Bernard Gert, *Morality: Its Nature and Justification* (New York; Oxford University Press, 1998), 191–195.

26. Ibid., 194.

27. Fraleigh, "Why the Good Foul," 269.

28. Kathleen Pearson, "Deception, Sportsmanship, and Ethics," in *Philosophic Inquiry in Sport*, ed. William J. Morgan and Klaus V. Meier (Champaign, Ill.: Human Kinetics Press, 1995), 184.

29. Ibid., 184.

30. The reason the penalty is needed is to insure fairness for other competitors who have not hit their shots into unplayable situations. Without the penalty, there would be no competitive disadvantage for hitting the bad shot that led to the unplayable lie. In a sense, the penalty compensates the other competitors.

31. This analysis might be disputed by an alternate internalist interpretation of basketball that did not view foul shooting as a basic skill of the game, or regarded the constant breaks in the flow of the game caused by strategic fouls not compatible with the best understanding of how the game should be played. For discussion, see Cesar Torres, "What Counts As Part of a Game?: A Look at Skill," *Journal of the Philosophy of Sport* 27 (2000): 81–92.

32. Sigmund Loland and Mike McNamee, "Fair Play and the Ethos of Sports: An Eclectic Philosophical Framework," *Journal of the Philosophy of Sport* 27 (2000): 63. The material in the parentheses is my own paraphrase of the original quotation.

33. Indeed, the distinction between sports and athletics, as made by Keating, will be questioned later in this chapter. For more extensive criticism, see Feezell, "Sportsmanship," 152–160.

34. Ken Johnson, "The Forfeit," *Dartmouth Alumni Review* Oct. 1990:8–16.

35. Those who would defend Colorado might reply that the Colorado quarterback, if he had known the true situation, would not have intentionally grounded a pass on what he thought was a third down play and therefore Colorado might have won if they had been apprised of the true situation. Because the situation was the same for both teams, fairness was preserved. But although an argument can be made in defense of Colorado and although it is clear that their players and coaches did not cheat, it also is unclear whether Colorado actually met the test set by the rules and therefore whether they deserved full credit for the victory.

36. Oliver Leaman, "Cheating and Fair Play in Sports," in *Philosophic Inquiry in Sport,* ed. William J. Morgan and Klaus V. Meier (Champaign, Ill.: Human Kinetics Press, 1995), 195.

37. Ibid., 196.

Chapter 4

1. See Tom Gerducci, "Totally Juiced," *Sports Illustrated* 96, no. 23 (2002): 34–48.

2. John Stuart Mill, *On Liberty* (1849), quoted from the Dolphin edition (Garden City, N.Y.: Doubleday, 1961), 484. Mill's Harm Principle, articulated in the quoted passage, also rules out interference with liberty to prevent acts that merely are offensive to

others or to interfere with acts on grounds of their alleged immorality, independent of any harm to others they may produce.

3. Ibid., 576.

4. Carolyn E. Thomas, *Sport in a Philosophic Context* (Philadelphia: Lea & Febiger, 1983), 198.

5. M. Andrew Holowchak, "'Aretism' and Pharmacological Ergogenic Aids in Sport: Taking a Shot At the Use of Steroids," *Journal of the Philosophy of Sport* 27 (2000): 40.

6. For an excellent discussion of different senses of "coercion," and an argument that we should think of coercion normatively as the *illegitimate* interference with the freedom of others, see Alan Wertheimer, *Coercion* (Princeton: Princeton University Press, 1989).

7. Norman Fost, "Let Them Take Steroids," *New York Times,* 9 September 1983, A19. But see also Wertheimer, op. cit., Chapter 1.

8. Roger Gardner, "On Performance-Enhancing Substances and the Unfair Advantage Argument," in *Philosophic Inquiry in Sport*, ed. William J. Morgan and Klaus V. Meier (Champaign, Ill.: Human Kinetics, 1995), 225.

9. Ibid. (for versions of this sort of argument).

10. Ibid., 229.

11. The idea of a veil of ignorance is presented by John Rawls as part of a complex argument for a conception of social justice in his monumental work, *A Theory of Justice* (Cambridge, Mass.: Harvard University Press, 1971). Part of his argument is that the principles of justice are those we would accept, if rational, from a position of choice in which we were ignorant of our personal characteristics or position in society. This would guarantee that choice was impartial and uninfluenced by such accidents of fate as the wealth of our parents or our genetic endowment.

12. Strictly speaking, athletes behind the veil will be ignorant even of their own values, but will have to take into account the possibility that in the real world they might have such values and vote accordingly.

13. My colleague Richard Werner suggests that a rule-consequentialist argument would lead to the same conclusion through a simpler argument; that is, a rule prohibiting the use of performance enhancers that are harmful to users would have better overall consequences than rules permitting use. However, such an approach would be open to objections of paternalism and, more important, would not explain the intuition of many of us that the use of performance enhancers is unfair. Moreover, the argument presented in the text can be presented without reliance on the "veil of ignorance" that, as Rawls sometimes seems to suggest, can be best viewed as a heuristic aid to impartial thinking. The main point of the argument is simply that if athletes disregard the personal benefits or harms that might accrue to them through steroid use, the use of steroids to enhance performance

makes no rational sense as a general practice. It provides the risk of significant harm to everyone who uses them but at best minimal relative gains in performance.

14. This sort of point has been made by Gardner, "On Performance-Enhancing Substances," 229.

15. Does this argument imply that we also should prohibit athletes from using glasses or contact lenses or from having LASIK surgery? Just when does a technological aid provide an unearned benefit and when should unearned benefits be prohibited? These are difficult questions. One kind of reply, worth exploring further, is that glasses do not modify the challenge of the sport or provide users with competitive advantages over others; they only allow athletes with poor vision to catch up with others. (Does this mean that steroids should be allowed, but only by weaker athletes to make them competitive with naturally stronger ones?)

16. This sort of antipaternalistic argument has been made in a series of articles by Miller Brown. See particularly W. M. Brown, "Paternalism, Drugs, and the Nature of Sport, *Journal of the Philosophy of Sport* 11 (1984): 14–22.

17. This point has been developed by Michael Lavin in his paper, "Drugs and Sports: Are the Cultural Bans Justified?" *Journal of the Philosophy of Sport* 14 (1987): 34–43. See also in the same issue (74–88) David Fairchild's paper "Sport Abjection: Steroids and the Uglification of the Athlete" for further reasons in favor of prohibition, as well as for some skeptical doubts about whether governing bodies in sport tend to be reasonable or nonarbitrary.

18. Frank DeFord, "An Encounter to Last an Eternity" *Sports Illustrated* (11 April 1983): 71. My account of the fight is based upon this article.

19. Ibid., 61.

20. John Stuart Mill, *On Liberty,* op. cit.

21. If Mill can be read here as advancing a rule utilitarian argument, he might avoid this objection. A society following a rule prohibiting paternalistic interference will actually promote utility more efficiently than one adopting a rule allowing it, for in the second society, the good produced by the few instances of justifiable paternalism will be swamped by the harm promoted by unjustifiable paternalistic interferences constantly carried out by utilitarian busybodies. Still, should the rule be followed blindly, even in special circumstances where paternalistic interference clearly would produce more good than harm?

22. Mill, *On Liberty*, 534.

23. The account of individual rights as political trumps has been advanced by Ronald Dworkin in *Taking Rights Seriously* (Cambridge: Harvard University Press, 1978). See particularly chapter 4, "Hard Cases."

24. Mill, *On Liberty*, 484.

25. An accessible discussion of the medical evidence on the effects of boxing on the health of the boxers, and of implications for policy, can be found in Robert H. Boyle

and Wilmer Ames, "Too Many Punches, Too Little Concern," *Sports Illustrated* (11 April 1983): 42–67.

26. The example of Mayhem is based on a similar illustration employed by Irving Kristol in his essay "Pornography, Obscenity, and the Case for Censorship," in *Philosophy of Law,* ed. Joel Feinberg and Hyman Gross (Encino, Calif.: Dickenson Publishing Company, 1975), 165–171.

27. *New York Times,* 14 December 1982, 30.

28. Important communitarian criticisms of liberalism and its supposed emphasis on the asocial individual include Alasdair MacIntyre, *After Virtue* (Notre Dame. Ind.: University of Notre Dame Press, 1984) and Michael Sandel, *Liberalism and the Limits of Justice* (New York: Cambridge University Press, 1982).

29. For extended critical discussion of communitarianism, see Amy Gutmann, "Communitarian Critics of Liberalism," *Philosophy & Public Affairs* 14 (1983): 308–322, and Robert L. Simon and Norman E. Bowie, *The Individual and the Political Order* (Lanham, Md.: Rowman and Littlefield, 1998), chaps. 4 and 5.

30. Paul Davis, "Ethical Issues in Boxing," *Journal of the Philosophy of Sport* 20–21 (1993–1994): 51.

31. Jack Tatum, with Bill Kushner, *They Call Me Assassin* (New York: Everest House, 1979), 12.

32. Ibid., 176.

33. Paul Hoch, *Rip Off the Big Game* (Garden City, N.Y.: Doubleday, 1972), 22.

34. A brushback pitch, designed to move hitters back from the plate, must be distinguished from a beanball, usually thrown behind batters (so that they will dodge right into it) with the intent to hit them.

35. For data supporting such a claim at a sample of highly selective universities and liberal arts colleges, see James L. Shulman and William G. Bowen, *The Game of Life* (Princeton: Princeton University Press, 2001), especially 55–56.

Chapter 5

1. Betty Spears, "Prologue: The Myth," in *Women in Sport: From Myth to Reality,* ed. Carol A. Ogelsby (Philadelphia: Lea and Febiger, 1978), 12.

2. *More Hurdles to Clear: Women and Girls in Competitive Athletics,* Clearinghouse Publication no. 63 (Washington D.C.: United States Commission on Civil Rights, 1980), 3. For a full account of development of women's athletics in the United States, see Ellen Gerber et. al., *The American Woman in Sport* (Reading, Mass.: Addison-Wesley, 1974).

3. Althea Gibson, *I Always Wanted to Be Somebody* (New York: Harper & Row, Perennial Library Edition, 1965), 42–43.

4. *More Hurdles to Clear,* 13, 22.

5. Annual Sports Participation Survey of the National Association of High School Federations (1997–1998), available online at www. Balliwick.lib.uiowa.edu/ge.

6. "Sport Is Unfair to Women," *Sports Illustrated* (28 May 1973).

7. Richard Wasserstrom, "On Racism and Sexism," in *Today's Moral Problems,* ed. Richard Wasserstrom (New York: Macmillan, 1979), 96–97.

8. Ibid., 10.

9. Eldon E. Snyder and Elmer A. Spreitzer, *Social Aspects of Sport* (Englewood Cliffs, N.J.: Prentice-Hall, 1978), 158.

10. Wasserstrom, "On Racism and Sexism," 104.

11. Pregnancy leaves seem a relevant exception, however, and may show that the assimilationist model should not extend to all areas of economic life or even that it requires severe modification.

12. Perhaps assimilationism can avoid this consequence by distinguishing between the fixed sexual preferences of many people and the social significance or importance attached to such preferences. In this view, the perhaps biological fact of fixed sexual attraction is neither just nor unjust but only given. What is just or unjust is the special significance and preferential status society attaches to such relationships, particularly heterosexual ones. On the other hand, given the facts that the assimilationist, in this interpretation, acknowledges literal blindness to the sex of other persons seems neither attainable nor desirable. That is, sexual assimilationism implies more than just nondiscrimination against people with different sexual preferences; it requires virtual blindness to the sex of persons, which seems to be quite another matter entirely.

13. Wasserstrom, "On Racism and Sexism," 97.

14. For a conflicting view, see Claudio Tamburrini, *The Hand of God: Essays in the Philosophy of Sports* (Gotesborg, Sweden: Acta Universitatis Gothoburgenis, 2000), 104ff.

15. See the discussion in Snyder and Spreitzer, *Social Aspects of Sport,* 155–161, on the association of certain sports with gender based stereotypes.

16. I am indebted here to Randy Carter's much fuller discussion in his unpublished paper, "Are 'Cosmic Justice' Worlds Morally Possible?"

17. For a critique of the identification of sex equality with sex blindness in areas other than sports and athletics, see Bernard Boxill, "Sexual Blindness," *Social Theory and Practice,* vol. 6, no. 3 (1980).

18. Betsy Postow, "Women and Masculine Sports," *Journal of the Philosophy of Sport* 7 (1980): 54.

19. Ibid., 273.

20. Jane English, "Sex Equality in Sports," *Philosophy & Public Affairs* 7, no. 3 (1978):275.

21. James Michener, *Sports in America* (New York: Random House, 1976), 20.

22. *Grove City College v. Bell,* 465 U.S. 555 1045 S. Ct 1211 (1984).

23. *Franklin v. Gwinnett County Public Schools,* 112 S. Ct. 1028 (1992).

24. An influential explication of fundamental rights in terms of equal concern and respect has been provided by Ronald Dworkin in *Taking Rights Seriously* (Cambridge, Mass.: Harvard University Press, 1987) in the course of a discussion of affirmative action. See particularly pp. 227–229.

25. *Final Report of the NCAA Gender Equity Task Force* (Overland Park, Kans.: National Collegiate Athletic Association, 1993).

26. Thus, according to the Annual Sports Participation Survey of the National Association of High School Federations, in 1997–1998, there were roughly 3,763,000 male participants in high school sports and 2,570,000 female participants. Although the total of female participants had grown since 1993, the disproportion in participation remained basically similar. Reports on participation rates can be found online at www. Balliwick.lib.uiowa.edu/ge.

27. For a critique of the effects of the proportionality requirement on men's sports, see Jessica Gavora, *Tilting the Playing Field: Schools, Sports, Sex and Title IX* (San Francisco: Encounter Books, 2001).

28. See for example Carol Gilligan's *In a Different Voice* (Cambridge, Mass.: Harvard University Press, 1982) and the vast critical literature it has generated. Gilligan argued that women tended to adopt a somewhat different form of moral reasoning than men. This has led to considerable debate in philosophy and psychology over whether there is a difference between an "ethic of care" presumably favored by women and a "justice perspective" presumably favored by men. For a useful account of and contribution to the debate, see Owen Flanagan and Kathryn Jackson, "Justice, Care and Gender: The Kohlberg-Gilligan Debate Revisited," *Ethics: An International Journal of Social, Political, and Legal Philosophy* 97, no. 3 (1987): 622–637.

29. The members of the advisory commission were divided on whether to radically restructure the proportionality requirement, and so were unable to agree on major changes in it. They did recommend some less fundamental revisions in the current interpretation of the law. See Diana Jean Schemo, "Advisory Panel Backs Easing Rules for Title IX," *New York Times,* 31 January 2003, D1.

30. James L. Shulman and William G. Bowen, *The Game of Life: College Sports and Educational Values* (Princeton: Princeton University Press, 2001), 245. See Daniel Fulks, *Revenues and Expenses of Division I and II Intercollegiate Athletic Programs: Financial Trends and Relationships—1997* (Indianapolis, Ind.: NCAA, 1998) for a study and figures provided by the NCAA.

31. What counts as a financial gain or loss can be controversial. For example, should a share of receipts from sale of apparel with a university logo be counted as revenue generated by athletics if sales would have been far less without the visibility of the university's athletic teams? Thus, different accounting decisions might well lead to a different evaluation of the financial gains and losses attributable to intercollegiate athletics. This point will be discussed in Chapter 6.

32. See John Rawls, *A Theory of Justice* (Cambridge, Mass.: Harvard University Press, 1971), 11–22, 60–83.

33. The operative concept here is Rawls's veil of ignorance, a major part of his argument in *A Theory of Justice.* Rawls suggested that just principles are those that would be accepted by rational persons reasoning as if behind a veil of ignorance that obscured from them their personal position in society, their own talents and abilities, and even their values. This would insure not only that they could not favor their own position but also that arbitrary contingencies, such as initial distributions of natural talents, would not unduly influence the choice of principles of justice. The use of the veil of ignorance has been highly influential and widely criticized, for example by allegedly requiring we adopt an impossible "view from nowhere," and has been de-emphasized in Rawls's later work. I suggest the concept is a useful tool of moral reasoning if used, perhaps in the way Rawls intended, as a device to assist us in reasoning about social arrangements not just from our own surely limited point of view but from the perspectives of others. As such, it surely does reflect a requirement of moral reasoning; namely, that we subject our own perspective as well as that of others to critical scrutiny and try to understand moral disagreements from a point of view that does not beg the question by implicitly building only our own prejudices and values into the principles we appeal to for adjudication.

Chapter 6

1. Rev. Jon Lo Shiavo, "Trying to Save a University's Priceless Assets," *New York Times,* 1 August 1982, S2.

2. Tates Locke and Bob Ibach, *Caught in the Net* (West Point, N.Y.: Leisure Press, 1982).

3. NCAA Infractions Report on the University of Minnesota, 24 October 2000, 2; available online at http://news.mpr.org/features/1999903/11_newsroom_cheating/infractionsreport.shtml.

4. Reports on graduation rates are issued annually by the NCAA and are broken down in various categories. The information in the text is from Steve Wieberg, "Off Court, Top Teams Fall Short," *USA Today,* 18 October 2002, 1c.

5. Lo Shiavo, "Trying to Save," S2.

6. John Stuart Mill is famous for defending freedom of thought and discussion in his *On Liberty* (1859) by arguing that such freedom gives us the opportunity of correcting our ideas when they are false and strengthening them, and therefore appreciating them more fully, when they are true.

7. Some observers would distinguish between elite programs such as those at Duke, North Carolina, Penn State, and Stanford, where athletes graduate at very high rates and those where graduation rates are dismal and the rigor of courses selected by many athletes is suspect.

8. Quoted in Ira Berkow, "College Factories and Their Output," *New York Times*, 18 January 1983, D25.

9. Based on NCAA statistics reported in "Graduation Rates for Male Basketball Players Falls to Lowest Levels in a Decade," *Chronicle of Higher Education*, vol. 48 (21 September 2001). NCAA methodology may tend to underestimate graduation rates, although perhaps not significantly. For example, if an athlete matriculates at Institution A and transfers to and graduates from Institution B, he or she counts as not graduating from A.

10. Harry Edwards, *Sociology of Sport* (Homeward, Ill.: The Dorsey Press), 198. See Edwards for a critique of genetic explanations for the disproportionate participation of African-American athletes in many sports.

11. Quoted in Eldon E. Snyder and Elmer A. Spreitzer, *Social Aspects of Sport* (Englewood Cliffs, N.J.: 1983), 189.

12. Jay Coakley, *Sport in Society* (St. Louis: C. V. Mosby Co., 1978), 295, quoted in Snyder and Spreitzer, *Social Aspects of Sport*, 190.

13. A Louis Harris Poll released in 1990 reported that 55 percent of black high school athletes expected to play ball in college and 43 percent said they could make it in professional sports. Only 39 percent of the whites thought they would play in college and just 16 percent thought they would compete at the professional level. In reality, only about 3 percent of high school athletes make it in college sports and only 1 in 10,000 go on to compete at the professional level. This poll was reported in the *NCAA News* 27, no. 41 (19 November 1990): 16. On the positive side, the survey also reported that participation in sports may help reduce racial barriers, as 70 percent of the responding athletes said they had become friends with team members from another racial or ethnic group. Moreover, 74 percent of black athletes, a higher percentage than for whites, claimed that participation in sports helped to keep them away from drugs.

14. See in particular John Hoberman, *Darwin's Athletes: How Sports Has Damaged Black America and Preserved the Myth of Race* (New York: Houghton Mifflin, 1998).

15. Former United States Senator Bill Bradley (and Princeton all-American basketball player and star of the professional New York Knicks) has expressed his views in a variety of forums, including television interviews and newspaper columns. See, for example, *Lexington (Kentucky) Leader*, 31 March 1982, C1. Senator Bradley's views have evolved over the years and he may no longer hold the views discussed in the text. The 2003 proposal was by Nebraska Senator Ernie Chambers. It is less comprehensive and would require that a stipend be paid to football players, subject to ratification by other states with state institutions in the Big 12. It is unclear whether paying such a stipend would make the players professionals. Reported on ESPN and at http:espn.go.com/ncf/news/2003/0212/1507801.html on 12 February 2003.

16. Harry Edwards, "Educating Black Athletes," *Atlantic Monthly* (August 1983): 36–37.

17. See the discussion of *The Game of Life* that follows later in this chapter.

18. For example, NCAA graduation statistics for the 1987–1992 period show 68 percent female athletes graduating compared to a roughly 58 percent for other female students. Male athletes, even in high-profile sports, graduate at high rates at such Division I scholarship institutions as Duke, Penn State, and Stanford.

19. For such a view, see Leslie P. Francis, "Title IX: Equality for Women's Sports?" in *Philosophic Inquiry in Sport,* ed. William J. Morgan and Klaus V. Meier (Champaign, Ill.: Human Kinetics Press, 1995), 305–315. Francis defends Title IX as necessary to provide fairness in an ethically suspect practice, intercollegiate athletics, but suggests that replacement of intercollegiate athletics by intramurals would in many contexts be desirable. See particularly p. 312 in Morgan and Meier.

20. Paul Weiss, *Sport: A Philosophical Inquiry* (Carbondale, Ill.: Southern Illinois University Press, 1969), 10–13.

21. Michael Oriad, "At Oregon State, Basketball Is Pleasing, Not Alarming," *New York Times,* 8 March 1981, S2.

22. James Shulman and William G. Bowen, *The Game of Life* (Princeton: Princeton University Press, 2001). Shulman and Bowen draw upon an extensive database involving cohorts of graduates from the institutions they study from the years 1951, 1976, 1989, and some recent but less complete studies from the 1990s. These institutions include academically respected Division I universities such as Duke and Penn State, the Ivy League schools, selective women's colleges such as Smith, and small coed selective liberal arts colleges such as Williams, Swarthmore, Denison, and my own institution, Hamilton. The same database was the basis for another widely discussed book, *The Shape of the River,* in which Bowen and former Harvard president, Derek Bok, defended affirmative action programs in the colleges and universities they studied. See William G. Bowen and Derek Bok, *The Shape of the River: Long-Term Consequences of Considering Race in College and University Admissions* (Princeton: Princeton University Press, 2000).

23. For a critical discussion of *The Game of Life* that focuses primarily on methodology, see Hal Scott, "What Game Are They Playing?" *Journal of College and University Law* 28, no. 3 (2002): 719–755. Material in the text is drawn from my own review of *The Game of Life* in the *Journal of the Philosophy of Sport* 29, no. 1 (2002): 87–95.

24. The failure to explore this issue is especially surprising. In *The Shape of the River,* the study of the effects of affirmative action based on material from the same database as that discussed in *The Game of Life,* Bowen and Bok did consider such a comparison, although admittedly not in depth. Their tentative conclusion was that students admitted under considerations of affirmative action were not displacing other applicants with vastly superior qualifications but were competing for spots with less qualified candidates (pp. 37–38). Although their discussion of this issue was quite brief, their tentative conclusion certainly is suggestive. For if it also is true to a significant extent that

preferred athletes generally are displacing other applicants who are relatively weak aca-demically, then it is far from clear that the effects of admission of athletes on the academic climate is as great as *The Game of Life* suggests.

25. For example, according to data from *The Game of Life,* in the 1989 cohort at coed liberal arts colleges, only 59 percent of the high-profile athletes had fathers with a bachelor's degree compared to 82 percent of students at large, and at the Division 1A private universities, only 53 percent of the athletes had fathers with a bachelor's degree compared to 78 percent of the students at large (see *Game of Life,* 51).

26. Shulman and Bowen have found that athletes with faculty mentors outperform other athletes academically, but are there institutional obstacles to the development of such a relationship? (see *Game of Life,* 71–74). If so, underperformance by athletes might be in significant part a result of experiences of indifference or rejection (as well as other institutional factors that might need to be considered) rather than being due largely to lack of academic commitment on their own part.

27. Albert Camus, "The Wager of Our Generation," in *Resistance, Rebellion, and Death*, trans. Justin O'Brien (New York: Vintage Books, 1960), 242.

Chapter 7

1. William J. Morgan, *Leftist Theories of Sport: A Critique and Reconstruction* (Chicago: University of Illinois Press, 1994), especially chap. 3.

2. James Michener, *Sports in America* (New York: Random House, 1976), 17.

3. Adrian Walsh and Richard Giulianotti, "This Sporting Mammon: A Normative Critique of the Commodification of Sport," *Journal of the Philosophy of Sport* 27, no. 1 (2002): 62.

4. Ibid.

5. For an account of the extent of use of performance-enhancing drugs among major league baseball players, see Tom Gerducci, "Totally Juiced," *Sports Illustrated* 96, no. 23 (2002): 34–48.

6. Morgan, "*Leftist Theories of Sport,*" 147.

7. Christopher Lasch, "The Degradation of Sport," in *Philosophic Inquiry in Sport*, ed. William J. Morgan and Klaus V. Meier (Champaign, Ill.: Human Kinetics Publishers, 1988), 407.

8. USDA Forest Service, 1982–1983, Nationwide Recreation Survey, and 1994–1995 National Survey on Recreation and the Environment, in Alison S. Wellner, *Americans At Play: Demographics of Outdoor Recreation and Travel* (Ithaca, N.Y.: New Strate-gist Publications, 1997), 3. Participation rates vary according to various demographic factors such as age, so caution must be used in evaluating the figures. Wellner provides a helpful discussion.

9. Ibid., 406.

10. This point also is made by Lasch, "Degradation of Sport," 405–407.

11. The distinction between scarce and basic benefits was to my knowledge introduced into discussions in the philosophy of sport by Jane English in her article, "Sex
Equality in Sports," *Philosophy & Public Affairs* 7, no. 3 (spring 1978): 269–277.

12. Milton Friedman, *Capitalism and Freedom* (Chicago: University of Chicago
Press, 1952), 133.

13. Robert A. Dahl, "A Prelude to Corporate Reform," in *Corporate Social Policy,* ed.
Robert L. Heilbroner and Paul London (Reading, Mass.: Addison-Wesley, 1975),
18–19, quoted by Norman E. Bowie, "Changing the Rules," in *Ethical Theory and Business,* ed. Norman E. Bowie and Tom L. Beauchamp, 2d ed. (Englewood Cliffs, N.J.:
Prentice-Hall, 1983), 103.

14. Ibid., 103.

15. A excellent account of stakeholder theory as well as an assessment and defense
of it is found in Thomas M. Jones, Andrew C. Wicks, and R. Edward Freeman, "Stakeholder Theory: The State of the Art," in *The Blackwell Guide to Business Ethics,* ed. Norman
E. Bowie (Malden, Mass.: Blackwell Publishers, 2002), 19–37.

16. For an important defense of a libertarian view, see Robert Nozick, *Anarchy,
State and Utopia* (New York: Basic Books, 1974), particularly chap. 7.

17. For fuller discussion, see Norman E. Bowie and Robert L. Simon, *The Individual and the Political Order* (Lanham, Md.: Rowman and Littlefield, 1998), particularly
chap. 3.

18. See John Rawls, *A Theory of Justice* (Cambridge, Mass.: Harvard University
Press, 1971) and the many discussions of it, as well as Rawls's later work, in the literature. A discussion of different approaches to justice is found in Bowie and Simon, "The
Individual and the Political Order"; and an analysis of different approaches to the justice
of social and economic institutions, including those of Rawls and the libertarians, can
be found in Christopher Heath Wellman, "Justice," in *The Blackwell Guide to Social and Political Philosophy,* ed. Robert L. Simon (Malden, Mass.: Blackwell Publishers, 2002),
60–84.

19. For a particularly important treatment of justice as mutual advantage that concludes such an approach is intellectually inferior to one that explicates justice in terms
of impartial agreement, see Brian Barry, *Theories of Justice* (Los Angeles: University of
California Press, 1989).

20. Gunnar Breivik, "Generosity as a Principle in Elite Sport" (paper presented at
the annual meeting of the International Association of the Philosophy of Sport, Pennsylvania State University, October 2002).

21. Many golfers consider breaking 90 the transition point from being a "hacker"
or "duffer" to being a golfer.

22. Moreover, unlike such informal arrangements between groups of recreational
golfers as allowing an extra shot off the first tee, a modification that an entire foursome
might agree to on the first tee (and which can be accommodated with USGA rules for

handicapping purposes), we can have golfer A playing a club that her partner, golfer B, refuses to use because its use violates USGA rules. Does B truly freely consent to being disadvantaged by allowing A to play the nonconforming club or will she feel pressured to agree and inwardly feel resentment at being cheated? So although golfers have modified rules in minor and mutually acceptable ways before, a marketing campaign to induce some golfers to make a much more fundamental change without mutual consent raises the ante. A difference in degree, when it becomes sufficiently great, becomes a difference in principle.

23. Again, this view resembles the "stakeholder" theory mentioned earlier. See Jones, Wicks, and Freeman, "Stakeholder Theory."

Chapter 8

1. Not all philosophers find such appeal to versions of the so-called Paradox of Relativism convincing or conclusive. According to the Paradox, relativists who assert that "there are no truths, only claims which hold within localized cultural, religious, or socioeconomic perspectives" are themselves making a claim, which is either true (thereby contradicting relativism) or is itself relative to some particular perspective and therefore need not be accepted by others. Some Marxists, for example, might seek to avoid the paradox by claiming that the socioeconomic perspective from which they make their own claims is more developed and comprehensive than earlier more parochial perspectives; that they have reached the point in history that comes closer to objectivity than ever before. But doesn't this strategy itself involve claims about which views are more comprehensive and developed than others that presuppose the possibility by comparing perspectives and making a judgment about them that purports to be objective? If so, unless Marxists are to exhibit blatant favoritism for their own views, the position of opponents who also claim to have reached such a point cannot simply be dismissed as false consciousness, but at least sometimes will have to be considered on its own merits.

2. Many contemporary writers who try to retrieve ideas of worth from the general body of Marx's work need not be reductionists or relativists at all, or accept the cruder deterministic aspects of some Marxist thought. For an example of such retrieval, see Richard Miller, "Marx's Legacy," in *The Blackwell Guide to Social and Political Philosophy*, ed. Robert L. Simon (Malden, Mass.: Blackwell Publishers, 2002), 131–153.

3. Drew A. Hyland, *Philosophy of Sport* (New York: Paragon House, 1990), 12.

4. Of course, various versions of utilitarianism or Kantian ethics based on respect for persons also can conflict with prevailing moral beliefs such as, for example, in a tyranny or repressive theocracy. The internal morality of sport overlaps with many aspects of Kantian ethics (and perhaps some forms of rule utilitarianism as well). The notion of respect for the opponent, for example, expresses a form of the Kantian injunction never to treat other persons merely as means to one's own goals. However,

the idea of athletic competition as a mutual quest for excellence presupposes a conception of respect for the opponent and suggests not only that sport can express a Kantian approach to treatment of others but also that sport provides independent support for such a moral perspective. And, of course, a tyrannical and oppressive society can reject the principle of respect for all persons in sport and throughout society as well.

5. For a discussion of the obligation of educational institutions to be neutral and nonpartisan, see Robert L. Simon, *Neutrality and the Academic Ethic* (Lanham, Md.: Rowman and Littlefield, 1994).

6. Thus, Carol Gilligan, in her book, *A Different Voice* (Cambridge, Mass.: Harvard University Press, 1982), has argued that emphasis on impartiality and universality in ethics expresses a moral perspective more associated with males than females in our society. The implications of a female-oriented approach to ethics is usefully explored by Virginia Held in her "Non-Contractual Society: A Feminist View," *Canadian Journal of Philosophy,* supplementary vol. 13 (1987): 111–137, and more recently in her "Feminism and Political Theory," in *The Blackwell Guide to Social and Political Philosophy,* ed. Robert L. Simon (Malden, Mass.: Blackwell Publishers, 2002), 154–176.

7. For a defense of a "core values" approach to moral education along these lines, see William J. Bennett and George Sher, "Moral Education and Indoctrination," *Journal of Philosophy* (1982): 665–677.

8. A very useful discussion of ethical dilemmas that may arise in coaching is found in Jeffrey P. Fry, "Coaching a Kingdom of Ends," *Journal of the Philosophy of Sport* 27 (2000): 51–62.

9. Must athletes *willingly* accept such benefits? What if an athlete does not want to be regarded as exhibiting moral virtues? My own view is that since good sport has an inner morality of its own, athletes who consent to participate and who try to be good competitors are freely committing to the virtues outlined in the text.

10. Plato, *Republic,* Book 3, line 412.

Index

Absolutism, 7, 11–13
Affirmative action, 230(nn 22, 24)
African American athletes, 138–139, 145,
   146–148, 153–154, 164, 229(n13)
Aggression, 111
Alcohol use, 72, 177, 213
Altruism, 22, 24–25
American College of Sports Medicine, 71
"Are Rules All an Umpire Has to Work
   With?" (Russell), 51–52
Aristotle, 13, 109
Armstrong, Lance, 182
Assimilationist model. *See under* Sex
   equality
Assumptions/presuppositions, 15, 21, 35,
   50, 54, 62, 82, 96, 98, 106, 130,
   155–156, 158, 162, 167, 185, 192,
   205–206, 207, 217(n7)
   assumptions about spectators and
     participating in sports, 175, 176
Athletics. *See* Intercollegiate athletics; *under*
   Sports
Atlantic Coast Conference, 138
Attendance, 119, 133
Autonomy, 95–96, 97, 99, 100, 114, 116,
   119, 186, 205, 208

Baseball, 18, 109, 116, 173, 176–177, 183
   balls/bats used in, 188–189, 194–195
   black players, 147
   brushback pitches in, 92, 104, 225(n34)

designated hitter rule in, 4, 48, 173, 196
home runs in, 174, 188
Louisville-Brooklyn game (1887), 51–52
spitball pitch in, 66
and steroid use, 69–70
umpires' rights in, 89
World Series of 1952 and 1986,
   181–182
Basketball, 18, 29, 58–59, 104, 109, 112,
   116, 117, 118, 122, 137, 139, 144,
   150, 161, 163, 177, 189, 222(n31)
   men's vs. women's games in, 120, 121,
     126–127
   National Basketball Association (NBA),
     134, 173
   NCAA Men's Basketball Championship,
     134, 137, 171
   professional, 146, 147, 148
   rule changes in, 180
   strategic fouling in, 43, 47, 48, 49, 55
   Women's National Basketball Association
     (WNBA), 133–134
Beauty, 37, 38
Bennett, William, 38
Bentham, Jeremy, 20
Berra, Yogi, 181
Bird, Sue, 119, 133, 182
Blood doping, 72
Bloom, Allen, 7
Bok, Derek, 230(nn 22, 24)
Boredom, 2

Boston Red Sox, 181

Bowen, William G., 22, 162, 164, 165, 230(nn 22, 24), 231(n26)

Bowie, Norman E., 185

Boxing, 90–91, 93–94, 96, 97–102, 107, 108

Bradley, Bill, 151, 229(n15)

Breivik, Gunnar, 190

Brooklyn Dodgers, 181

Bryant, Kobe, 146

Buckner, Bill, 181–182

Budgets. *See under* Intercollegiate athletics

Bush administration, 132

Butcher, Robert, 50–51

California Institute of Technology, 140

Callaway, Ely, 191, 192

Campanella, Roy, 181

Camus, Albert, 168

Carbohydrate loading, 80, 84, 85

Caught in the Net (Locke), 138

Causation, 22, 105, 167, 196

Challenge(s), 27, 28, 29, 30–31, 34, 35–36, 37, 38, 39, 42, 54, 64, 70, 111, 120, 160, 166, 168, 178, 189, 203, 209

   and sports equipment, 80, 191, 193, 194

   and steroid use, 83, 85

Chambers, Ernie, 229(n15)

Character development, 21–23, 37, 38–39, 204

Chastain, Brandy, 41

Cheating, 19, 24, 42, 61, 108, 150, 202, 213

   and incompatibility thesis, 46, 56, 143

   as not always wrong, 65–66

   in recruitment, 138

   and steroid use, 73, 79, 81

   See also under Strategic fouling

Chicago, University of, 140

Children, 4, 74, 96, 99, 187, 204, 212, 213

Choices, 33, 34, 35, 76, 86, 87, 95, 96, 100, 114, 186, 223(n11)

   constrained choices, 77–79, 80

free/informed choices, 74, 75, 81, 82, 97, 98, 101, 102. *See also* Informed consent

Cincinnati, University of, 145

Civil rights/liberties, 88, 89, 90, 96, 115, 122, 123. *See also* Office of Civil Rights

Civil Rights Restoration Act (1988), 124

Clemson University, 138–139

Closing of the American Mind, The (Bloom), 7

Coaches, 98, 106–107, 131, 138, 143, 144, 153, 155, 158, 161, 162, 167, 169

   role of, 205, 206, 207, 208–210, 214

Coercion, 75–77, 78, 98

College students, 11–12, 22, 163, 166

Commercialization. *See under* Sports

Commercials, 173

Commissioner of Baseball, 183

Communitarianism, 100–101, 102, 205

Competition, 17–39, 44, 67, 83, 85, 108, 110, 173, 178, 190, 192, 195, 200

   consequences of, 20–23, 24, 38, 167

   criticism of, 18, 19, 20, 24, 27–28, 31, 32, 34, 202, 206

   derogatory terms concerning, 34

   economic, 24, 200

   enhancing, 47

   ethical issues concerning, 4, 205

   improper competitive pressures, 77

   nonconsequentialist critics of, 24

   in non-sport areas, 2

   with self, 28–31, 219(n18)

   women's need for, 111

   See also Quest for excellence; Winning

Conformity, 106, 114

Connecticut, University of, 120, 133, 135, 137, 150

Consequences, 94, 95, 128. *See also* Sports, educational/social consequences of; *under* Competition

Consistency, 14

Conventions/conventionalism, 48–49, 56, 57, 59, 60, 62, 64, 66

Cooperation, 24, 25, 27, 28, 30, 31, 32, 167

Corporations, 183–185, 187

Corruption. *See under* Sports

Cost-benefit analysis, 20, 192

Courage, 23, 32, 37, 38, 91, 101

Crenshaw, Ben, 24–25

Crime, 57, 139, 148, 180, 211, 213

Critical perspective, 15

Culture of athletics, 162, 165–166

Curry, Wesley, 51–52

Dahl, Robert A., 185

Damn Yankees, 173

Dancers, 31

Davis, Benjamin, 90–91

Delattre, Edwin, 26–27

Democracy, 167, 168, 195

Diet, 80, 84, 85, 86, 87, 94, 97

Discipline, 21, 106, 201, 202, 205, 206, 207

Diversity, 13, 156, 164, 166, 218(n8)

Dogmatism, 7, 11, 12

Dominance, 2

Drugs (addictive), 97, 212, 213, 229(n13)

Drug testing, 88–89, 90. *See also*
    Performance-enhancing drugs

Duke University, 138, 150, 162, 228(n7)

Duval, David, 34–35, 53

Dworkin, Ronald, 33, 50, 52, 125

Edwards, Harry, 23, 153–154

Elite athletes, 87, 88, 172, 176, 179, 180, 192, 196, 210

Emory University, 140

English, Jane, 121–122

Equal opportunity, 114, 118, 121, 148
    vs. equal expenditures, 125, 133, 136

Equal Rights Amendment, 113–114

Equal treatment vs. treatment as an equal, 33

Ethics, 2–5, 168, 213
    objectivity of, 7, 8, 234(n6)

rationality of, 6–7, 8, 11, 15, 217(n7).
    See also Moral reasoning

and sports management, 183–190

Euthyphro (Plato), 5

Evans, Janet, 158

Evashevski, Forest, 17

Exploitation of athletes, 145–146, 152, 154, 155

Externalism, 45, 49

Extreme Football League, 188

Fair play, 2, 24, 25, 32, 39, 63, 67, 82, 107, 150, 168, 172, 192, 205. *See also*
    Sportsmanship; *under* Rules

"Fair Play As Respect for the Game"
    (Butcher and Schneider), 50–51

Fans, 2, 4, 100, 103, 121, 133, 151–152, 155, 171, 173, 187, 188, 189

fan-player relationships, 174, 181–182.
    See also Role models

as non-participating spectators, 175–177

sportsmanship for, 178

Felonies, 57. *See also* Crime

Feminists, 111, 121, 123

Fencing, 102

Feudal society, 200

Fielding, Michael, 24

Financial aid, 154. *See also* Scholarships

Florida, University of, 137, 145

Football, 18, 91, 92, 102–107, 122, 137, 150, 183

Cornell—Dartmouth game (1940), 62–63

criticism of, 103, 137–138, 144, 145–146, 200

Extreme Football League, 188

Fiesta Bowl game of 20003

institutional resources shifted from, 128, 129

National Football League, 183

professional, 146, 147, 148

strategic fouling in, 55

University of Colorado—University of
    Missouri game (1990), 42–43,
    61–62, 63–64, 64–65, 222(n35)
    violence in, 187–188
    Yale-Princeton game(1895), 25–26
Formalism, 46–48, 49, 56
    interpretive, 50
Fouls. *See* Strategic fouling
Fraleigh, Warren, 55, 56, 57
Francis, Leslie P., 230(n19)
Franklin v. Gwinnett County Public Schools,
    124
Freedom, 9, 73, 77, 94, 95, 228(n6). *See
    also* Autonomy; Civil rights/liberties
Friedman, Milton, 184
Fundamentalism, 9

Game of Life, The (Shulman and Bowen), 22,
    23, 162, 163, 164, 166, 168, 169,
    230(n22), 231(nn 25, 26)
Games, 3, 46
    "It's only a game," 37
    zero-sum, 18, 24, 28
Gardner, Roger, 79, 80
Gender equity, 110, 112, 113, 116–123,
    124, 132, 136
    presumptive approach to, 126
    See also Sex equality; Title IX of
        Education Amendments of 1972
Genocide, 12
Gert, Bernard, 54–55
Giamatti, A. Bartlett, 27, 31
Gibson, Althea, 110
Gilligan, Carol, 227(n28), 234(n6)
Girls, 2, 110, 120, 124
Golf, 3, 18, 24–25, 34–35, 47, 48, 51,
    112, 116, 117, 128, 164, 183, 195,
    208
    Balkanization of, 192
    equipment for, 79, 80, 84, 85, 191, 192,
        193, 233(n22)
    men's vs. women's contests in, 120–121

Professional Golfers Association (PGA),
    117, 183
    United States Golf Association (USGA),
        48, 191, 195, 232–233(n22)
    unplayable lie rule in, 57–58
    See also under Rules
Good life (the), 54
Grades, 153, 154, 157, 193
Graduation rates, 139, 145, 154, 156, 158,
    228(n7), 229(n9)
    female, 151, 159, 230(n18)
Green Bay Packers, 17
Greening of America, The, (Reich), 38
Grove City v. Bell, 124
Gymnastics, 121–122, 128

Hamm, Mia, 41
Hare, R. M., 14
Harlem Globetrotters, 189
Harmon, Butch, 208
Harm Principle. *See under* Mill, John Stuart
Harms vs. wrongs, 190
Hart, H. L. A., 48, 50
Haskins, Clem, 139
Health issues, 172, 178. *See also* Steroids,
    side effects
High diving, 122
Hill, Grant, 182
Hobbes, Thomas, 192, 194, 195
Hoch, Paul, 103, 200
Hockey, 2, 91, 108
    and killing of coach by parent in 2001, 4,
        92
Hodges, Gil, 181. 182
Holdsclaw, Chamique, 119, 133
Holowchak, M. Andrew, 78
Hyland, Drew, 201

Identity crisis, 22–23
Impartiality, 14
In a Different Voice (Gilligan), 227(n28),
    234(n6)

Income taxes, 186, 211

Indoctrination, 204, 205, 207

Inequalities, 32–35, 111, 126, 127, 135. *See also* Gender equity; Sex equality

Informed consent, 74, 75, 76. *See also* Choices, free/informed choices

Injuries, 91, 97, 188, 195
   deliberate, 34, 35, 53, 107, 225(n34)

Intercollegiate athletics, 110, 112, 120, 123, 127, 128, 129, 130, 131, 137–169, 208–209
   and academic fraud, 139, 143, 146, 150, 155, 209
   and academic standards, 157, 158
   budgets for, 123, 131, 132. *See also* Equal opportunity, vs. equal expenditures
   corruption of, 144–149. *See also* Sports, corruption of
   criticism of, 137–138, 148–149, 157, 160, 162
   de-emphasis of, 155
   as enhancing academics, 159–169
   and Incompatibility Thesis, 140, 141, 143–144, 166
   and practicing, 157–158, 165, 207
   professionalization of, 151–152
   reforming, 149–159
   as revenue producing, 134, 135, 144, 150, 152, 154–155, 168, 171, 210, 227(n31)
   role in universities, 140–144, 169
   See also Gender equity; Sex equality; Title IX of Education Amendments of 1972

Internalism, 45–46, 49, 222(n31)
   broad internalism, 50–52, 54, 58, 63, 174
   See also Formalism

International Olympic Committee (IOC), 82, 86

IOC. *See* International Olympic Committee

Iowa, 120

Ivy League, 138, 141, 154, 162, 165

Jogging/walking, 176

Johnson, Ben, 69

Jones, K. C., 138

Jordan, Michael, 70, 137, 138, 146, 175, 182, 213

Kantian ethics, 233–234(n4)

Keating, James W., 43–44, 53, 61

Lacrosse, 112, 116, 117, 164

Lasch, Christopher, 175, 176

Law(s), 50, 57, 88, 103, 110

Leftist Theories of Sport (Morgan), 46

Legal positivists, 50

Lending sports equipment, 47, 49, 51, 52

Lewis, Carl, 69

Liberal arts education, 23, 141–142, 159, 162, 165, 167, 168

Libertarianism, 186

Life style, 94

Literacy, 145

Locke, Tates, 138–139

Loland, Sigmund, 60

Lombardi, Vince, 17

Loyalty, 21, 23, 106, 155, 177, 178, 200, 206

MacArthur, Douglas, 19

Mack, Reddy, 51

Mantle, Mickey, 181

Marxism, 200, 201, 233(nn 1, 2)

Maryland, University of, 139

Mayhem (imaginary sport), 99, 102

Media, 124, 133, 134, 144, 146, 172, 175, 176, 178, 212
   commercials in, 173

Mencken, H. L., 74

Mentors, 231(n26)

Methodology, 163, 229(n9)

Michener, James, 123, 172, 175, 178
Mill, John Stuart, 20, 73, 224(n21),
    228(n6)
  Harm Principle of, 74, 76, 89, 94,
    96–99, 101, 222(n2)
Miller, Ralph, 161
*Miller Lite Report on American Attitudes Towards
    Sport,* 217(n1)
Minnesota, University of, 139, 143, 209
Moral principles and moral examples,
    14–15, 39
Moral reasoning, 6–7, 82, 130, 205,
    227(n28), 228(n33)
  criteria for, 13–15
  See also Ethics, rationality of
Moral responsibility, 208–214
Morgan, William J., 46, 52, 174
Multiculturalism, 12–13

National Amateur Athletic Federation,
    Women's Division, 110
National Association of High School
    Federations, 227(n26)
National Collegiate Athletic Association
    (NCAA), 82, 86, 125, 138, 229(n9),
    230(n18)
  Gender Equity Task Force, 127
  Men's Basketball Championship, 134,
    137, 139
  reform movement within, 152–154, 157
  See also Rules, NCAA rules
National Football League, 183
Nationalism, 4
NBA. *See* Basketball, National Basketball
    Association
NCAA. *See* National Collegiate Athletic
    Association
NESCAC. *See* New England Small Colleges
    Athletic Conference
Nevada, University of, 145
New England Small Colleges Athletic
    Conference (NESCAC), 138

New Mexico Golden Gloves, 90–91
New York Mets, 181
New York Yankees, 173, 181
Nike, 183
North Carolina, University of, 137, 138,
    150, 228(n7)
Notre Dame, 137, 150
Nozick, Robert, 29

Obedience, 106, 143
Obesity, 172
OCR. *See* Office of Civil Rights
Office of Civil Rights (OCR), 123,
    124–126, 127, 128, 129
Officials/referees, 25, 51–52, 58, 59, 89,
    125, 173
  mistakes by, 42, 61, 63
  role of, 63, 89
Oklahoma, University of, 139, 145
Olympics (Summer 1988), 69
O'Neal, Shaquille, 146
On Liberty (Mill), 94–96, 228(n6)
Oregon State University, 161
Oriad, Michael, 161

Page, Alan, 145
Parents, 4, 32, 98, 231(n25)
Partisanship, 204, 205, 206
Paternalism, 73–74, 76, 94–96, 99,
    223(n13), 224(n21)
Pearson, Kathleen, 55–56, 57
Penalties, 3, 217(n2), 222(n30)
  as sanctions vs. prices for options,
    57–61, 64, 66
Penn State, 137, 145, 150, 228(n7)
Performance-enhancing drugs, 3–4, 6, 11,
    98, 174, 195
  defining, 72
  See also Steroids; *under* Quest for
    excellence
PGA. *See* Professional Golfers Association
Philosophy, 5–6. *See also* Philosophy of sport

Philosophy of sport, 1, 6
 actual and ideal in, 66–67, 107–108,
  118
Physical education classes, 172
Plato, 5, 215
Play, 3
Pleasure, 20, 44
Pluralism. *See* Sex pluralism
Pole vaulting, 84, 146–147, 193
Policy issues, 108, 109, 113, 116, 123,
  184, 207. *See also* Title IX of
  Education Amendments of 1972
Political correctness, 12
Postow, Betsy, 119, 121
Poverty, 98, 146, 181, 187
Premises of arguments, 9
Presuppositions. *See*
  Assumptions/presuppositions
Privacy, 88
Professional Golfers Association (PGA),
  117, 183
Proportionality. *See under* Sex equality

Quest for excellence, 18, 21, 24–28, 30,
  37, 52, 53, 62, 63, 65, 66, 67, 104,
  107, 108, 159, 172, 178, 188, 189,
  202, 203, 205, 209, 213, 215,
  234(n4)
 and academic excellence, 140, 166, 167
 and performance-enhancing drugs,
  70–71

Racial issues, 114, 123, 146, 181, 201,
  229(n13)
Rationality. *See under* Ethics
Rawls, John, 14, 81–82, 135, 186, 223(nn
  11, 13), 228(n33)
Reagan, Ronald, 114
Reciprocity, 185
Recruiting athletes, 138, 144, 148, 155,
  157, 164, 165, 166, 173
Reductionist thesis. *See under* Values

Reese, Pee Wee, 181
Reforms, 49, 102, 107, 108
 incremental, 154, 155–156, 157, 159
 See also Intercollegiate athletics,
  reforming; National Collegiate
  Athletic Association, reform
  movement within; Rules, changes in
Reich, Charles, 38
Relativism
 and absolutophobia, 11–13
 critique of, 8–11
 descriptive, 7–8, 8–9, 10
 ethical, 8, 10–11, 205, 218(n8)
 Paradox of Relativism, 233(n1)
Religion, 9, 12, 115–116
Republic (Plato), 215
Respect, 50–51, 115, 125, 134, 136, 184,
  194, 205, 206, 210, 214,
  233–234(n4)
 for opponents, 107, 108, 168, 178, 192,
  203
Revenues. *See* Sports, as revenue producing
Rice, Grantland, 17
Riflery, 113
Rights, 96, 114, 134, 150, 185, 187, 200
 welfare rights, 186
 See also Civil rights/liberties
Right-wing politicians, 12
Rip Off the Big Game (Hoch), 103
Risk taking, 73, 78, 91, 97, 102, 104,
  220(n19)
Rizzuto, Phil, 181
Robinson, Jackie, 181
Role models, 146, 211–214
Roosevelt, Theodore, 137–138
Rose, Pete, 211, 213
Royal and Ancient, 48, 191
Rules, 3, 18–19, 32, 39, 41, 42, 43, 55, 59,
  62, 173, 206
 changes in, 4, 48, 49, 52, 58, 172–173,
  180, 194, 195–196
 constitutive, 19, 25, 46, 57, 221(n10)

enforcing, 88–90
and fair play, 44, 45
in golf, 57–58, 191, 192, 193–194,
232–233(n22)
interpreting, 51–52
and legal systems, 50
NCAA rules, 140, 144, 148, 158
permitting/prohibiting steroid use, 81,
87, 223(n13)
rule-governed violence, 103
rule-making/governing bodies, 82, 86,
87, 88, 90, 173, 183, 188, 191
Russell, Bill, 138
Russell, J. S., 51–52

Safety issues, 194–195. *See also* Injuries
Sanctions, 53. *See also* Penalties, as sanctions
vs. prices for options
San Francisco, University of (USF), 138,
139
Sarazen, Gene, 84
SAT scores, 153–154, 157
Scandals, 137, 138
Schaar, John, 24
Schneider, Angela, 50–51
Scholarships, 125, 129, 138, 140, 145,
147, 148, 154–157, 158, 162
Scurry, Briana, 3, 41–42, 47, 59, 60–61,
64–65
Self-discovery, 26, 28, 160
Self-esteem, 194
Self-expression, 37, 39
Self-improvement, 28, 29–30, 37
vs. achievement, 31
Self-interest, 14, 31, 81, 190, 220(n19)
Selfishness, 24, 25, 28, 31–32
Separate but equal doctrine, 121, 123
Sex, 7
Sex blindness, 113, 114, 115, 116–117,
118, 122–123, 136, 226(n12)
Sex differences, 116, 117, 118, 119,
121–122, 136, 234(n6)

and interest in participating in athletics,
130, 131
Sex discrimination, 112, 115, 127. *See also*
Title IX of Education Amendments of
1972
Sex education, 204
Sex equality, 113–116, 119, 121, 122
assimilationist model of, 114, 115,
116–117, 118, 123, 136, 226(nn 11,
12)
and proportionality, 126, 127–132, 136,
227(n29)
See also Gender equity; Sex pluralism;
Title IX of Education Amendments of
1972
Sex pluralism, 113, 115–116, 117–122
Sex roles, 114–115, 116, 117, 118, 119
Sexual preferences, 115, 226(n12)
Shape of the River, The (Bowen and Bok),
230(nn 22, 24)
Shiavo, John Lo, 138, 139
Shulman, James L., 22, 162, 164, 165,
230(n22), 231(n26)
Skepticism, 8, 13, 65, 217(n7)
and descriptive relativism, 10
Skis, cross-country, 193
Slavery, 12
Snider, Duke, 181
Soccer, 2, 48, 112, 116
Arsenal FC-Sheffield United (England),
60
World Cup (1999), 3, 41–42, 47, 59,
60–61, 64
Social change, 104
Social contract, 186, 210
Socialization, 130
Socrates, 5—6, 215
Sorenstam, Annika, 117, 119, 182
Sports
vs. athletics, 44, 61–62, 63
basic and scarce benefits of, 178–179,
180, 213

change in girls' and women's roles in
1970s/1980s, 110
commercialization of, 171–197
contact sports, 91, 102, 105, 107, 112,
116. *See also individual sports*
corruption of, 144–149, 172–183, 190,
196–197
definitions, 3
and discharge of aggression, 111
educational/social consequences of, 132,
149–151, 156, 159–169, 190, 196,
199, 201
ethical issues in, 2–5, 183–190. *See also*
Ethics
expressive function of, 23, 45, 85, 167,
168, 201, 213
high school athletics, 110, 120, 123,
124, 127, 227(n26), 229(n13)
imaginary. *See* Mayhem
inner morality of, 201–204, 206, 213,
214, 233(n4), 234(n9)
intercollegiate/interscholastic. *See*
Intercollegiate athletics
internal/external goods of, 178–180,
202, 203
and moral education, 204–208
as noncompetitive, 18, 38
professional, 146, 147, 148, 173, 185,
187, 189, 197, 203
respect for interests of, 50–51
role in universities, 140–144. *See also*
Intercollegiate athletics
rule-making/governing bodies, 82, 86,
87, 88, 90, 173, 183, 188, 191,
195
spectators vs. participants in, 175–177,
178
women in, 109, 110, 119–120, 124,
130, 131, 133, 150, 156, 163, 164,
176, 227(n26). *See also* Gender
equity; Graduation rates, female; Sex
equality; Soccer, World Cup (1999)

women's sports as inferior, 119–120
See also Intercollegiate athletics
Sports equipment, 79–80, 83, 84–85, 86,
125, 183, 190–194, 224(n15)
and making game too easy, 191, 193
See also Lending sports equipment
Sports Illustrated, 111
Sports in America (Michener), 172
Sports management, 183–190
Sportsmanship, 41–67, 108, 172, 205
definitions, 43
See also Fair play
Standards, 157, 158, 215
Stanford University, 138, 162, 228(n7)
Stereotypes, 118, 130, 176
Steroids, 3–4, 8, 14, 69–70, 71–90,
223(n13)
as permissible, 78, 79, 81, 83–84, 85–86
reasons for athletes not using, 72–73,
86–88
side effects, 71, 74
stanozolol, 69
as unfair, 79, 82
use of compared with use of superior
equipment, 79–80, 84, 86, 87
See also Cheating, and steroid use;
Performance-enhancing drugs
Stimulants, 77, 80
Stingley, Darryl, 103
Strategic fouling, 47, 48, 108, 222(n31)
and cheating, 47, 48, 54–57, 59, 60–61
defense of, 57, 64, 67. *See also*
Conventions/conventionalism
See also Soccer, World Cup (1999); *under*
Basketball
Stress, 97
Suits, Bernard, 221(n10)
Supreme Court, 124
Swimming, 115, 128, 158, 176

Tactics vs. strategy, 9
Tatum, Jack, 103, 104, 105

Teachers, 206–207, 214

Teamwork, 22, 23, 45, 167, 200, 205

Technology. *See* Sports equipment

Television. *See* Media

Tennessee, University of, 120, 133, 137, 150

Tennis, 18, 25, 29, 84, 92, 104, 112, 116, 128, 164, 193, 208

men's vs. women's games in, 120–121

Theory of Justice, A (Rawls), 135, 223(n11), 228(n33)

They Call Me Assassin (Tatum), 103

Thompson, John, 153

Ticket prices, 173, 174

Title IX of Education Amendments of 1972, 110, 111–113, 132–133, 136, 176, 230(n19)

development of, 123–124

test for compliance with, 125–126, 127, 128, 129, 131

Tolerance, 11, 12

Track-and-field sports, 109, 112, 114, 117

Training, 76, 77, 78, 84, 87, 91, 131, 146, 166, 167, 207, 209

Umpires. *See* Officials/umpires

United States Golf Association (USGA), 48, 191, 195, 232–233(n22)

Universities, function of, 141–142, 148–149, 161, 167, 169

Urinalysis, 88

Use of force. *See under* Violence

USF. *See* San Francisco, University of

USGA. *See* United States Golf Association

Utilitarianism, 20–21, 24, 94–96, 149, 150, 168, 184, 192, 193, 203, 218(n5), 233(n4)

act and rule utilitarianism, 219(n5), 224(n21)

Values, 2, 4, 7, 12, 13, 19, 23, 38, 43, 67, 83, 86, 96, 100, 102, 108, 172, 187, 188, 189–190, 199–215

academic vs. athletic, 141, 143, 150, 153, 162, 166–168, 209

and commercialization of sports, 196

conservative, 105–106, 107, 166

market values, 174

and reductionist thesis, 199–201, 202

taught in schools, 204

universal, 9, 203

worst, 103

See also Conventions/conventionalism; Externalism; Internalism

Veil of ignorance, 81, 82, 223(nn 11, 12, 13), 228(n33)

Violence, 4, 90–108, 138, 177, 180, 187–188

characterized, 92–93

and use of force, 92, 93, 104, 105, 108

Vitamins, 87

Vulnerability Principle (VP), 104–105

Wade, Louis, 90–91

Wasserstrom, Richard, 114, 115

Weiss, Paul, 160

Werner, Richard, 223(n13)

West, Jerry, 29

Whaley, Suzy, 117

Williams, Venus and Serena, 119, 120

Winning, 1–2, 4, 6, 17, 23, 24, 31, 32, 33, 39, 46, 71, 108, 139, 143, 144, 177, 184, 202, 209, 220(n19)

importance of, 35–38, 148, 200, 210

pride in victory, 36, 63

WNBA. *See* Basketball, Women's National Basketball Association

Women, 227(n28). *See also* Sex equality; *under* Sports

Woods, Tiger, 34–35, 53, 70, 182, 208, 213

Work ethic, 182

World Cup. *See under* Soccer

Wrestling, 128, 188, 189

Ying, Liu, 3, 41–42